The Pre-History of Western Mexico

Allen Schery

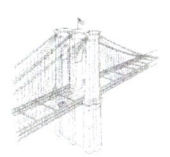

Brooklyn Bridge Books

Copyright 2025 by Allen Schery

All rights reserved.

No portion of this book may be reproduced in any form without written permission from the publisher or author, except as permitted by U.S. copyright law.

Contents

About the Author	V
Preface	VII
1. Theoretical Foundations and Methodological Innovations	1
2. Environmental Context and Cultural Ecology	20
3. The Deep Past – Paleoindian and Archaic Foundations (13,000-1500 BCE)	37
4. The Shaft Tomb Revolution – Mortuary Complexity and Social Stratification (1500 BCE-400 CE)	56
5. Obsidian Mastery and Trade Networks (200 BCE–900 CE)	73
6. The Teuchitlán Tradition – Circular Cosmologies and Social Complexity (300 BCE-900 CE)	93
7. The Turquoise Trail – Mesoamerica and the American Southwest	114
8. The Metallurgical Revolution – Copper, Bronze, and Cultural Innovation (900-1200 CE)	129

9.	Religious Systems and Cosmological Frameworks	146
10.	The Tarascan Empire – Political Complexity and Cultural Synthesis (1350–1530 CE)	158
11.	Colonial Encounters and Cultural Resilience (1530-1750 CE)	173
12.	Art, Symbolism, and Cultural Expression	197
13.	Social Organization and Cultural Dynamics	223
14.	Comparative Analysis and Theoretical Synthesis	239
15.	Legacy and Contemporary Significance	260
Bibliography		278
Index		318
Endnotes		328

About the Author

Allen Schery is intimately connected to Pedro Armillas, Phil Weigand and Garman Harbottle. Armillas was his mentor for two years having one on one classes with Armillas throughout this time. One summer Armillas took Allen for a tour of Mexican sites from Cholula through Yucatan, At Palenque Sr. Segovia took Armillas and Allen to view Lord Pakal's tomb beneath the Temple of the Inscriptions, in Chiapas, Mexico to view his headstone. Their last stop was Tulum.

Phil and Allen lived together with the Tepehuan Indians in Azqueltan, Jalisco, Mexico on the Rio Bolanos River, Allen vividly remembers red ant bites while writing down names and dates from grave markers to use to determine lineages. At night while sleeping on straw petates *Arizona Bark Scorpions (*Centruroides sculpturatus) danced by their heads. They are the most venomous scorpion in North America. Jalapenos grown in the local red soils were so hot that one bite numbed one's lips as if a shot of Novocain from a dentist. Mezcal grown and produced locally and dark yellow in color burned one's throat while going down. There were endless prickly pear tunas to eat but the payback was fingers laced with Glochids which serve as a passive evolutionary defense system, deterring animals and humans from handling the fruit without caution. We dug holes in the sand and waited for water to filter through for our drinking water. Our benefactor was Don Salvador Escobedo de Torres who was visibly touched and cried when we left

When the Turquoise project started, I worked at Brookhaven National Labs several days a week for two years preparing the ampules for insertion into the nuclear reactor for neutron activation. "Gar" and I were sports car enthusiasts. He had a British racing green 1962 Jaguar XKE While I drove a silver big block Corvette. When I got married, he was there to support me. As you can see these three men were an important part of my life. Phil never closed the loop by writing a book so my good friend I spent over two years writing this tome as a salute to you. I fashion myself as a Philosophical Anthropologist and used that approach in the construction of this book. Of my sixteen books written one can find "The Dragon's Breath the Human Experience", "The Primate Principle" and "The Pattern Seeking Ape" All are anthropology and philosophy based as I have endeavored to explain what it means to be a human in all times and places. At 77 I thought I would circle back to the beginning to thank and give tribute to these three great men-all sorely missed.

Preface
Toward a Philosophical Anthropology of Western Mexican Prehistory

This work represents a comprehensive attempt to understand the prehistoric cultural development of Western Mexico through the lens of philosophical anthropology, integrating rigorous archaeological evidence with theoretical frameworks that honor both scientific method and indigenous ways of knowing. It emerges from the recognition that Western Mexico's prehistory has long been marginalized within Mesoamerican studies, relegated to a peripheral position that obscures its profound contributions to human cultural achievement and its distinctive pathways to social complexity. To address this neglect, the present study confronts the persistent theoretical challenges that continue to shape archaeological interpretation. The lingering influence of center–periphery models distorts our understanding of cultural development by privileging certain regions and traditions while dismissing others as derivative or incomplete. Environmental determinism, despite decades of critique, still colors interpretations of human–environment relationships in ways that deny indigenous agency and sophisticated ecological knowledge. Similarly, evolutionary frameworks, when applied uncritically, impose linear progressions that fail to capture the diverse pathways through which human societies achieve complexity and meaning.

Against these reductive tendencies, this work advocates for a philosophical anthropological approach that recognizes cultural development as fundamentally creative, diverse, and meaningful human activity. Drawing on phenomenological and hermeneutic traditions, it seeks to understand prehistoric societies as communities of meaning-makers whose material productions reflect sophisticated philosophical and cosmological systems. Such a perspective requires moving beyond simple functional explanations to engage with the symbolic dimensions of material culture and the worldview systems that informed ancient practice. The methodological foundation for this approach rests on the pioneering collaborative research of Phil Weigand, Pedro Armillas, and Garman Harbottle, whose friendship and scientific partnership established new standards for interdisciplinary archaeological research. Their integration of field archaeology, ecological anthropology, and scientific analytical techniques demonstrates how humanistic interpretation can be strengthened rather than undermined by rigorous empirical methods, providing a framework for defending against potential criticisms while maintaining theoretical sophistication.

Weigand's systematic regional surveys and architectural documentation established the empirical foundation for understanding Western Mexico's unique cultural achievements. His recognition of the circular pyramid complexes challenged fundamental assumptions about Mesoamerican cultural development and demonstrated the necessity of understanding regional traditions on their own terms rather than as variants of better-known patterns. Building on his documentation, this work extends theoretical interpretation to encompass broader questions of human cultural creativity and alternative pathways to social complexity. Armillas's ecological anthropology provides crucial theoretical frameworks for understanding human–environment relationships without falling into deterministic explanations. His analysis of agricultural systems, water management, and landscape modification demonstrates how indigenous communities achieved sustainable relationships with challenging environments through sophisticated technological and social innovations. From this perspective, Western Mexican societies appear not as passive respondents to environmental constraints but as creative agents in landscape transformation. Harbottle's innovations in archaeometry and provenance analysis, meanwhile, offer precise analytical tools for reconstructing ancient trade networks and cultural connections. His collaboration with Weigand on turquoise provenance studies revealed previously unknown patterns of interregional exchange that connected Mesoamerica to the American Southwest through Western Mexican intermediation. These discoveries challenge traditional boundaries between culture areas while demonstrating the sophisticated organization required for long-distance trade and cultural exchange.

The theoretical stance of this work also anticipates and addresses several potential lines of philosophical criticism. Against relativism, it maintains that while cultural diversity and alternative pathways to complexity must be emphasized, cross-cultural comparison and evaluation remain both possible and necessary. The archaeological record provides objective evidence for technological achievements, organizational sophistication, and cultural innovations that can be assessed using consistent analytical frameworks. The unique circular architecture, sophisticated metallurgy, and extensive trade networks of Western Mexico represent genuine achievements that contributed to human cultural development and deserve recognition alongside better-known civilizational traditions. Against environmental determinism, this study demonstrates that although ecological factors influenced cultural development, human agency remained paramount in shaping responses to opportunities and constraints. Indigenous knowledge systems, innovative technological solutions, and sustainable resource management practices reflect creative adaptation rather than simple environmental response, and the diversity of cultural solutions across Western Mexico's varied ecological zones provides compelling evidence of this creativity. Against evolutionary reductionism, the work insists on the importance of understanding each cultural tradition within its own terms and contexts. The circular pyramid complexes represent an alternative pathway to architectural monumentality that cannot be understood as an incomplete version of developments elsewhere, while the shaft tomb tradition reflects sophisticated concepts of death, ancestry, and social organization that deserve analysis as complex meaning systems rather than mere markers of evolutionary stages. Against center–periphery models, the evidence demonstrates that Western Mexico developed distinctive forms of social complexity characterized by unique architectural traditions, innovative technologies, and extensive trade networks. These were indigenous innovations, not peripheral adaptations of central Mexican developments, and they influenced broader Mesoamerican development while contributing to continental-scale cultural integration. Finally, against positivist reductionism, this work argues that while empirical rigor and scientific method remain essential, interpretive frameworks must also accommodate the symbolic and meaningful dimensions of human cultural activity. The archaeological record provides evidence not only for technological and organizational achievements but also for sophisticated philosophical and cosmological systems that guided human action and gave meaning to material culture.

Equally important, this work seeks to honor indigenous knowledge systems and contemporary indigenous communities while maintaining scholarly rigor and theoretical sophistication. The archaeological traditions documented here remain significant to contemporary indigenous peoples, particularly the Huichol (Wixáritari), who maintain cultural and territorial connections to many of the areas studied. Their ongoing ceremonial practices, oral traditions, and ecological knowledge provide crucial insights into the symbolic and philosophical dimensions of prehistoric cultural systems. Contemporary indigenous perspectives challenge archaeological interpretation to move beyond purely academic concerns and to engage with questions of cultural heritage, community identity, and environmental sustainability. The sophisticated agricultural systems, sustainable resource management practices, and alternative social organizational models documented in Western Mexico's prehistory offer insights relevant to contemporary environmental and social challenges, extending the relevance of this study beyond academic interest to encompass practical applications for sustainable development, community organization, and cultural preservation.

The structure of the argument proceeds through systematic analysis of Western Mexico's prehistoric development from earliest settlement through Spanish contact, maintaining theoretical coherence while documenting empirical evidence for distinctive cultural achievements. Temporal analysis reveals patterns of innovation, continuity, and transformation over more than three millennia, illustrating diverse pathways to social complexity from Archaic hunter-gatherer adaptations through complex circular pyramid societies to imperial integration. Spatial analysis demonstrates both local distinctiveness and interregional connection, showing how Western Mexican traditions emerge clearly when compared to developments elsewhere, while evidence for extensive trade networks reveals sophisticated integration with broader American cultural systems. Thematic analysis of architecture, technology, social organization, religious systems, and artistic expression reveals consistent patterns of innovation and distinctive approaches to universal human challenges, with circular architecture, advanced metallurgy, and elaborate mortuary systems reflecting coherent cultural solutions grounded in philosophical and cosmological principles. Theoretical synthesis integrates empirical evidence with frameworks derived from philosophical anthropology, ecological anthropology, and comparative civilizational analysis, producing new insights into human cultural potential and alternative pathways to social complexity.

Ultimately, this work contributes to ongoing discussions within anthropological theory and archaeological interpretation by demonstrating that sophisticated forms of social organization can emerge through pathways quite different from those documented elsewhere. The emphasis on circular architecture, alternative approaches to political organization, and sustainable resource management offers insights relevant to contemporary debates on social alternatives and environmental sustainability. The methodological integration pioneered by Weigand, Armillas, and Harbottle provides a model for interdisciplinary research that combines scientific rigor with humanistic interpretation, while the philosophical anthropological framework employed here contributes to efforts to develop archaeological interpretation that honors both indigenous perspectives and scholarly rigor. By emphasizing the symbolic and meaningful dimensions of material culture while maintaining commitment to empirical evidence, this approach offers a path toward more inclusive and comprehensive understanding of human cultural development.

The evidence presented here challenges persistent biases within Mesoamerican studies and broader archaeological theory, demonstrating the necessity of understanding regional traditions within their own contexts while recognizing their contributions to broader patterns of human cultural achievement. Western Mexico's prehistory deserves recognition not as a peripheral variant of better-known developments but as a distinctive and sophisticated cultural tradition that expanded the range of human cultural possibility. This work stands as both a scholarly contribution and an advocacy for more inclusive understanding of human cultural achievement. The prehistoric peoples of Western Mexico created distinctive solutions to universal human challenges, developed sophisticated forms of social organization, and established cultural traditions that influenced continental-scale patterns of development. Their achievements deserve recognition alongside better-known civilizational traditions and offer crucial insights into human cultural potential and alternative pathways to social complexity. Through systematic analysis of empirical evidence integrated with theoretical frameworks that honor both scientific rigor and indigenous ways of knowing, this study seeks to contribute to a more comprehensive understanding of human cultural development while advocating for recognition of Western Mexico's distinctive and profound contributions to human cultural achievement. The pages that follow present the evidence and arguments that support these claims, offering readers a comprehensive examination of Western Mexico's prehistoric heritage that combines scholarly rigor with respect for indigenous knowledge and contemporary relevance.

Chapter One
Theoretical Foundations and Methodological Innovations

The philosophical foundations of archaeological interpretation have undergone fundamental transformations over the past century, moving from positivist frameworks that sought to establish universal laws of cultural development toward more nuanced approaches that recognize the creative and meaningful dimensions of human cultural activity. The prehistory of Western Mexico provides a particularly compelling case study for examining these theoretical developments, as the region's distinctive cultural traditions challenge conventional interpretive frameworks while offering rich evidence for alternative pathways to social complexity. Understanding these achievements requires theoretical approaches that can accommodate both empirical rigor and interpretive sophistication, frameworks capable of recognizing indigenous innovation while maintaining scholarly standards for evidence and argument.

The phenomenological tradition within philosophical anthropology offers crucial insights for understanding prehistoric cultural systems as meaningful human constructions rather than mere adaptive responses to environmental or evolutionary pressures. Drawing on the work of philosophers like Edmund Husserl and Maurice Merleau-Ponty, phenomenological approaches emphasize the importance of understanding human experience from the perspective of the experiencing subject, recognizing that material culture emerges from intentional human action directed toward meaningful goals within culturally constructed worlds. This perspective proves particularly relevant for interpreting the distinctive architectural traditions of Western Mexico, where circular ceremonial complexes reflect cosmological principles and social organizational patterns that differ fundamentally from those documented elsewhere in Mesoamerica. The circular pyramids of Teuchitlán cannot be understood simply as functional responses to environmental constraints or as incomplete versions of developments elsewhere, but must be recognized as intentional creations that embody distinctive approaches to sacred space, ceremonial organization, and community integration.

The hermeneutic tradition provides additional theoretical resources for interpreting material culture as symbolic communication across temporal and cultural boundaries. Following the insights of philosophers like Hans-Georg Gadamer and Paul Ricoeur, hermeneutic interpretation recognizes that understanding prehistoric cultures requires engaging with their material productions as meaningful texts that can be interpreted through careful attention to context, symbolic systems, and cultural patterns. The elaborate ceramic traditions of Western Mexico's shaft tomb culture, with their detailed depictions of daily life, ceremonial activities, and mythological narratives, exemplify the rich symbolic dimensions of material culture that require interpretive rather than purely functional analysis. These ceramic figurines and vessels communicate complex information about social roles, religious beliefs, and cultural values that can be accessed through systematic iconographic analysis informed by comparative ethnographic and ethnohistorical research.

Structural-functional analysis provides complementary theoretical frameworks for understanding how cultural systems integrate symbolic meaning with practical social organization. Drawing on the work of anthropologists like Claude Lévi-Strauss and Talcott Parsons, structural-functional approaches examine how cultural elements serve both practical and symbolic functions within integrated systems of meaning and social organization. The settlement patterns of Teuchitlán tradition sites reveal sophisticated integration of ceremonial centers with residential areas and agricultural zones, suggesting forms of social organization that balanced centralized ceremonial authority with dispersed economic and domestic activities. This pattern reflects underlying principles of social organization that emphasized collective ceremony combined with household autonomy, principles that can be understood through structural analysis of architectural relationships and settlement hierarchies.

Critical examination of center-periphery models reveals persistent biases within archaeological interpretation that have systematically marginalized regions like Western Mexico despite evidence for sophisticated cultural achievements and distinctive contributions to broader patterns of Mesoamerican development. These models, originally developed to explain patterns of political and economic domination in modern world systems, have been inappropriately applied to prehistoric contexts where different forms of cultural interaction and regional specialization operated. The archaeological evidence from Western Mexico demonstrates that the region developed distinctive forms of social complexity characterized by unique architectural traditions, innovative technologies, and extensive trade networks that influenced rather than simply responded to developments elsewhere in Mesoamerica. The turquoise trade networks that connected central Mexico to the American Southwest through Western Mexican intermediation provide compelling evidence for the region's role in facilitating continental-scale cultural integration rather than serving as a passive recipient of external influences.

The collaborative research paradigm established by Phil Weigand, Pedro Armillas, and Garman Harbottle demonstrates the potential for interdisciplinary integration of field archaeology, ecological anthropology, and scientific analytical techniques to produce more comprehensive understanding of prehistoric cultural systems while maintaining both empirical rigor and theoretical sophistication. Their friendship and professional partnership, spanning more than four decades of research, established new standards for archaeological collaboration while producing fundamental discoveries that transformed understanding of Western Mexico's role in Mesoamerican civilization. Weigand's systematic documentation of circular ceremonial complexes provided the empirical foundation for recognizing Western Mexico's distinctive cultural traditions, while Armillas's ecological anthropological framework offered theoretical tools for understanding human-environment relationships without falling into deterministic explanations, and Harbottle's innovations in archaeometry enabled precise reconstruction of ancient trade networks and cultural connections.

Phil Weigand's contributions to Western Mexican archaeology began with the serendipitous discovery of Los Guachimontones in 1970, when he and his wife Acelia García encountered the mysterious circular pyramids that would revolutionize understanding of the region's prehistory. Weigand's immediate recognition of the site's significance, combined with his systematic approach to documentation and regional survey, established the empirical foundation for understanding the Teuchitlán tradition as a distinctive Mesoamerican cultural development rather than a peripheral variant of better-known patterns. Over four decades of research, the Weigands identified and recorded over 2,000 archaeological sites throughout Western Mexico, creating the first comprehensive database of the region's prehistoric occupation while demonstrating the systematic nature of circular ceremonial architecture across the broader region. This comprehensive approach enabled Weigand to formulate and test hypotheses about settlement patterns, economic organization, and cultural development that could be evaluated against extensive empirical evidence rather than relying on limited site-specific data.

Weigand's theoretical contributions emphasized the importance of understanding Western Mexican societies within their own cultural and environmental contexts rather than as derivative versions of central Mexican civilizations. His recognition that the Teuchitlán tradition represented a parallel development of social complexity, one that achieved sophisticated levels of organization through different means than those employed elsewhere in Mesoamerica, required new analytical frameworks that could accommodate cultural diversity within broader Mesoamerican patterns while recognizing fundamental distinctiveness. This perspective challenged persistent center-periphery models within Mesoamerican studies while demonstrating the necessity of regional approaches to understanding cultural development. Weigand's integration of architectural analysis with settlement pattern studies, combined with systematic attention to environmental context and resource distribution, established methodological standards that influenced subsequent research throughout the region while providing models for understanding cultural adaptation and innovation in diverse environmental settings.

The methodological innovations introduced by Weigand included systematic regional survey techniques that enabled comprehensive documentation of settlement hierarchies and territorial organization across broad geographical areas. His approach combined intensive site excavation with extensive regional reconnaissance, creating databases that could support analysis of cultural development at multiple spatial and temporal scales. The integration of topographic mapping, architectural documentation, and artifact analysis provided comprehensive records of site organization and cultural patterns that enabled comparative analysis across the region while supporting detailed interpretation of specific sites and cultural phases. This systematic approach demonstrated how comprehensive empirical documentation could support sophisticated theoretical interpretation while maintaining rigorous standards for evidence and analysis.

Pedro Armillas García brought to Mesoamerican archaeology a sophisticated theoretical framework that integrated ecological, economic, and social factors in explaining cultural development, establishing foundations for ecological anthropological approaches that remain influential in contemporary research. Born in Spain but educated in Mexico following the Spanish Civil War, Armillas developed theoretical perspectives influenced by historical materialism and cultural ecology that emphasized the dynamic relationships between human societies and their environments. His landmark research on irrigation systems and agricultural intensification at sites like Teotihuacan demonstrated how systematic excavation could reveal evidence for sophisticated technological systems and environmental management practices that supported complex urban civilizations. These methodological innovations established new standards for studying the relationship between agricultural systems and social complexity throughout Mesoamerica while providing analytical tools for understanding how societies achieved sustainability in challenging environmental settings.

Armillas's theoretical framework emphasized human agency in landscape modification and environmental adaptation, challenging deterministic approaches that portrayed cultural development as simple response to environmental constraints. His research demonstrated that Mesoamerican civilizations actively transformed their environments through sophisticated technological and organizational innovations, creating agricultural systems that could support dense populations and complex social institutions over extended periods. The theoretical perspective developed through this research proved particularly relevant for understanding Western Mexican societies, which achieved complex forms of organization in volcanic environments that required different technological and social solutions than those documented in the highland valleys where most Mesoamerican research had focused. Armillas's emphasis on agricultural systems, water management, and landscape modification provided analytical frameworks for understanding how Western Mexican societies developed sustainable relationships with their diverse environments while achieving sophisticated levels of social organization and cultural elaboration.

The methodological contributions of Armillas included systematic approaches to documenting ancient agricultural systems, irrigation networks, and environmental management practices that had been largely invisible to previous archaeological research. His excavations at Teotihuacan revealed sophisticated canal systems, terraced fields, and water management installations that supported the city's population while maintaining soil fertility and agricultural productivity over centuries. These discoveries demonstrated the necessity of understanding urban civilizations within broader regional contexts that included agricultural hinterlands and resource management systems, perspectives that influenced subsequent research throughout Mesoamerica while establishing new standards for integrating environmental and cultural analysis in archaeological interpretation.

The theoretical implications of Armillas's work extended beyond methodological innovation to encompass fundamental questions about the relationship between human societies and their environments. His research challenged simple environmental determinism by demonstrating how human communities actively shaped their environments through technological innovation and social organization, while also recognizing the importance of environmental factors in influencing cultural development. This perspective enabled more sophisticated understanding of human-environment relationships that recognized both environmental constraints and human creativity in cultural adaptation, frameworks that proved essential for interpreting the diverse cultural traditions of Western Mexico within their varied ecological contexts.

Garman Harbottle's revolutionary contributions to archaeological research emerged through his pioneering application of nuclear analytical techniques to problems of provenance determination and cultural exchange, establishing archaeometry as a crucial subdiscipline within archaeological research while demonstrating the potential for interdisciplinary collaboration between physical scientists and anthropologists. Working at Brookhaven National Laboratory from 1949 to 1997, Harbottle developed instrumental neutron activation analysis (INAA) as a powerful tool for tracing the sources of archaeological materials and reconstructing ancient trade networks with unprecedented precision and reliability. His collaboration with archaeologists like Phil Weigand produced fundamental discoveries about long-distance cultural connections that challenged traditional assumptions about the geographical scope and organizational sophistication of prehistoric exchange systems while establishing new standards for empirical rigor in archaeological research.

Harbottle's scientific approach to archaeology exemplified the potential for interdisciplinary collaboration to address fundamental questions about cultural development, technological innovation, and inter-regional interaction in prehistoric societies. His development of sophisticated analytical techniques enabled archaeologists to trace specific objects to their geological sources with remarkable precision, revealing patterns of exchange and cultural interaction that would have been impossible to document through traditional archaeological methods alone. The databases created through decades of systematic analysis provided unprecedented opportunities for comparative research across broad geographical areas while establishing empirical foundations for testing hypotheses about cultural diffusion, technological transfer, and economic organization in prehistoric societies.

The collaboration between Harbottle and Weigand on turquoise provenance analysis produced one of the most significant discoveries in Mesoamerican archaeology, providing definitive evidence for systematic trade relationships between central Mexico and the American Southwest through analysis of over 2,000 turquoise artifacts from 28 archaeological sites compared with samples from over 40 mining areas. This massive analytical effort revealed that turquoise artifacts found in Mexican sites could be traced to specific mines more than 1,000 miles away in New Mexico, Arizona, and Nevada, demonstrating the existence of formal commercial relationships rather than casual exchange and indicating sophisticated organizational systems for long-distance trade and cultural interaction. The systematic nature of turquoise importation, evidenced by the large quantities of raw material found at sites like Alta Vista in Zacatecas, revealed that this trade facilitated broader cultural exchanges between Mesoamerica and the American Southwest, with reciprocal influences affecting art, architecture, and religious practices across vast distances.

The theoretical implications of Harbottle's research extended beyond specific discoveries about trade relationships to encompass fundamental questions about the technological and organizational capabilities of prehistoric societies. His work on medieval European sculpture, ancient Chinese musical instruments, and Mesoamerican artifacts demonstrated that prehistoric and historic societies possessed sophisticated understanding of materials science and maintained complex networks of technological and cultural exchange that operated across continental scales. This perspective challenged traditional assumptions about the limitations of prehistoric technological systems while providing empirical evidence for the sophisticated organizational capabilities required to maintain long-distance trade and cultural exchange over extended periods.

The methodological innovations developed by Harbottle included sophisticated statistical methods for handling large datasets produced by INAA, enabling researchers to identify patterns of similarity and difference among archaeological materials with unprecedented precision. The Mahalanobis Distance search algorithms developed at Brookhaven represented novel approaches to pattern recognition in archaeological data that could accommodate the complex multivariate relationships among chemical compositions while providing statistically reliable methods for provenance determination. These analytical techniques established new standards for empirical rigor in archaeological research while demonstrating how sophisticated quantitative methods could be integrated with qualitative interpretation to produce more comprehensive understanding of cultural processes and historical relationships.

The integration of multiple theoretical perspectives within a coherent philosophical anthropological framework requires careful attention to the relationships among different levels of analysis and the compatibility of different methodological approaches. Phenomenological interpretation of symbolic meaning systems must be grounded in empirical evidence about actual cultural practices and material productions, while structural-functional analysis of social organization must acknowledge the creative and meaningful dimensions of human cultural activity that cannot be reduced to simple adaptive functions. The hermeneutic interpretation of material culture as symbolic communication requires systematic attention to archaeological context and comparative analysis, while ecological anthropological analysis of human-environment relationships must recognize both environmental constraints and human agency in cultural adaptation and innovation.

The collaborative research model established by Weigand, Armillas, and Harbottle demonstrates how different analytical approaches can be integrated to produce more comprehensive understanding while maintaining theoretical coherence and empirical rigor. Their synthesis of field archaeology, ecological analysis, and scientific analytical techniques created synergistic effects that enabled discoveries and interpretations that none could have achieved alone. Weigand's systematic documentation of architectural and settlement patterns provided the empirical foundation for understanding regional cultural development, while Armillas's theoretical framework offered analytical tools for understanding human-environment relationships and social organizational patterns, and Harbottle's analytical chemistry enabled precise reconstruction of trade networks and cultural connections that revealed previously unknown patterns of inter-regional interaction.

Contemporary anthropological theory offers additional theoretical resources for understanding cultural development and change that complement and extend the foundations established by these pioneering scholars. Practice theory, developed by anthropologists like Pierre Bourdieu and Anthony Giddens, provides frameworks for understanding how individual agency and structural constraints interact in cultural reproduction and transformation, perspectives that prove particularly relevant for understanding how Western Mexican societies maintained distinctive cultural traditions while participating in broader patterns of Mesoamerican development. Agency theory offers analytical tools for understanding how human actors navigate structural constraints while pursuing meaningful goals within culturally constructed worlds, frameworks that enable more sophisticated understanding of cultural innovation and adaptation than simpler evolutionary or functional models.

World systems theory and its archaeological applications provide additional perspectives on inter-regional interaction and cultural exchange that complement provenance studies and trade network reconstruction while avoiding the deterministic implications of center-periphery models. Archaeological world systems approaches examine how different regions participate in broader networks of interaction while maintaining distinctive cultural identities and contributing specialized products or services to inter-regional exchange systems. The Western Mexican case provides compelling evidence for this type of complex inter-regional relationship, with the region serving as a crucial corridor for cultural and commercial exchange between Mesoamerica and North America while developing distinctive cultural traditions that influenced broader patterns of continental development.

Postcolonial theory and indigenous archaeology offer crucial perspectives for developing more inclusive and ethically responsible approaches to interpreting prehistoric cultures, particularly those that continue to be significant to contemporary indigenous communities. These theoretical approaches challenge traditional archaeological practices that treat indigenous pasts as objects of study rather than recognizing contemporary indigenous peoples as stakeholders in archaeological research and interpretation. The Huichol (Wixáritari) communities who maintain cultural and territorial connections to many areas of Western Mexico studied by archaeologists provide contemporary perspectives on the significance and meaning of prehistoric cultural traditions that must be incorporated into scholarly interpretation while respecting indigenous intellectual property and cultural sovereignty.

The philosophical implications of archaeological interpretation extend beyond academic concerns to encompass fundamental questions about human nature, cultural development, and the possibilities for alternative forms of social organization. The evidence from Western Mexico's prehistory demonstrates that sophisticated forms of social complexity can emerge through pathways quite different from those documented elsewhere, suggesting that human cultural potential encompasses greater diversity than previously recognized. The circular ceremonial architecture, sustainable agricultural systems, and alternative approaches to political organization documented in Western Mexico provide insights relevant to contemporary discussions about social alternatives and environmental sustainability while challenging linear evolutionary models that privilege certain forms of cultural development over others.

The methodological integration demonstrated by Weigand, Armillas, and Harbottle establishes standards for contemporary interdisciplinary research that combines scientific rigor with humanistic interpretation while maintaining respect for indigenous perspectives and contemporary community interests. Their collaborative approach demonstrates how different analytical methods can be integrated to produce more comprehensive understanding while avoiding the reductionism that often characterizes attempts to apply single theoretical frameworks to complex cultural phenomena. The emphasis on systematic empirical documentation combined with sophisticated theoretical interpretation provides models for contemporary research that seeks to advance scholarly understanding while maintaining ethical responsibility to indigenous communities and contemporary stakeholders.

The theoretical foundations established through this collaborative research continue to influence contemporary archaeological practice while providing frameworks for addressing new questions about cultural development, technological innovation, and inter-regional interaction in prehistoric societies. The integration of field archaeology, ecological analysis, and scientific analytical techniques established methodological standards that remain relevant for contemporary research while demonstrating the potential for interdisciplinary collaboration to produce discoveries and interpretations that advance both scholarly understanding and practical applications for contemporary cultural and environmental challenges. The Western Mexican case provides compelling evidence for theoretical arguments about cultural diversity, indigenous innovation, and alternative pathways to social complexity while offering insights relevant to contemporary discussions about sustainability, community organization, and cultural preservation that extend beyond purely academic interests to encompass practical applications for addressing contemporary social and environmental challenges.

Chapter Two
Environmental Context and Cultural Ecology

The environmental foundations of Western Mexico's cultural development encompass an extraordinary diversity of ecological zones, topographic features, and resource distributions that created both opportunities and constraints for human adaptation over more than three millennia of prehistoric occupation. This geographical complexity, extending from Pacific coastal plains through volcanic highlands to the edges of the central Mexican plateau, provided the environmental context within which indigenous communities developed distinctive cultural traditions while maintaining sophisticated relationships with diverse natural systems. Understanding these environmental relationships requires theoretical frameworks that can accommodate both the material constraints imposed by natural systems and the creative agency demonstrated by indigenous communities in landscape modification, resource management, and technological innovation. The archaeological evidence reveals that

Western Mexican societies achieved remarkable success in developing sustainable adaptations to challenging environments while creating cultural systems of exceptional sophistication and distinctiveness within the broader Mesoamerican tradition.

The physical geography of Western Mexico encompasses dramatic topographic contrasts that created diverse opportunities for human settlement and resource exploitation while establishing natural corridors and barriers that influenced patterns of cultural interaction and regional development. The region extends from sea-level coastal plains along the Pacific Ocean through intermediate highlands and volcanic plateaus to elevations exceeding 4,000 meters in the volcanic mountains of the Trans-Mexican Volcanic Belt. This vertical zonation creates corresponding climatic and ecological gradients that support dramatically different plant and animal communities within relatively short geographical distances, enabling human communities to access diverse resource bases through seasonal movement or specialized exchange relationships. The volcanic landscapes that dominate much of the region reflect relatively recent geological activity that created fertile soils while also imposing constraints through rugged topography and periodic seismic activity that influenced settlement patterns and architectural traditions.

The coastal plains of Nayarit and Jalisco provided rich marine resources, fertile alluvial soils, and access to long-distance maritime transportation that connected Western Mexico to broader Pacific trade networks extending from South America to the North American Southwest. Archaeological evidence indicates sophisticated exploitation of marine resources including fish, shellfish, and salt production that supported both local consumption and long-distance trade, while the fertile coastal soils enabled intensive agricultural production that supported dense populations and complex social institutions. The seasonal patterns of coastal resource availability required sophisticated scheduling and storage technologies that are reflected in archaeological site distributions and architectural features designed for processing and storing marine products. The coastal zone also provided access to distinctive raw materials including marine shells used for ornament production and specialized tools, materials that appear in inland archaeological contexts throughout Western Mexico and beyond, indicating extensive trade networks and cultural exchange relationships.

The highland volcanic landscapes of central Jalisco and adjacent areas provided the environmental context for the most distinctive cultural developments in Western Mexico's prehistory, including the circular ceremonial complexes of the Teuchitlán tradition and the sophisticated agricultural systems that supported these complex societies. The volcanic soils of these areas, derived from relatively recent ash deposits and lava flows, provided exceptional fertility when properly managed, while the rugged topography created numerous microenvironments that supported diverse plant and animal communities within limited geographical areas. The highland lakes and seasonal wetlands provided additional resources including waterfowl, fish, and aquatic plants, while also serving as focal points for settlement and ceremonial activity. The archaeological evidence indicates sophisticated water management systems including canals, terraces, and drainage facilities that enabled intensive agricultural production while maintaining soil fertility over extended periods, demonstrating remarkable ecological knowledge and sustainable land management practices.

The transitional zones between highland and lowland areas provided crucial corridors for human movement and cultural exchange while also supporting distinctive adaptive strategies that combined highland and lowland resource exploitation patterns. These intermediate elevations often provided optimal conditions for agriculture while maintaining access to both highland and lowland resources through seasonal movement or exchange relationships. The archaeological distribution of sites in these transitional zones suggests that they served as crucial nodes in regional settlement systems, facilitating interaction between highland and coastal communities while supporting local populations through diverse resource bases. The topographic complexity of these areas also provided natural defensive advantages that influenced settlement patterns and political organization, with many sites positioned to control access routes between different ecological zones.

Pedro Armillas's pioneering research on environmental relationships and cultural adaptation in Mesoamerica established theoretical frameworks that prove particularly relevant for understanding Western Mexican cultural development within its diverse environmental contexts. His emphasis on human agency in landscape modification challenged simplistic environmental determinism while recognizing the important role of environmental factors in influencing cultural development and adaptation strategies. Armillas demonstrated that Mesoamerican societies actively transformed their environments through technological innovation and social organization rather than simply responding to environmental constraints, creating agricultural systems that could support complex social institutions while maintaining long-term sustainability. This perspective proves essential for understanding Western Mexican societies, which developed distinctive cultural traditions within environmental contexts that differed significantly from those of central Mexico where most Mesoamerican research had focused.

The theoretical framework developed by Armillas emphasized the dynamic relationships between human societies and their environments, recognizing that cultural adaptation involves continuous interaction between environmental constraints and human creativity in developing technological and organizational solutions. His research on irrigation systems, agricultural intensification, and landscape modification demonstrated that understanding cultural development requires systematic attention to environmental relationships while avoiding deterministic explanations that reduce cultural phenomena to simple environmental responses. The Western Mexican archaeological record provides compelling evidence for this perspective, revealing sophisticated environmental management systems that enabled sustainable adaptation to diverse and challenging ecological conditions while supporting the development of complex social institutions and distinctive cultural traditions.

Armillas's methodological innovations in documenting ancient agricultural systems and environmental management practices established analytical approaches that remain relevant for contemporary research on human-environment relationships in prehistoric societies. His systematic excavation of irrigation canals, terraced fields, and water management installations at sites like Teotihuacan revealed the sophisticated technological knowledge required for intensive agriculture in challenging environments while demonstrating the organizational capabilities necessary for coordinating large-scale landscape modification projects. These methodological approaches enabled detailed reconstruction of ancient environmental management systems while providing analytical tools for understanding the relationship between agricultural intensification and social complexity that proved crucial for interpreting similar developments in Western Mexico.

The ecological zones of Western Mexico created distinctive resource bases that required different technological and organizational solutions while also providing opportunities for specialization and exchange that facilitated cultural interaction and regional integration. The diversity of environmental conditions within relatively limited geographical areas enabled human communities to develop sophisticated strategies for exploiting multiple ecological niches while maintaining cultural coherence across diverse environmental settings. Archaeological evidence indicates that Western Mexican societies developed specialized technologies for exploiting specific environmental resources while maintaining exchange relationships that provided access to materials and products from different ecological zones. This pattern of ecological specialization combined with cultural integration appears throughout Western Mexico's prehistory, suggesting fundamental principles of environmental adaptation that influenced social organization and cultural development over extended periods.

The highland volcanic environments that supported the most complex cultural developments in Western Mexico required particularly sophisticated environmental management strategies that are reflected in archaeological evidence for agricultural intensification, water management, and sustainable land use practices. The circular ceremonial complexes of the Teuchitlán tradition were supported by agricultural systems that included terraced fields, irrigation canals, and sophisticated soil management techniques that maintained fertility while supporting dense populations and monumental construction projects. Archaeological surveys have documented extensive systems of agricultural terraces, water control features, and soil conservation installations that demonstrate remarkable ecological knowledge and long-term planning capabilities. These environmental management systems enabled sustainable intensification of agricultural production while maintaining landscape stability and soil fertility over centuries of continuous occupation.

The obsidian resources of Western Mexico provided crucial raw materials for tool production and long-distance trade while also requiring sophisticated geological knowledge and extraction technologies that demonstrate advanced understanding of natural systems and resource management principles. The region's volcanic activity created numerous obsidian sources with different characteristics that required specialized knowledge for identification and exploitation, while the scale of obsidian production indicated sophisticated organizational systems for coordinating extraction, processing, and distribution activities. Archaeological evidence indicates that Western Mexican societies controlled over 1,000 obsidian sources and produced an estimated 14,000 tons of obsidian tools and raw materials, suggesting systematic approaches to resource management that maintained sustainable extraction rates while supporting extensive trade networks and technological specialization.

The mineral resources of Western Mexico, including copper ores, turquoise, and various stone materials, provided additional opportunities for technological innovation and cultural exchange while requiring sophisticated geological knowledge and extraction techniques. The development of metallurgy in Western Mexico during the Postclassic period demonstrates advanced understanding of geological processes and materials science that enabled innovation in both utilitarian and ceremonial object production. Archaeological evidence indicates systematic exploitation of mineral resources through specialized mining operations that required coordination of labor, technical knowledge, and distribution systems while maintaining sustainable extraction practices that could operate over extended periods. The integration of mineral exploitation with broader cultural systems reveals sophisticated understanding of resource management principles that balanced immediate needs with long-term sustainability.

The diverse climatic patterns of Western Mexico reflect both regional topographic complexity and broader atmospheric circulation patterns that create seasonal and annual variations requiring adaptive strategies and environmental management techniques. The region experiences both Pacific maritime influences and continental weather patterns that create complex seasonal cycles affecting resource availability, agricultural scheduling, and human settlement patterns. Archaeological evidence indicates that Western Mexican societies developed sophisticated understanding of climatic patterns and seasonal cycles that enabled effective scheduling of agricultural activities, resource exploitation, and ceremonial events while maintaining adaptive flexibility for responding to climatic variation and environmental change. The integration of astronomical observations with agricultural and ceremonial calendars suggests advanced knowledge of seasonal patterns and their cultural significance for community organization and ritual practice.

The hydrological systems of Western Mexico, including highland lakes, seasonal wetlands, and river drainages, provided crucial water resources while also creating opportunities for intensive agriculture through irrigation and water management techniques. The archaeological evidence for sophisticated water control systems, including canals, dams, and drainage facilities, demonstrates advanced hydraulic engineering capabilities that enabled agricultural intensification while maintaining watershed stability and water quality. These water management systems required detailed understanding of hydrological processes, seasonal patterns, and landscape relationships that enabled sustainable water use while supporting dense populations and intensive agricultural production. The integration of water management with settlement patterns and ceremonial architecture suggests that hydrological knowledge was embedded within broader cultural systems that recognized water as both practical resource and sacred element.

The vegetation communities of Western Mexico reflect the complex interactions between topographic diversity, climatic patterns, and soil conditions that create distinctive plant assemblages requiring specialized knowledge for effective exploitation and management. Archaeological evidence indicates sophisticated understanding of plant ecology and sustainable harvesting practices that enabled systematic exploitation of wild plant resources while maintaining ecosystem stability and resource availability over extended periods. The development of agriculture required detailed knowledge of plant biology, soil relationships, and water requirements that enabled successful cultivation of domestic crops while maintaining diverse wild plant resources through careful land management practices. The integration of agricultural and wild resource management demonstrates holistic approaches to environmental relationships that recognized the interconnectedness of natural systems and the importance of maintaining ecological diversity for long-term sustainability.

The animal resources of Western Mexico included both terrestrial and aquatic species that required different hunting and management strategies while providing crucial protein sources, raw materials, and symbolic elements for cultural expression and religious practice. Archaeological evidence indicates sophisticated hunting technologies and wildlife management practices that maintained sustainable harvest rates while providing consistent access to animal resources for both subsistence and ceremonial purposes. The domestication of dogs and turkeys required advanced understanding of animal behavior and breeding techniques that enabled systematic production of animal protein while maintaining genetic diversity and health in domestic populations. The integration of hunting, fishing, and animal husbandry within broader subsistence systems demonstrates comprehensive approaches to animal resource management that balanced immediate needs with long-term sustainability while recognizing the spiritual and symbolic significance of animal relationships.

The concept of sacred landscapes provides crucial theoretical frameworks for understanding how Western Mexican societies integrated environmental knowledge with cosmological beliefs and ceremonial practices that gave spiritual meaning to geographical features and natural processes. Archaeological evidence indicates that mountains, lakes, caves, and other distinctive landscape features served as focal points for ceremonial activity and pilgrimage that connected local communities with broader regional sacred geography. The circular ceremonial architecture of Western Mexico appears to reflect cosmological principles that emphasized the sacred significance of natural cycles and landscape relationships while providing architectural expressions of these spiritual concepts. The integration of astronomical observations with landscape features and ceremonial architecture suggests sophisticated understanding of natural cycles and their spiritual significance for human community organization and cultural identity.

The ethnographic and ethnohistorical evidence for contemporary indigenous environmental knowledge and land management practices in Western Mexico provides crucial insights into the persistence and transformation of environmental relationships that may reflect continuities with prehistoric cultural systems. The Huichol (Wixáritari) communities maintain sophisticated ecological knowledge and ceremonial practices that recognize the spiritual significance of natural systems while providing practical guidance for sustainable resource management and landscape stewardship. Their contemporary practices include systematic attention to seasonal cycles, water management, plant cultivation, and animal relationships that demonstrate the persistence of indigenous environmental knowledge systems despite centuries of cultural disruption and environmental change. The integration of practical environmental management with spiritual practice and community organization provides models for understanding how prehistoric societies may have embedded environmental knowledge within broader cultural systems.

The theoretical implications of environmental relationships in Western Mexico's prehistory extend beyond regional concerns to encompass fundamental questions about human-environment relationships, sustainable development, and the cultural dimensions of ecological adaptation. The archaeological evidence demonstrates that sophisticated forms of social complexity can emerge through sustainable environmental relationships that maintain ecosystem integrity while supporting dense populations and complex cultural institutions. The environmental management systems developed by Western Mexican societies provide historical examples of sustainable development that achieved long-term cultural continuity while maintaining environmental quality and resource availability. These historical precedents offer insights relevant to contemporary environmental challenges while demonstrating the potential for human societies to achieve sustainable relationships with natural systems through appropriate technologies, social organization, and cultural values.

The comparative analysis of environmental relationships across different regions and time periods reveals both universal patterns and distinctive innovations in human environmental adaptation that provide broader theoretical insights into the possibilities and limitations of sustainable development. The Western Mexican case demonstrates that environmental diversity can serve as a foundation for cultural innovation and regional distinctiveness while also facilitating cultural exchange and integration through specialization and trade relationships. The ability of Western Mexican societies to maintain cultural coherence across diverse environmental settings while developing distinctive adaptive strategies for different ecological zones provides important insights into the relationship between environmental diversity and cultural development that remain relevant for understanding contemporary patterns of cultural and environmental change.

The methodological approaches developed for studying environmental relationships in Western Mexico's prehistory provide models for contemporary interdisciplinary research that integrates archaeological evidence with environmental science, ethnographic research, and indigenous knowledge systems. The systematic documentation of ancient agricultural systems, water management installations, and resource extraction sites requires collaboration between archaeologists, environmental scientists, and indigenous community members that can produce more comprehensive understanding while respecting indigenous intellectual property and cultural values. The integration of multiple analytical approaches and knowledge systems provides more robust interpretations while establishing ethical frameworks for contemporary research that recognizes indigenous communities as partners rather than subjects in archaeological investigation.

The contemporary relevance of Western Mexico's prehistoric environmental relationships extends beyond academic concerns to encompass practical applications for sustainable development, cultural preservation, and environmental restoration that address current social and environmental challenges. The sophisticated environmental management systems documented in the archaeological record provide historical examples of sustainable practices that maintained ecosystem integrity while supporting human welfare over extended periods. The integration of traditional ecological knowledge with contemporary environmental science offers opportunities for developing more effective approaches to environmental management that combine indigenous wisdom with modern analytical capabilities while respecting cultural values and community autonomy. The Western Mexican case demonstrates the potential for archaeological research to contribute to contemporary environmental challenges

ALLEN SCHERY

while honoring indigenous knowledge and supporting cultural continuity in indigenous communities.

Chapter Three

The Deep Past – Paleoindian and Archaic Foundations (13,000-1500 BCE)

The earliest human presence in Western Mexico extends deep into the Late Pleistocene, when mobile hunter-gatherer bands first crossed the dramatically different landscapes that would later support some of Mesoamerica's most distinctive cultural developments. These Paleoindian pioneers, arriving between 13,000 and 11,000 years ago, encountered vast pluvial lakes, expanded grasslands, and megafaunal populations that provided rich subsistence opportunities while demanding sophisticated adaptive strategies and technological innovations. The philosophical implications of this earliest chapter in Western Mexico's human story extend far beyond simple chronological priority, encompassing fundamental questions about human creativity, environmental adaptation, and the origins of the cultural traditions that would eventually produce the region's unique architectural and social achievements. Understanding these deep foundations requires theoretical frameworks capable of recognizing both universal patterns of human adaptation and the specific environmental and cultural circumstances that shaped Western Mexico's distinctive trajectory within broader American prehistory.

Archaeological evidence for Paleoindian occupation throughout Western Mexico includes distinctive fluted projectile points that connect the region to the continent-wide Clovis cultural tradition, while also revealing regional adaptations that presage later patterns of local innovation within broader cultural frameworks. The El Bajío site in Sonora, containing nine Clovis points collected from a single location, represents the largest known Clovis site in western North America and demonstrates the importance of Western Mexico within early continental settlement patterns. Located in a large basin bounded by mountains and hills approximately eighty kilometers northeast of Hermosillo, El Bajío provides stratigraphic evidence for the transition from Late Pleistocene to Holocene environments, including the distinctive "black mat" layer found at Clovis sites throughout western North America. The artifacts recovered from this and related sites reveal sophisticated lithic technologies adapted to diverse hunting and processing tasks, indicating that Paleoindian groups possessed advanced knowledge of stone tool manufacture and maintenance that enabled effective exploitation of varied environmental resources.

The distribution of Clovis points throughout Western Mexico, from Guaymas northward through Sonora and extending south to Jalisco, suggests occupation zones that followed natural corridors between highland and coastal environments while maintaining technological and cultural connections to broader continental networks. Thirteen documented Clovis sites and twenty-one isolated point occurrences in Sonora alone indicate systematic rather than sporadic occupation, revealing settlement patterns that took advantage of diverse ecological zones within relatively compact geographical areas. The Pacific coastal corridor appears to have played a particularly important role in facilitating southward movement of Paleoindian groups, providing access to marine resources while maintaining connections to inland hunting territories and raw material sources. This pattern of coastal-inland integration would persist throughout Western Mexico's prehistory, influencing trade networks, settlement distributions, and cultural exchange relationships that continued into historic periods.

Paleoindian technology in Western Mexico reveals sophisticated understanding of lithic raw materials and tool manufacture techniques that enabled effective adaptation to diverse environmental challenges while maintaining cultural connections to broader technological traditions. Typical Clovis points from the region exhibit the characteristic fluted lanceolate form, measuring between one and two inches wide and approximately four inches long, with carefully pressure-flaked edges and distinctive concave flutes removed from one or both blade surfaces. The technical skill required for flute removal, combined with evidence for systematic blade resharpening and tool recycling, demonstrates advanced technological knowledge that supported extended use-lives for valuable stone tools while enabling adaptation to varied hunting and processing requirements. Associated lithic assemblages include large bifacial knives, scrapers, and specialized tools for hide processing, bone working, and plant processing that reveal diverse subsistence strategies extending beyond the big-game hunting traditionally associated with Clovis cultures.

The environmental context for Paleoindian occupation in Western Mexico differed significantly from contemporary conditions, with cooler and drier climates supporting vegetation communities and animal populations that required different adaptive strategies than those employed by later prehistoric groups. Late Pleistocene environments included expanded grasslands, higher elevation pine forests, and pluvial lakes that provided rich but seasonally variable resource bases requiring sophisticated knowledge of environmental cycles and resource scheduling. Archaeological evidence suggests that Paleoindian groups developed comprehensive understanding of these environmental patterns, timing their movements to take advantage of seasonal resource availability while maintaining technological flexibility for responding to environmental variation and resource unpredictability. The success of these early adaptations provided the foundation for subsequent cultural developments while establishing patterns of environmental knowledge and technological innovation that would characterize Western Mexican cultures throughout prehistory.

The transition from Paleoindian to Archaic cultural adaptations in Western Mexico reflects both continental-scale climatic changes and regional environmental transformations that required fundamental adjustments in subsistence strategies, settlement patterns, and technological systems. Beginning around 10,000 years ago, Holocene warming and the extinction of Pleistocene megafauna eliminated many traditional Paleoindian resources while creating new opportunities for exploitation of smaller game, plant resources, and marine environments. This transition, rather than representing cultural replacement or demographic discontinuity, appears to reflect adaptive flexibility within continuing human populations that developed new technological and organizational strategies for succeeding in transformed environmental contexts. Archaeological evidence indicates gradual rather than abrupt changes in projectile point styles, lithic technologies, and site distributions, suggesting cultural continuity combined with innovative responses to changing environmental opportunities and constraints.

Early Archaic adaptations in Western Mexico emphasized increased reliance on locally available wild plant resources and small game animals that required different hunting technologies and processing techniques than those employed during Paleoindian periods. Small-stemmed dart points and atlatl technology replaced fluted points and associated hunting systems, while grinding stones, manos, and metates became increasingly important for processing plant foods that assumed greater dietary significance. Archaeological sites from this period reveal diverse tool assemblages including specialized implements for plant processing, hide working, and wood working that indicate expanding technological repertoires adapted to more intensive exploitation of local environmental resources. Settlement patterns shifted toward greater residential stability, with repeated occupation of favorable locations that provided access to diverse resource zones while supporting larger group sizes and longer occupation episodes than typically associated with Paleoindian mobility patterns.

The development of early agricultural systems during the Late Archaic period represents one of the most significant transformations in Western Mexico's prehistory, establishing the subsistence foundations that would support all subsequent cultural elaborations while fundamentally altering human relationships with environmental systems. Archaeological evidence indicates that cultivation of maize, beans, and squash began around 7,000 years ago in Mesoamerica generally, with Western Mexico participating in this continental-scale agricultural revolution through adoption and local adaptation of domesticated crops originally developed in other regions. The integration of these domesticates with continuing wild resource exploitation created mixed subsistence systems that provided greater security and surplus production capacity while maintaining adaptive flexibility for responding to environmental variation and resource fluctuations. This agricultural transition required sophisticated understanding of plant biology, soil management, water control, and seasonal scheduling that represented fundamental expansions in environmental knowledge and technological capability.

The Three Sisters agricultural complex of maize, beans, and squash achieved particular significance throughout Western Mexico and broader American regions due to the ecological and nutritional complementarity of these crops, which provided complete protein when consumed together while supporting soil fertility through nitrogen fixation. Archaeological evidence indicates that these crops were typically cultivated using companion planting techniques that maximized productive efficiency while minimizing soil depletion, demonstrating sophisticated understanding of ecological relationships and sustainable agricultural practices. Maize served as a natural trellis for climbing beans, while squash provided living mulch that retained soil moisture and suppressed weed growth, creating integrated agricultural systems that achieved high productivity with minimal external inputs. The successful adaptation of these crops to Western Mexico's diverse environmental conditions required detailed knowledge of local climate patterns, soil conditions, and water availability that enabled agricultural expansion throughout the region's varied ecological zones.

Early ceramic traditions in Western Mexico emerged during the Late Archaic period as part of broader technological innovations associated with increased sedentism and agricultural intensification, providing new capabilities for food storage, processing, and serving that supported larger group sizes and more complex social organization. The earliest ceramics were relatively simple brown wares with minimal decoration, designed primarily for utilitarian functions including cooking, storage, and water transport that addressed practical needs of increasingly settled communities. Technological analysis reveals sophisticated understanding of clay preparation, temper selection, firing techniques, and vessel construction that enabled production of durable containers adapted to specific functional requirements while expressing emerging aesthetic preferences and cultural identities. The gradual elaboration of ceramic technologies and decorative systems provides evidence for increasing technological specialization and artistic innovation that would culminate in the spectacular ceramic traditions of later periods.

Settlement patterns during the Archaic period reveal increasing commitment to particular locations and environmental zones, with repeated reoccupation of favorable sites that provided access to diverse resources while supporting growing populations through intensified subsistence strategies. Early villages emerged around 3,000 BCE in protected highland valleys where reliable water sources, fertile soils, and diverse resource bases enabled year-round occupation while supporting the agricultural experimentation and technological innovation that characterized this transitional period. These early settlements featured simple residential structures, storage facilities, and communal work areas that indicate increasing social cooperation and coordination while maintaining the egalitarian social organization typical of hunter-gatherer societies. The gradual expansion of these villages and the emergence of site hierarchies suggest developing social complexity and territorial organization that would provide the foundation for later political and ceremonial elaboration.

Mortuary practices during the Archaic period provide crucial insights into emerging concepts of social identity, spiritual beliefs, and community organization that would influence later cultural developments throughout Western Mexico. Early burial practices included simple pit interments with minimal grave goods, but gradually developed greater complexity and elaboration that suggests emerging social differentiation and spiritual sophistication. The inclusion of ground stone tools, shell ornaments, and other material goods in burial contexts indicates developing concepts of personal identity and social roles that persisted beyond death, while the careful arrangement of bodies and grave goods reveals emerging ritual protocols and spiritual beliefs. Some sites provide evidence for cremation practices that presage later mortuary traditions, suggesting that fundamental spiritual concepts and ritual practices had deep historical roots in Western Mexican cultural development.

Rock art sites throughout Western Mexico provide additional evidence for emerging symbolic systems and spiritual practices that connected local communities with broader landscape features and cosmological concepts. Painted and pecked designs in caves and rock shelters include human figures, animals, and geometric motifs that suggest ritual landscapes where shamanic practices, seasonal ceremonies, and spiritual journeys connected individual and community experience with broader cosmic cycles. The sophisticated artistic techniques and complex iconographic systems evident in these rock art traditions indicate advanced symbolic thinking and aesthetic sensibilities that would influence later artistic developments while providing insight into prehistoric worldview systems and religious practices. The association of many rock art sites with water sources, distinctive topographic features, and astronomical alignments suggests integration of artistic expression with practical knowledge of environmental and celestial cycles that guided community activities and spiritual observances.

The use of ochre and other mineral pigments for both artistic and ceremonial purposes provides evidence for sophisticated understanding of geological resources and their cultural significance that would continue throughout Western Mexico's prehistory. Archaeological evidence from underwater caves in the Yucatán reveals extensive Paleoindian ochre mining operations that required advanced planning, technological innovation, and social coordination to extract high-quality pigments from dangerous underground environments. The sophisticated mining techniques documented at La Mina, including the use of stone tools fashioned from cave formations and the establishment of navigation markers and hearth features hundreds of meters from cave entrances, demonstrate remarkable technological capabilities and organizational sophistication among early populations. The investment of time, energy, and risk required for these mining operations indicates that ochre held profound cultural significance extending beyond simple utilitarian applications to encompass spiritual, social, and artistic dimensions that influenced community identity and individual status.

Technological innovations during the Archaic period established many of the fundamental technical capabilities that would support later cultural elaborations throughout Western Mexico while demonstrating continuing human creativity and adaptive flexibility. Ground stone technology became increasingly sophisticated, with specialized tools for plant processing, hide working, and woodworking that enabled more intensive resource exploitation and expanded craft production capabilities. Basketry, textile production, and other perishable technologies, though poorly preserved archaeologically, appear to have achieved considerable sophistication during this period, providing essential capabilities for food storage, transport, and processing that supported increased sedentism and population growth. The development of specialized tools and techniques for obsidian working, shell ornament production, and other craft activities indicates emerging technological specialization and trade relationships that would become increasingly important in later periods.

The integration of technological innovation with environmental management reveals sophisticated understanding of ecological relationships and sustainable resource use that enabled long-term cultural continuity while supporting growing populations and increasing social complexity. Archaeological evidence indicates that Archaic populations developed effective techniques for managing wild plant resources through selective harvesting, controlled burning, and other interventions that enhanced productivity while maintaining ecosystem stability. These management practices required detailed ecological knowledge and careful coordination among community members, suggesting developing social institutions and collective decision-making processes that would influence later political and social organization. The success of these early environmental management systems provided crucial foundations for later agricultural intensification and population growth while establishing principles of sustainable resource use that would characterize Western Mexican societies throughout prehistory.

Cultural transmission during the Archaic period operated through both vertical inheritance within lineage groups and horizontal exchange among neighboring communities, creating dynamic networks of technological and cultural innovation that facilitated regional integration while maintaining local distinctiveness. Seasonal gatherings for resource procurement became venues for social interaction, mate exchange, and cultural transmission that spread innovations across broad geographical areas while maintaining cultural connections among dispersed communities. The exchange of exotic materials including marine shells, highland obsidian, and specialized manufactured goods indicates developing trade networks that would become increasingly elaborate and extensive in later periods while providing mechanisms for cultural communication and technological diffusion. These early exchange systems established patterns of inter-regional interaction that would influence Western Mexico's role in broader Mesoamerican cultural networks while maintaining the region's distinctive character and innovative capabilities.

Philosophical implications of Archaic cultural developments extend beyond immediate practical concerns to encompass fundamental questions about human nature, cultural creativity, and the relationship between tradition and innovation that would characterize Western Mexican societies throughout prehistory. The successful adaptation to post-Pleistocene environmental changes demonstrates remarkable human flexibility and creativity, revealing cultural systems capable of maintaining coherent identities while continuously adapting to changing circumstances through technological and organizational innovation. The development of agricultural systems represents not merely economic change but fundamental transformation in human-environment relationships that involved new concepts of time, responsibility, and community obligation extending beyond immediate survival needs to encompass future generations and landscape stewardship. These philosophical dimensions of cultural development established conceptual foundations that would influence later religious systems, social organization, and architectural traditions while demonstrating the creative potential and adaptive capability that would distinguish Western Mexican cultural achievements within broader Mesoamerican civilization.

Social organization during the Archaic period maintained essentially egalitarian structures while developing increasing coordination capabilities and collective decision-making processes that would provide foundations for later political complexity and social stratification. Archaeological evidence suggests that leadership roles were primarily situational and task-specific rather than permanent or hereditary, with different individuals assuming authority for hunting expeditions, agricultural activities, or ceremonial events depending on their particular expertise and community recognition. The development of specialized knowledge systems for environmental management, technological production, and ritual practice created opportunities for individual distinction and social recognition while maintaining community cohesion and collective resource access. These early patterns of social organization established principles of earned authority and specialized expertise that would influence later political systems while maintaining cultural values emphasizing community welfare and collective responsibility.

Gender roles and family organization during the Archaic period reveal complex divisions of labor and social responsibility that integrated economic efficiency with cultural reproduction and community continuity. Archaeological evidence suggests that men typically assumed primary responsibility for hunting, tool manufacture, and long-distance travel, while women focused on plant resource processing, textile production, and child care, though these divisions were flexible and situational rather than rigid and absolute. Both men and women participated in agricultural activities, with gender-specific roles in different aspects of crop production, processing, and storage that required coordination and cooperation between family members and community groups. The importance of women's knowledge systems for plant biology, food processing, and resource management suggests significant female authority and influence in community decision-making processes, particularly regarding subsistence strategies and resource allocation that affected community welfare and survival.

Territorial organization and resource management during the Archaic period reveal developing concepts of landscape ownership and community boundaries that balanced exclusive access rights with reciprocal obligations and sharing arrangements. Archaeological site distributions suggest that communities maintained preferred access to particular resource zones while recognizing similar rights of neighboring groups and establishing protocols for shared use of seasonal or specialized resources. The development of these territorial systems required sophisticated understanding of resource distributions, seasonal availability patterns, and sustainable harvest levels that could support community needs while maintaining long-term resource productivity. These early concepts of territory and resource management established precedents for later political organization while demonstrating the integration of practical resource management with social and spiritual concepts that recognized landscape features as sacred spaces with intrinsic value beyond immediate economic utility.

Trade networks and cultural exchange during the Archaic period established patterns of inter-regional interaction that would influence Western Mexico's distinctive role within broader American cultural systems while facilitating technological and cultural innovation through contact with diverse traditions. Archaeological evidence indicates systematic exchange of marine shells from Pacific coastal sources, obsidian from highland volcanic sources, and manufactured goods including stone tools, textiles, and ornamental objects that connected Western Mexican communities with trading partners across continental distances. The scale and systematic nature of these early exchange systems required sophisticated organizational capabilities, standardized value systems, and reliable transportation networks that enabled effective coordination across diverse cultural and linguistic boundaries. These early trading relationships established Western Mexico's role as a cultural corridor connecting Mesoamerican civilizations with North American societies while facilitating the cultural innovations and technological developments that would characterize the region throughout prehistory.

Continuities and transformations in cultural development reveal complex patterns of innovation and tradition that established the fundamental characteristics distinguishing Western Mexican societies within broader Mesoamerican civilization. Archaeological evidence indicates that basic subsistence strategies, technological systems, and social organization patterns established during the Archaic period provided stable foundations that supported later cultural elaborations while maintaining adaptive flexibility for responding to changing environmental and social circumstances. The integration of agricultural intensification with continuing wild resource exploitation created resilient subsistence systems that could support growing populations and increasing social complexity while maintaining environmental sustainability and cultural continuity. These patterns of adaptive innovation within traditional frameworks would characterize Western Mexican cultural development throughout prehistory, enabling the distinctive architectural traditions, social systems, and cultural achievements that would distinguish the region within Mesoamerican civilization while maintaining connections to broader continental cultural networks.

The foundations established during the Paleoindian and Archaic periods thus provided both material and conceptual prerequisites for the remarkable cultural florescence that would characterize later Western Mexican prehistory, demonstrating human creative potential while establishing sustainable relationships between cultural and environmental systems that would support sophisticated civilizational achievements. The successful adaptation to diverse and changing environmental conditions revealed innovative capabilities and adaptive flexibility that would enable later cultural innovations while maintaining cultural continuity and regional distinctiveness. The development of agricultural systems, technological specializations, and social institutions during these early periods established organizational capabilities and knowledge systems that would support the architectural monumentality, artistic sophistication, and social complexity that would emerge during subsequent cultural phases. Most importantly, the integration of practical adaptation with symbolic and spiritual dimensions of cultural life established conceptual frameworks recognizing the meaningful and creative dimensions of human cultural activity that would distinguish Western Mexican societies as innovative and sophisticated contributors to broader patterns of human cultural development and civilizational achievement.

Chapter Four
The Shaft Tomb Revolution – Mortuary Complexity and Social Stratification (1500 BCE - 400 CE)

The development of the shaft tomb tradition in Western Mexico represents one of the most dramatic mortuary innovations in prehistoric Mesoamerica, establishing architectural and social foundations that would distinguish the region for over eighteen centuries while providing unprecedented insights into ancient concepts of death, ancestry, and social organization. This remarkable burial tradition, characterized by deep vertical shafts opening into subterranean chambers containing multiple interments and elaborate grave goods, emerged initially at El Opeño in Michoacán around 1500 BCE before spreading throughout the western states of Jalisco, Nayarit, and Colima during the centuries immediately preceding the

Common Era. The philosophical implications of shaft tomb construction extend far beyond mere mortuary practice to encompass fundamental questions about human relationships with death, the persistence of social identity beyond biological existence, and the role of monumental labor investment in creating and maintaining social hierarchies within emerging complex societies. Understanding this tradition requires theoretical frameworks capable of recognizing both the universal human concerns with death and afterlife that motivate mortuary elaboration and the specific cultural innovations that made Western Mexican shaft tombs unique within broader patterns of Mesoamerican cultural development.

The earliest manifestation of shaft tomb architecture at El Opeño in northwestern Michoacán provides crucial evidence for the origins and initial development of this distinctive mortuary tradition while demonstrating its antiquity relative to other Mesoamerican cultural achievements. Dating to approximately 1600-1200 BCE, the El Opeño tombs represent the oldest known mortuary monuments in Mesoamerica, predating even the emergence of Olmec civilization and challenging traditional assumptions about the temporal and geographical origins of complex society in ancient Mexico. Each tomb contained multiple individuals of both sexes interred over extended periods, suggesting family or lineage crypts that were reused across generations while accumulating elaborate assemblages of grave goods that indicate significant wealth differentiation and social stratification. The labor investment required for tomb construction—vertical shafts extending 3-7 meters into volcanic tuff with carefully excavated chambers measuring up to 4 by 4 meters—demonstrates organizational capabilities and economic surplus that enabled monumental construction projects reserved for elite members of society.

The ceramic assemblages from El Opeño reveal sophisticated artistic traditions and technological capabilities that established precedents for later developments throughout Western Mexico while providing insights into early concepts of personal identity and social differentiation. The pottery includes plain bowls and small vessels decorated with linear incisions, punctuation, and appliqué techniques similar to contemporary ceramics from Tlatilco in central Mexico, suggesting broad cultural connections and shared technological traditions across Mesoamerica during the Early Formative period. The presence of negative painted decoration, rendered in red and black pigments, may represent the earliest predecessor of the negative painting techniques that would characterize later Tarascan pottery, indicating remarkable continuity in technological and aesthetic traditions across more than two millennia of cultural development. The quality and variety of ceramic grave goods, combined with evidence for specialized production techniques and exotic materials, demonstrate emerging craft specialization and economic differentiation that supported the social hierarchies reflected in differential burial treatment.

The geographic distribution and temporal development of shaft tomb traditions throughout Western Mexico reveal complex patterns of cultural diffusion, local innovation, and regional adaptation that shaped the distinctive characteristics of mortuary practices in different areas while maintaining underlying conceptual and architectural continuities. The tradition spread from its origins in Michoacán northward into Jalisco, Nayarit, and Colima during the Late Formative period, reaching its greatest elaboration between 300 BCE and 400 CE in the highland valleys around Teuchitlán, Jalisco, which constitute the "undisputed core" of the shaft tomb tradition. Regional variations in tomb architecture, ceramic styles, and burial practices reflect local environmental conditions, cultural preferences, and social organizational patterns while maintaining common elements that indicate shared cosmological concepts and mortuary ideologies. The persistence of shaft tomb construction across such extensive geographical and temporal ranges demonstrates the enduring significance of the underlying cultural concepts and social functions that motivated this distinctive form of mortuary elaboration.

The architectural characteristics of Western Mexican shaft tombs reveal sophisticated engineering capabilities and detailed understanding of geological conditions that enabled construction of durable subterranean monuments in challenging volcanic environments. Typical tombs feature vertical or nearly vertical shafts ranging from 3 to 20 meters in depth, excavated through often challenging volcanic tuff using stone tools and human labor coordinated through complex organizational systems. The base of each shaft opens into one or more horizontal chambers with carefully constructed walls and low ceilings that create intimate spaces for burial ceremonies and ongoing mortuary activities. The technical skill required for shaft excavation, chamber construction, and structural stability demonstrates advanced understanding of geological processes, soil mechanics, and construction techniques that enabled creation of permanent underground spaces suitable for repeated use over extended periods.

The association of shaft tombs with overlying buildings and surface architecture reveals integrated approaches to mortuary commemoration that connected subterranean burial spaces with above-ground ceremonial and residential activities. Archaeological evidence indicates that many tombs were deliberately positioned beneath important structures, creating vertical relationships between burial chambers and surface buildings that enabled ongoing interaction between the living and the dead through ritual activities and ancestral veneration. This architectural integration suggests sophisticated concepts of sacred space that recognized death as transition rather than termination while providing mechanisms for maintaining social relationships across the boundary between life and afterlife. The coordination required for such complex construction projects demonstrates social organizational capabilities and collaborative labor systems that enabled community mobilization for monumental construction while expressing collective identity through shared mortuary traditions.

The mortuary practices documented within shaft tombs provide detailed insights into ancient concepts of death, social identity, and spiritual transformation that reveal sophisticated philosophical frameworks for understanding human existence and its continuation beyond biological death. Multiple burials in each chamber, with evidence for tomb reuse over extended periods, indicate concepts of collective identity and family continuity that transcended individual lifespans while creating enduring monuments to lineage identity and social status. The careful arrangement of bodies and grave goods according to consistent patterns suggests standardized ritual protocols and spiritual beliefs that guided mortuary treatment while expressing social roles and personal identities through material culture. The inclusion of elaborate ceramic figurines, personal ornaments, utilitarian objects, and food offerings reveals concepts of afterlife that required continued access to material culture and social relationships while providing mechanisms for maintaining connections between living and deceased community members.

The ceramic figurine traditions associated with shaft tombs represent some of the most sophisticated and expressive artistic achievements in prehistoric Mesoamerica, providing unprecedented insights into ancient social life, cultural values, and spiritual beliefs while demonstrating remarkable technical and aesthetic capabilities. These hollow ceramic sculptures, ranging from small portrait-like figures to elaborate multi-figure tableaux depicting complex social scenes, capture details of daily life, ceremonial activities, and mythological narratives with remarkable precision and artistic sophistication. The naturalistic rendering of human subjects, attention to individual characteristics and social roles, and depiction of emotional states reveal advanced understanding of human psychology and social relationships while providing ethnographic insights into ancient community life that would otherwise remain inaccessible through archaeological evidence. The technical mastery demonstrated in ceramic construction, surface treatment, and firing techniques indicates specialized craft production and artistic training that supported full-time artisans capable of creating masterworks for elite patrons.

Regional stylistic variations in shaft tomb ceramics reflect local cultural preferences and artistic traditions while maintaining underlying thematic and conceptual continuities that indicate shared mythological and spiritual frameworks throughout Western Mexico. The Ameca style of Jalisco features elongated faces with high foreheads, prominent braided or turban-like headgear, aquiline noses, and wide staring eyes created through applied clay fillets that produce distinctive expressions suggesting spiritual states or ritual transformation. Colima ceramics emphasize smooth, rounded forms rendered in warm brown-red slips, with particular emphasis on animal subjects including the famous plump dogs that served as psychopomps guiding souls through afterlife journeys. Nayarit traditions include elaborate multi-figure compositions depicting architectural complexes, ceremonial activities, and social gatherings that provide detailed insights into ancient building techniques, ritual practices, and community organization. These regional variations demonstrate local innovation within shared cultural frameworks while providing evidence for inter-regional exchange and cultural communication across Western Mexico.

The subject matter and iconographic content of shaft tomb ceramics reveal sophisticated narrative traditions and mythological systems that provided frameworks for understanding human experience, social relationships, and cosmic order within ancient Western Mexican societies. Common themes include ancestor pairs depicting male and female figures that may represent founding couples or deceased relatives, emphasizing the importance of marriage relationships and gender complementarity in social organization and spiritual beliefs. Ceramic tableaux show multiple figures engaged in various activities including food preparation, musical performance, ball game participation, and ceremonial gatherings that provide ethnographic insights into ancient social life while expressing cultural values and community identity. The frequent depiction of shamanic figures, warriors, and individuals with physical anomalies suggests complex social hierarchies and specialized roles while revealing cultural concepts of spiritual power, physical difference, and social integration that influenced community organization and individual identity.

The ceramic dog figurines found throughout Western Mexican shaft tombs provide particularly rich insights into ancient concepts of death, spiritual transformation, and human-animal relationships that reveal sophisticated philosophical frameworks for understanding consciousness, identity, and the persistence of being beyond biological existence. These plump, hairless dogs, often depicted in naturalistic poses that capture individual personality and emotional states, served as psychopomps responsible for guiding human souls through dangerous afterlife journeys while providing companionship and protection in unfamiliar spiritual realms. The consistent presence of openings in ceramic dog figurines—through mouths, tails, or specially constructed funnels—indicates concepts of spiritual receptacles that could house human souls during afterlife transitions while enabling ongoing relationships between deceased individuals and their animal companions. The religious significance of dogs as emissaries of Xolotl, the Aztec deity associated with death and the underworld, suggests continuity in spiritual concepts that connected Western Mexican traditions with broader Mesoamerican cosmological frameworks while maintaining distinctive regional characteristics.

The social implications of shaft tomb construction and use reveal complex hierarchical societies with significant wealth differentiation, specialized craft production, and elaborate status display systems that challenge traditional assumptions about social organization during the Late Formative period in Western Mexico. The enormous labor investment required for tomb construction, combined with the wealth and quality of grave goods, demonstrates that shaft tombs were reserved exclusively for elite members of society while providing mechanisms for expressing and perpetuating social distinctions across generations. Archaeological analysis of tomb contents reveals systematic differences in burial treatment, grave good assemblages, and architectural elaboration that reflect complex social hierarchies with multiple levels of status differentiation and specialized roles within emerging complex societies. The evidence for family or lineage-based tomb use suggests hereditary status systems and corporate group organization that enabled wealth accumulation and power concentration within elite families while maintaining social control through ideological and ceremonial mechanisms.

The chronological development of shaft tomb traditions reveals evolving social complexity and changing mortuary practices that reflect broader cultural transformations in Western Mexican societies during the transition from village-based communities to hierarchical chiefdoms and early state-level organization. Early phases of the tradition emphasized relatively simple tomb architecture and modest grave good assemblages, while later developments featured increasingly elaborate underground chambers, sophisticated ceramic art, and wealth accumulations that indicate growing social stratification and economic specialization. The peak of shaft tomb elaboration during the Late Formative and Early Classic periods coincides with evidence for population growth, settlement hierarchy development, and the emergence of monumental surface architecture that suggests coordinated regional political systems and centralized authority structures. The gradual decline of shaft tomb construction after 400 CE coincides with the rise of the Teuchitlán tradition's circular ceremonial complexes, suggesting fundamental changes in social organization and ideological systems that shifted emphasis from lineage-based ancestor veneration to community-based ceremonial integration.

The relationship between shaft tombs and emerging monumental architecture in Western Mexico reveals complex interactions between mortuary practices and public ceremonial systems that reflect evolving concepts of authority, community identity, and sacred landscape organization. Archaeological evidence indicates that some shaft tombs were deliberately positioned in relationship to surface buildings and ceremonial spaces, creating integrated sacred complexes that connected subterranean burial spaces with above-ground ritual activities. The transition from shaft tomb emphasis to circular ceremonial architecture during the Early Classic period suggests fundamental changes in social organization that shifted from lineage-based ancestor veneration to community-based ceremonial integration while maintaining underlying spiritual concepts and ritual practices. This transformation reflects broader patterns of political centralization and ideological change that would characterize the development of complex societies throughout Mesoamerica while maintaining distinctive regional characteristics that distinguished Western Mexican cultural achievements.

Comparative analysis of Western Mexican shaft tombs with mortuary traditions elsewhere in Mesoamerica reveals both universal patterns in the development of social complexity and distinctive innovations that contributed to the diversity of cultural solutions for expressing and maintaining social hierarchies. The labor investment, wealth accumulation, and artistic sophistication evident in shaft tomb construction parallels developments in other Mesoamerican regions while demonstrating alternative approaches to monumental construction and elite display that emphasized subterranean rather than above-ground architectural elaboration. The emphasis on family or lineage-based mortuary commemoration reflects broader Mesoamerican patterns of ancestor veneration and corporate group organization while revealing distinctive approaches to expressing kinship relationships and maintaining social continuity across generations. The integration of artistic expression with mortuary practice demonstrates shared Mesoamerican values emphasizing the importance of aesthetic achievement and cultural sophistication while revealing regional innovations in ceramic technology and narrative art that contributed to broader traditions of Mesoamerican artistic achievement.

The philosophical implications of shaft tomb traditions extend beyond immediate mortuary concerns to encompass fundamental questions about human consciousness, social identity, and the persistence of being that influenced broader cultural development throughout Western Mexico. The elaborate mortuary preparations, ongoing ritual activities, and architectural investments evident in shaft tomb construction reveal sophisticated concepts of personal identity that persisted beyond biological death while maintaining social relationships and community membership through material culture and ceremonial interaction. The integration of individual identity with family or lineage affiliation demonstrates concepts of collective selfhood that balanced personal autonomy with corporate group membership while providing mechanisms for maintaining social continuity and cultural transmission across generations. The artistic traditions associated with shaft tombs reveal aesthetic sensibilities and narrative capabilities that influenced broader cultural development while establishing precedents for later artistic achievements throughout Western Mexican prehistory.

The technological innovations evident in shaft tomb construction and associated ceramic production demonstrate sophisticated understanding of geological processes, materials science, and artistic techniques that established foundations for later cultural achievements throughout Western Mexico. The engineering capabilities required for deep shaft excavation in challenging volcanic environments reveal advanced understanding of soil mechanics, structural stability, and construction coordination that enabled complex architectural projects while supporting specialized craft production and technological innovation. The ceramic technologies developed for figurine production, including hollow construction techniques, sophisticated firing methods, and complex surface treatments, established technical traditions that would influence pottery production throughout Western Mexican prehistory while demonstrating innovative solutions to artistic and functional challenges. The integration of technological innovation with aesthetic achievement reveals cultural values that emphasized both practical capability and artistic sophistication while providing foundations for continued cultural development and regional distinctiveness.

The cultural transmission and diffusion processes evident in shaft tomb traditions reveal complex networks of social interaction, technological exchange, and ideological communication that connected Western Mexican communities with broader Mesoamerican cultural systems while maintaining distinctive regional characteristics. The spread of shaft tomb architecture and associated mortuary practices from Michoacán northward through Jalisco, Nayarit, and Colima demonstrates systematic cultural communication and adaptation that enabled local innovation within shared conceptual frameworks. The stylistic variations and technological adaptations evident in different regions reflect creative responses to local environmental conditions, cultural preferences, and social organizational patterns while maintaining underlying continuities in spiritual concepts and ritual practices. The evidence for long-distance trade in exotic materials, artistic influences, and technological innovations indicates participation in extensive exchange networks that connected Western Mexico with cultural developments throughout Mesoamerica while enabling the distinctive achievements that would characterize the region throughout prehistory.

The contemporary significance and continuing relevance of shaft tomb traditions encompass both scholarly insights into the development of social complexity and practical lessons about sustainable community organization, cultural continuity, and the integration of individual and collective identity within coherent social systems. The evidence for hereditary status systems combined with community-based ceremonial integration provides insights into alternative forms of political organization that balanced elite authority with collective participation while maintaining social cohesion and cultural identity across extended periods. The emphasis on lineage-based identity and ancestor veneration demonstrates mechanisms for maintaining social continuity and cultural transmission that remain relevant for contemporary discussions of community organization and cultural preservation. The artistic achievements and technological innovations evident in shaft tomb traditions provide examples of cultural creativity and aesthetic sophistication that contributed to human cultural heritage while demonstrating the potential for regional distinctiveness within broader patterns of civilizational development.

The shaft tomb revolution thus established fundamental patterns of social organization, cultural expression, and spiritual practice that would influence Western Mexican cultural development throughout prehistory while contributing distinctive innovations to broader Mesoamerican civilization. The sophisticated mortuary architecture, elaborate artistic traditions, and complex social hierarchies evident in shaft tomb construction demonstrate remarkable human creativity and organizational capability while providing insights into alternative pathways to social complexity that expanded the range of possibilities for civilizational achievement. The philosophical frameworks and spiritual concepts embedded in shaft tomb traditions reveal sophisticated understanding of human nature, social relationships, and cosmic order that influenced broader cultural development while establishing foundations for the distinctive achievements that would characterize Western Mexican societies throughout their prehistoric trajectory. Most importantly, the integration of individual identity with collective belonging, technological innovation with aesthetic achievement, and local distinctiveness with broader cultural participation established principles of cultural development that would enable Western Mexican societies to make fundamental contributions to human civilizational achievement while maintaining their distinctive character and innovative capabilities throughout the challenges and opportunities of their remarkable prehistoric development.

Chapter Five
Obsidian Mastery and Trade Networks (200 BCE–900 CE)

In the volcanic landscapes of Western Mexico, obsidian was more than a stone. It was the sharp edge of survival, the medium of ritual sacrifice, the currency of long-distance exchange, and the foundation of political authority. Between 200 BCE and 900 CE, communities across Jalisco, Nayarit, Colima, and Michoacán transformed obsidian into the backbone of their economies and the connective tissue of their societies. To understand the prehistory of this region is to understand the mastery of obsidian: how it was located and claimed, quarried and refined, standardized and distributed, sacralized and monopolized—and how those processes braided the technological, political, and cosmological strands that held Western Mexico together. This chapter follows those strands across quarry floors and workshop courtyards, along ridge-top roads and littoral canoe routes, through ceremonial circles and elite compounds, tracing an industrial logic that grew to scale and an ideological order that turned black glass into power. It also honors the decisive clarity of Phil C. Weigand, whose tireless mapping of sources, reading of landscapes, and defense of Western Mexico's centrality forced a pivot in how scholars narrate this region. In Weigand's hands, obsidian stops being a passive material and becomes a system—a federated network of extraction, specialization, exchange, and meaning.

Western Mexico is marked by volcanic abundance. More than a thousand obsidian sources dot its highlands and intermontane basins, a density unmatched elsewhere in Mesoamerica. The distribution is not uniform, nor is it trivial: nodules and flows vary widely in color, clarity, fracture quality, and inclusion profile, which means not all obsidian is equal in knapping potential or aesthetic value. Communities confronted this mosaic as a strategic landscape. Identifying a high-quality source was the first move; claiming it, defending it, and organizing labor around it were the next. Access was never simply environmental. It was political, and in many places it was ritualized. The path to a quarry might pass through a ceremonial precinct; offerings might mark entrances or boundaries; extraction might be calendrically staged. Phil Weigand's surveys across Jalisco and adjacent areas revealed that many sources were embedded in arrangements of territorial control—rules of passage, signs of ownership, a choreography of who could quarry and when. It is a mistake to think of obsidian as an open commons. In Western Mexico, it was a contested domain, folded into alliance and enmity, tribute and protection, mediation and force.

The scale of production across these centuries was astonishing. A conservative reconstruction places regional output in the realm of tens of thousands of metric tons of tools and preforms. The numbers matter less as crude totals than as windows into organization: middens of debitage rising like berms, floors varnished with microflakes, exhausted cores tossed to the edges of workshops by the dozens, then by the hundreds. At Teuchitlán and neighboring centers, knapping debris accumulates in layers that read as calendars of production intensity—quiet phases of learning and maintenance, crescendos of standardized blade-making that imply coordination across many hands. In highland ridges around Magdalena and in uplands of northern Jalisco, quarry faces bear scars of repeated strike sequences; slopes carry talus that, when sieved, still sound like broken glass. Such noise—the percussion of hammerstones and antler tines, the controlled shiver of conchoidal fracture—was the daily rhythm of places organized around obsidian. The analogy with steel is not indulgent. Obsidian is not malleable, yet it was indispensable: for clearing fields and processing agave, butchering game and crafting domestic implements, equipping warriors and sanctifying altars. Its ubiquity made it the silent infrastructure of social reproduction. Control of that infrastructure—who owned the quarry and the road; who trained knappers and managed quality; who stored preforms and monetized blades—was not incidental to politics. It was politics.

Technological mastery in Western Mexico was not derivative, and it was not static. By 200 BCE, experienced knappers were already working through complex reduction sequences, balancing percussion and pressure flaking to produce bifaces, points, and cutting implements suited to varied tasks. By the turn of the millennium, standardized prismatic blade technology—drawing on prepared polyhedral cores, striking with attention to platform angle and scar geometry—anchors production. The prismatic blade revolution is both a technical and an organizational achievement. It requires careful core preparation, trained muscle memory, and consistent platform rejuvenation; it also presupposes an environment in which hundreds or thousands of blades per week can be used or exported. The technology travels, but it is also localized. Western Mexico's knappers adapted platform widths to local obsidian fracture profiles, altered blade thickness for tools intended for wet coastal versus dry upland tasks, and learned to bend the line between efficiency and durability depending on the market. Phil Weigand saw this as dialogue, not imitation: a technical conversation that linked Western Mexico with Central Mexican centers, sharing innovations, borrowing methods, and asserting independence through style. The adoption of prismatic blade cores did not flatten local traditions. In many workshops one sees parallel sequences: blade core reduction in one corner, bifacial work two benches away, with apprentices circulating and masters supervising, each technique anchored in its own microculture of tools, gestures, and pedagogy.

These workshops were not haphazard. The organization of extraction and processing shows a proto-industrial logic. Extraction teams quarreled nodules with consistent spacing, then staged initial reduction near the quarry mouth to reduce weight and weed out flawed material. Donkeys or human porters ferried preforms to workshops where finishing happened under a different regime: with light, with peers, with quality control. Some workshops specialized, producing only blades or only points; others were polyvalent, adjusting output to demand. Inventories had rhythms: dry-season production feeding planting tools, and times of martial tension padding caches of points. Tool standardization implies measurement—if not with rulers then with repeated hand calibrations and a master's corrections—and it implies storage and accounts. Knapping is tactile and visual, but when scaled it becomes administrative. Where blades were destined for redistribution, one finds evidence of bundling: sets wrapped in fiber, preforms stacked in baskets. This movement from quarry to bench to market maps onto political organization. It insinuates craft specialists whose economic identity is defined by skill and production, and it implies oversight by elites who turn obsidian into revenue.

Exchange systems radiated outward from these production nodes. Within Western Mexico, highland sources fed lowland communities whose work—the fishing economy of coastal Colima, the salt-making along brackish lagoons, the horticultural zones of river valleys—required cutting and scraping implements, and whose own products were desirable up-slope. The exchange is ecological, but it is also institutional. Phil Weigand tracked predictable artifact distributions that point to regularized routes: not the occasional passing barter but routinized flows with guardianship and scheduling. Roads, often ridge-tracing, connected ceremonial and residential clusters; smaller tracks slipped into drainages and out to coastal landing points. Along these routes, obsidian moved alongside maize and agave products, shell ornaments and copper precursors, ceramics and fermented beverages. Exchange was social embeddedness as much as commerce: kin networks brokered deals; ritual calendars underwrote fairs; marriage alliances shaped who supplied whom.

The reach extended beyond the region. Obsidian from Western Mexico threads into Central Mexican contexts that signal long-distance caravans, nodal markets, and ideological circuits. The mechanics of transport varied. Overland portage moved prefabricated cores;

coastal canoe navigation moved packaged tools up and down the Pacific littoral; riverine corridors linked interior points to ocean channels. The existence of such flows makes two claims. First, Western Mexico was fully integrated into pan-Mesoamerican exchange, not isolated or marginal. Second, the integration was not only economic. It was cosmological and political. Obsidian is a ritual material, a choice for bloodletting and sacrifice, a polished mirror for divination and reflection. When blades and mirrors circulate, they carry ideology. They bring the ritual grammar of other centers and export Western Mexico's own iconographies and practices outward, making exchange a vehicle for shared liturgies and contested meanings. Weigand's reframing of Western Mexico hinges on this: the region participates in, and helps produce, the broader civilizational pattern.

Monopoly emerges in the wake of such flows as a structure of power. Control of source access, workshop production schedules, and route security converts material into advantage. Elites do not simply own quarries; they modulate supply, privilege allies and punish enemies, extract tribute payable in bundles of blades and point lots, enforce standards to protect reputation, and reserve ritual-grade obsidian for liturgical performance. In political economics terms, obsidian is a currency of governance. It pays for building projects in ceremonial centers, underwrites maintenance of retainers and patrols, anchors gift economies that cement alliances, and moves in and out of elite residences as a sign of curated abundance. When crisis strikes—drought, border conflict, leadership transition—control of obsidian allows elites to act: lowering prices to ease subsistence strain, stockpiling to prepare for war, staging ritual distributions to signal continuity. The power is real, but it is never total. Master knappers carry their own leverage. Their skill, embodied and slow to learn, cannot be mass-produced by fiat. Good knappers are valued; their apprenticeship lines are curated; their allegiance has to be negotiated. In this equilibrium, technological knowledge is not just a means of production; it is social capital, held by bodies and taught across generations, mobilized as a resource in its own right.

Craft specialization thus blooms into occupational identity. Knappers are not generic laborers; they are bearers of technique and reputation. In many places they form guild-like clusters—kin-based, apprentice-structured, with rules about teaching and tool use. The room where blades are made has an ethic: the apprentice's first pressures are supervised and their mistakes corrected; the master's eye tracks platform angles and scar patterns; failures are discarded and successes celebrated. Such communities of practice are not only economic. They are political subjects subject to elite oversight and popular respect, and they are cultural producers generating aesthetic norms and ritual possibilities. If obsidian is the backbone of the economy, knappers are the spinal column's discs: they absorb pressure and help the whole bend without breaking.

As obsidian courses through regional networks, inequality deepens its grooves. Elites accumulate material and symbolic capital by controlling obsidian flows. They preside over ritual uses that sanctify their authority, stage displays that reorder social vision, and equip warriors whose force sustains the political order. Commoners labor in quarries, carry loads, and cut their fingers learning to pressure flake. The gap is not only in possession but in access. Those who can reach high-quality obsidian have better tools, make better yields, and live under different daily conditions than those who cannot. Yet inequality is not uniform. Periods of political limitation or ideological generosity open access via periodic fairs or redistribution ceremonies, and some communities build strength by leveraging coastal trade to counterbalance highland monopolies. Even within elite circles, competition can unsettle concentration: lineages vie for the right to stage obsidian-rich rituals, and the public's memory of generosity or austerity becomes a vote in the next succession. Obsidian sits at the center of these contests; its glitter is never neutral.

All this speaks to the agency of technology in human life. Obsidian cuts, and its sharpness shapes what people do. It is brittle, and its fragility disciplines how tools are wielded and stored, where they can be repaired and when they must be replaced. It invites innovation because it demands it: a point that breaks at the shoulder forces redesign; a blade that shatters under torque teaches the limits of pressure; a nodule with internal banding requires a different approach to core preparation. Obsidian's qualities do not act alone; they act in concert with human bodies, with learned gestures and tacit techniques, with cosmologies that interpret the break as a sign and the polish as a mirror. In this sense, obsidian is not passive. It participates in history by affording and constraining actions, by pushing communities toward certain forms of organization and not others, by knitting technological learning to social identity. Philosophically, this is technological agency—not as anthropomorphic projection, but as recognition that material properties have historical force when entangled with human practice.

Innovation travels through those entanglements. The spread of prismatic blade technology is the conspicuous example, but smaller innovations matter: platform rejuvenation tricks that extend core life, polishing techniques that improve mirror quality, pressure grips that reduce apprentice injuries, transport packages that lower loss rates on long routes. Innovations are not abstract; they are embodied in sequences of movement, words of instruction, and social rituals of achievement. Many are apprenticeships coded with status. A master's willingness to teach a particular trick is a gift, a covenant, sometimes a control mechanism that binds talent to place. Cultural transmission here is not copying; it is creative revision under constraint, a dialogue in which peripheral communities are not mere recipients but co-authors. Western Mexico's dialogue with Central Mexico is not dependency. It is co-invention, framed by different landscapes and market ecologies, each side bringing obsidian into its own cosmological orbit.

As exchange and production intensify, environmental questions surface. Quarrying is not agriculture, but it has ecological footprints: cutting paths, eroding slopes, churning talus, concentrating human traffic around brittle landscapes. Workshops leave their own traces: tool dust, human waste, concentrated activity that alters small ecologies over decades. Western Mexico's abundance—the sheer number of sources and the varying scales at which they were used—may have buffered depletion, but abundance did not make exploitation costless. Communities learned how to rotate extraction points, how to rest a quarry face, how to balance immediate demand against long-run sustainability. The lessons are pragmatic; they are also cosmological. If obsidian is ritually marked, extraction is ritually policed. A quarry is not a mere hole in earth; it is an entrance to a domain that demands respect. Ritual closures and ceremonial openings do practical work: they slow use, govern timing, and make people attend to limits. Sustainability in this context is not modern resource management. It is a tapestry where practical, ritual, and political threads are woven together.

Turn now to places, to flesh the general dynamics with case evidence. The Teuchitlán Tradition in Jalisco anchors the narrative with its circular ceremonial centers—architectural forms that align with ritual choreography, social ordering, and economic coordination. These circles, sometimes complex with multiple concentric rings, are not only liturgical spaces but hubs where redistribution occurs, where markets gather under elite supervision, and where obsidian's movement is made legible. Workshops cluster around such centers and along approach roads; middens of knapping debris mark neighborhoods where production is concentrated. The proximity is not accidental. It is managerial, enabling elite oversight of quality and volume, and it is symbolic, tying production of blades used in ritual to the precincts where ritual validates rule. Phil Weigand's interpretations of these centers emphasized their integrative function: they bring together ceremony and economy, governance and craft, making the circular space a technology of social coordination as much as an expression of cosmology.

Elsewhere, production landscapes sketch variations on this theme. In the uplands of northern Jalisco and into Zacatecas, sites like La Quemada show defensive architecture and evidence of long-distance exchange, with obsidian signaling ties into Western Mexican sources and Central Mexican markets. The setting—hilltop fortifications, visual command of surrounding valleys—suggests a political ecology in which control of movement matters. Blades and points found here register both local use and passing trade, and the rhythm of production debris implies fluctuating intensity tied to security demands and seasonal pulses. Further west, in Nayarit and Colima, coastal communities carry obsidian inland and return marine products, salt, and decorative shellwork. The balance is not simple. In some periods, coastal routes outcompete inland ridge roads for speed and safety; in others, seasonal storms and conflict make ridge paths more reliable. Along those paths, small redistribution nodes act as buffers and brokers, aggregating obsidian from multiple workshops and shipping standardized packages onward. A node's success turns on trust and reputation. If a package arrives with blades chipped or points fragile, a node's name suffers and elites reconsider contracts.

Michoacán's obsidian, notably from Ucareo and Zinapécuaro, enters this Western system as both complement and competitor. Sourcing studies show Western material circulating into Michoacán and Michoacán material flowing west. Where they meet, one sees choices: tools made of different sources for different tasks, mirror production clustered around sources with suitable clarity, and status signaling through selection—an elite might prefer a particular obsidian for its color or provenance to mark distinction. Such choice is not trivial. It tells a story about taste, ideology, and the grammar of value. It also tells a story about integration: Western Mexico's obsidian world is not sealed; it is porous and dynamic, plugging into adjacent regions and recalibrating as political tides and ritual fashions shift.

Within communities, the human texture of production gives the chapter its pulse. Picture a workshop at mid-morning. The master sits at the center, cores arranged to his left, hammerstones and pressure flakers to his right. Apprentices squat in a ring, watching every movement. The master's hands are quick but not hurried; he strikes, and a blade peels away clean, the scar on the core neat, the platform still viable. He turns the core, measures angle by feel, strikes again. He pauses to show a grip, to correct a wrist, to explain why an earlier platform failed. Apprentices try, and their mistakes are noisy—platforms crushed, blades shattering. The master shakes his head, smiles, and returns to demonstration. This is a social scene, and a pedagogical one. Authority is gentle but firm. Knowledge is scarce but reproducible only through patience. The economics are visible in the edges of the room: baskets of finished blades, piles of rejects, bundles destined for a trader who will arrive in an hour. In another corner, a knapper works quietly on a biface intended for a ceremonial deposit. The piece is fine; he uses a different tool, polishes the face, checks symmetry like a sculptor. In the afternoon, a trader arrives and counts bundles, inspects a few blades, nods, pays in goods that will be redistributed: maize, salt cakes, cotton thread, a glazed pot requested by a knapper's wife. The trader leaves. The workshop returns to its rhythm. This scene repeats across Western Mexico, with local variations, contributing to a regional hum that is not audible to the past but is readable in debris and distribution.

The politics of this hum can be sharp. Elites extend oversight, sometimes as patrons who invest in workshop spaces and provide tools, sometimes as regulators who enforce quality or levy taxes, sometimes as monopolists who aim to capture surplus. There is tension here. A master knapper's authority in his domain can strain under elite demands, and apprentices' loyalty can shift if another patron offers better terms. Where elites are wise, they treat knappers as precious resources; where they are vain or cruel, they lose control as craft clusters drift or as quality declines under punitive policies. Political equilibrium depends on senses of fairness and shared interest, and it is periodically recalibrated through ritual. When an elite stages a ritual distribution of blades—placing bundles on the ground in a ceremonial circle, inviting commoners to take tools, announcing the gift as a sign of abundance—the economy rejoices and politics strengthen. But ritual distribution carries risk. If bundles are thin or quality is poor, the symbolism backfires. People whisper. Knappers frown. Reputation erodes. Obsidian makes or breaks faces, and faces make or break regimes.

Ritual itself is a thick layer of meaning here. Obsidian blades open skin for bloodletting, a foundational act in many Mesoamerican liturgies. The material participates in sacrificial practice, sometimes as instrument, sometimes as offering. Mirrors made from polished obsidian serve divinatory functions, a depth of black that becomes a portal for seeing. These uses are not peripheral to political economy; they center it. Ritual provides legitimacy; obsidian enacts ritual and makes it visible. Elite control of obsidian for ritual stages ideology: it reads as access to the gods, as mastery over the material that cuts into the body and the veil. Yet ritual also democratizes. In simpler ceremonies, commoners use obsidian tools to mark life passages, to clear fields as offerings, to prepare foods for feasts. Obsidian's presence in these acts ties everyday reproduction to cosmological frameworks. The material is a thread binding domestic cycles to ceremonial cycles, an intimacy that gives politics its endurance.

In building this story, the figure of Phil C. Weigand walks through the archive and the field. Weigand's legacy is not just the mapping of sources and the identification of flows; it is the insistence that Western Mexico belongs at the center of Mesoamerican prehistory. He fought a narrative of peripherality by refusing to let obsidian be local and small. He demonstrated density, showed standardization, traced routes, and interpreted the Teuchitlán Tradition not as quaint or isolated but as complex, integrated, and decisive. In academic terms, he changed the default. Scholars now read Western Mexico as a zone of co-creation, not simply influence from the great Central Mexican centers. Practically, he gave future archaeologists a toolkit: source catalogs, expectations about workshop debris, hypotheses about trade nodes. Philosophically, he asked us to see technology not as external to society but intertwined, with obsidian as an agent of social order. His intuition that obsidian could reframe whole arguments holds in this chapter. Without obsidian, Western Mexico looks different; with it, the region comes into focus as a civilization-making engine.

The final turn is reflective. Between 200 BCE and 900 CE, obsidian was the lifeblood of Western Mexico. It underwrote survival in direct ways—hewing agave, dressing game, carving wood, preparing food—and in social ways—structuring identities, binding communities, stabilizing exchange, legitimizing power. It brought the region into broader circuits of commerce and cosmology, connecting rites and markets, roads and rivers, uplands and coasts. It trained bodies, crafted hands, made ears sensitive to fracture noise and eyes tuned to scar patterns. It was material and metaphor, mundane and sacred. Its mastery required technical skill and organizational intelligence, its trade demanded trust and force, its ritual use needed choreography and belief. This range is why obsidian makes sense as the spine of a chapter and the spine of a civilization. The argument is not that Western Mexico was only obsidian. It is that obsidian illuminates how the region worked: how people turned material into meaning, meaning into order, and order into endurance across seven centuries of change.

If we attend closely, we can see the everyday and the extraordinary overlapping in obsidian's course. An apprentice watches a master, failing, learning, bleeding a little, coming back tomorrow with a better grip. A trader shoulders a basket and walks the ridge road, humming, thinking of salt in his mouth at the coast, trading blades for fish. An elite sits in a circle's interior, holding a polished mirror in both hands, seeing himself and something beyond, staging a distribution ritual that will echo in talk for years. A quarry continues to give, and a slope grows bare, and a community debates closing it for a season to let the earth rest, telling a story about a deity who demands patience. These scenes are not decorative. They are analytic, pulling the technological, economic, social, and philosophical threads through time into a single fabric. Obsidian cuts that fabric into pieces—tools, weapons, mirrors, offerings—and in doing so it reveals the pattern from which those pieces came.

Western Mexico's obsidian world holds lessons beyond its time. It suggests that technology's agency must be read with care: neither an external force that moves humans like puppets nor a neutral substrate on which humans make arbitrary choices, but a co-actor with properties that pull and push within specific ecologies of practice. It suggests that monopoly is relational rather than absolute, dependent on the skill and allegiance of those who make value possible. It suggests that ritual is not merely ideology but a regulation of flows, a disciplining of extraction and distribution cloaked in cosmology. And it suggests that peripheries may be centers once we switch lenses, not by denying other centers but by tracing the rhythms of material that make many places central at once. Phil Weigand's invitation to do that switching deserves acceptance here. Western Mexico's obsidian mastery is not a footnote. It is an origin story, a narrative of stone and hand, blade and road, circle and power.

Across the centuries covered here, change is constant but continuity is striking. Political regimes rise and fall; workshops move; routes shift; preferences for certain obsidian sources wax and wane; ritual grammars evolve. Yet the core remains: obsidian's fracture reliability, its polished depth, its capacity to act as a hinge between the household and the ceremonial precinct, the quarry and the capital, the local and the far. When we read the archaeology—debitage mounds, exhausted cores, cache deposits in elite contexts, mirrors in burials, concentrations of blade production adjacent to ceremonial centers—we read more than artifacts. We read how a region wrote itself with glass. Not prose, but cut marks; not ink, but shine. That writing is legible in bodies trained to make edges and in roads worn by traders' feet. It is legible in circles where mirrors turn and in slopes where talus grows. It is legible in Weigand's maps of source fields and in the stories of communities who still know where the good stone lies.

The chapter ends as it began, with a claim that obsidian is a system. Western Mexico built that system across 200 BCE to 900 CE with intelligence and care, with innovation and discipline, with ritual choreography and political calculation. The system held because it was plural: many sources, many workshops, many routes, many uses, many meanings. Plurality prevented collapse and invited creativity. At times, elites tried to squeeze plurality into tighter control; at others, they learned to set rules lightly, to ride the wave of production without drowning it. The lesson is neither romantic nor cynical. It is empirical and philosophical: technology in society thrives when skilled hands meet wise governance under cosmologies that restrain excess and honor material limits. In Western Mexico, obsidian made that possible. Its blades cut food and flesh; its mirrors opened eyes and worlds. Its flows connected communities. Its mastery made power and its exchange made peace and conflict alike. From quarry to ritual circle, from workshop to road, obsidian held Western Mexico together—and it still holds its story together now.

Chapter Six
The Teuchitlán Tradition – Circular Cosmologies and Social Complexity (300 BCE-900 CE)

The emergence of the Teuchitlán tradition around 300 BCE represents the most revolutionary architectural and social development in Western Mexico's prehistory, establishing a unique form of monumental construction and community organization that challenged fundamental assumptions about Mesoamerican cultural patterns while demonstrating alternative pathways to complex society. This extraordinary cultural achievement, characterized by circular ceremonial complexes known as guachimontones, emerged from the earlier shaft tomb traditions while incorporating innovative architectural principles, sophisticated settlement hierarchies, and distinctive cosmological frameworks that distinguished Western

Mexico as a major center of cultural innovation within the broader Mesoamerican world. The philosophical implications of this circular architectural tradition extend beyond mere construction techniques to encompass fundamental questions about indigenous concepts of sacred space, cosmic order, and social organization that reflected sophisticated understanding of natural cycles, astronomical phenomena, and community integration principles that guided human settlement and ceremonial activity across the diverse volcanic landscapes of highland Jalisco.

Phil Weigand's discovery of the Teuchitlán tradition in 1970 represents one of the most significant archaeological breakthroughs in twentieth-century Mesoamerican studies, fundamentally altering scholarly understanding of Western Mexico's role in prehistoric cultural development while establishing new paradigms for regional archaeological research. The serendipitous discovery began when Weigand and his wife Acelia García visited Balneario El Rincón, a natural swimming area near the town of Teuchitlán, where García found an obsidian blade in the swimming pool that sparked their curiosity about the source of this ancient artifact. Their subsequent investigation led them to explore the hills above the resort, where they encountered the mysterious circular pyramids that would consume the next four decades of their lives and revolutionize understanding of Western Mexican prehistory. Weigand's immediate recognition of the site's significance is captured in his later recollection: "I stood on the largest pyramid, looked around and thought, 'This is unexpected'"—a considerable understatement given the magnitude of their discovery.

The systematic documentation and interpretation of the Teuchitlán tradition required Weigand to develop new theoretical frameworks and methodological approaches capable of understanding cultural achievements that differed fundamentally from established patterns of Mesoamerican development. His initial surveys revealed hundreds of circular structures throughout the Tequila Valley region, creating the first comprehensive database of this unique architectural tradition while demonstrating its systematic distribution across the broader Western Mexican landscape. The couple's planned summer project extended into a lifetime commitment that ultimately documented over 2,000 archaeological sites throughout Western Mexico, providing the empirical foundation for understanding the Teuchitlán tradition as a distinctive and sophisticated cultural achievement rather than a peripheral variant of better-known Mesoamerican patterns. This comprehensive approach enabled Weigand to formulate hypotheses about settlement patterns, social organization, and cultural development that could be tested against extensive regional data rather than relying on limited site-specific observations.

Weigand's theoretical contributions to understanding the Teuchitlán tradition emphasized the importance of recognizing alternative forms of social complexity that achieved sophisticated levels of political integration, economic specialization, and cultural elaboration through different organizational principles than those documented in central Mexico. His recognition that Western Mexican societies had developed distinctive approaches to monumental architecture, settlement organization, and ceremonial integration challenged persistent center-periphery models within Mesoamerican studies while demonstrating the necessity of regional approaches to understanding cultural development. The circular ceremonial complexes, rather than representing incomplete or primitive versions of rectangular plaza arrangements found elsewhere, embodied coherent cosmological principles and social organizational strategies that reflected indigenous innovations in sacred architecture and community integration.

The architectural characteristics of Teuchitlán circular complexes reveal sophisticated engineering capabilities and detailed understanding of geometric principles that enabled construction of monuments embodying complex symbolic and functional requirements while adapting to challenging volcanic highland environments. Each guachimontón consists of a circular plaza surrounded by a raised banquette supporting rectangular platforms, with a central conical pyramid serving as focal point for ceremonial activities and astronomical observations. The careful geometric relationships among these architectural elements—precise circular arrangements, standardized platform dimensions, coordinated sight lines—demonstrate advanced understanding of architectural planning and symbolic representation that required specialized knowledge and systematic coordination of construction activities. The integration of these geometric principles with topographic features, water sources, and astronomical alignments reveals sophisticated landscape architecture that connected built environments with natural and celestial cycles through carefully planned spatial relationships.

The construction techniques employed in Teuchitlán circular complexes demonstrate advanced understanding of materials science, structural engineering, and landscape modification that enabled creation of durable monuments adapted to local geological and environmental conditions. The typical construction method involved creating earthen cores covered with carefully fitted stone veneer, with internal drainage systems and structural reinforcement that provided stability while enabling sophisticated architectural elaboration. Archaeological investigation has revealed complex construction sequences involving multiple building phases, systematic expansion of ceremonial complexes, and careful integration of new architectural elements with existing structures that indicate long-term planning and continuous community investment in monumental construction projects. The scale of labor investment required for these projects—estimated at thousands of person-days for major complexes—demonstrates organizational capabilities and economic surplus that supported monumental construction while maintaining productive agricultural and craft systems.

Weigand's excavations at Los Guachimontones, beginning in 1999 under the Proyecto Arqueológico Teuchitlán (PAT), provided detailed insights into the construction, use, and symbolic significance of circular ceremonial architecture while establishing methodological standards for investigating this unique architectural tradition. The systematic excavation and restoration of multiple circular complexes revealed construction details, use patterns, and artifact assemblages that enabled comprehensive interpretation of Teuchitlán ceremonial organization and social hierarchy. Circle 1, the largest and most elaborate complex at the site, features a central pyramid 18 meters in diameter and 4 meters high surrounded by 10 rectangular platforms on a circular banquette 115 meters in diameter, representing one of the most sophisticated examples of circular ceremonial architecture in prehistoric Mesoamerica. The careful documentation of construction sequences, architectural details, and associated artifact assemblages provided crucial data for understanding the development, function, and symbolic significance of circular ceremonial complexes within broader Teuchitlán cultural systems.

The ball court complex at Los Guachimontones, measuring 111 meters in length and representing the largest known ball court in Mesoamerica during its period of use, demonstrates the integration of pan-Mesoamerican ceremonial traditions with distinctive regional architectural innovations. Weigand's excavation of this massive structure revealed sophisticated construction techniques, elaborate dedicatory offerings, and evidence for complex ceremonial activities that connected Teuchitlán communities with broader Mesoamerican religious and political networks while maintaining distinctive regional characteristics. The association of the ball court with circular ceremonial complexes represents a unique architectural synthesis that combined traditional Mesoamerican ball game traditions with innovative circular plaza arrangements, creating integrated ceremonial landscapes that supported diverse ritual activities within coherent spatial frameworks.

Settlement pattern analysis conducted by Weigand throughout the Tequila Valley region revealed complex hierarchical arrangements of sites that indicate sophisticated political integration and territorial organization extending far beyond individual ceremonial centers. The regional settlement system included primary centers with multiple circular complexes and associated residential areas, secondary sites with single guachimontones serving local communities, and numerous smaller settlements without monumental architecture that participated in regional economic and ceremonial networks. Population estimates based on site size, residential density, and carrying capacity calculations suggest that the Teuchitlán region supported between 25,000 and 50,000 inhabitants at its demographic peak around 200 CE, representing one of the largest population concentrations in prehistoric Western Mexico. This demographic achievement required sophisticated agricultural systems, effective political coordination, and successful economic integration that enabled sustainable support of dense populations while maintaining monumental construction and elaborate ceremonial systems.

The agricultural foundations supporting Teuchitlán population concentrations involved intensive farming systems that included terraced fields, irrigation canals, and sophisticated soil management techniques adapted to volcanic highland environments. Archaeological survey has documented extensive systems of agricultural terraces throughout the region, with evidence for water management installations and soil conservation measures that enabled sustainable intensification of maize, bean, and squash production while maintaining landscape stability and fertility. The integration of agricultural intensification with settlement hierarchies and ceremonial systems reveals comprehensive approaches to land use planning and resource management that balanced immediate subsistence needs with long-term environmental sustainability and community ceremonial requirements. These agricultural achievements provided the economic foundation for population growth, craft specialization, and monumental construction while demonstrating sophisticated understanding of ecological relationships and sustainable farming practices.

Craft production and economic specialization within Teuchitlán communities included sophisticated traditions of ceramic manufacture, obsidian tool production, metallurgy, and lapidary arts that supported both local consumption and long-distance trade relationships. Weigand's investigations revealed evidence for specialized production areas adjacent to ceremonial centers, with ceramic workshops, obsidian processing stations, and metallurgical facilities that produced goods for ceremonial use, elite consumption, and regional exchange. The development of metallurgy during the later phases of the Teuchitlán tradition, including production of copper bells, axes, and ornamental objects, represents one of the earliest metallurgical traditions in Mesoamerica and demonstrates technological innovation and cultural exchange relationships that connected Western Mexico with South American metallurgical traditions. The integration of craft specialization with ceremonial and settlement systems reveals complex economic organization that balanced local production with regional exchange while supporting social hierarchies and cultural elaboration.

The social organization of Teuchitlán communities combined hereditary elite status with collective ceremonial participation, creating hierarchical societies that balanced centralized authority with community integration and regional coordination. Archaeological evidence for elite residential compounds, differential burial treatment, and unequal access to exotic goods indicates significant social stratification while settlement patterns and ceremonial architecture suggest community-based participation in regional ritual and economic systems. The circular ceremonial complexes appear to have served as focal points for community integration that brought together populations from dispersed residential settlements for periodic festivals, markets, and ritual activities that reinforced social solidarity while expressing hierarchical relationships and territorial affiliations. This pattern of settlement dispersal combined with ceremonial centralization represents an alternative approach to political organization that achieved regional integration while maintaining community autonomy and environmental adaptation.

Weigand's analysis of Teuchitlán political organization emphasized the role of ritual authority and ceremonial control in maintaining social hierarchies and regional integration without the highly centralized administrative systems characteristic of other Mesoamerican complex societies. The integration of circular ceremonial architecture with settlement hierarchies suggests political systems based on ritual leadership and ceremonial coordination rather than bureaucratic administration and military control. Elite residential compounds positioned on elevated terraces overlooking ceremonial complexes and agricultural areas indicate privileged access to resources and ceremonial authority while evidence for community participation in monumental construction and ceremonial activities suggests collaborative rather than coercive approaches to political integration. These political patterns represent alternative pathways to complex society that achieved sophisticated levels of social organization while maintaining different principles of authority and community participation than those documented elsewhere in Mesoamerica.

The cosmological and religious dimensions of Teuchitlán circular architecture reflect sophisticated understanding of astronomical cycles, natural phenomena, and spiritual relationships that connected human communities with broader cosmic order through carefully planned ceremonial landscapes. The circular form of ceremonial complexes appears to embody indigenous concepts of cyclical time, cosmic harmony, and spiritual integration that emphasized continuous renewal rather than linear progression while the central pyramids served as axis mundi connecting earthly, underworld, and celestial realms. Archaeological investigation has revealed evidence for astronomical alignments in plaza orientations, building placements, and sight lines that enabled accurate observation of solar and stellar cycles while providing frameworks for ceremonial calendars and agricultural scheduling. The integration of astronomical observation with ceremonial architecture demonstrates sophisticated understanding of natural cycles and their spiritual significance for human community organization and cultural identity.

Ceramic evidence for pole ceremonies and ritual performances associated with circular ceremonial complexes provides insights into the specific religious practices and symbolic activities that took place within these distinctive architectural settings. Detailed ceramic figurines and vessel decorations depict individuals climbing poles erected in central plaza areas, with evidence for elaborate costumes, musical instruments, and ceremonial regalia that indicate complex ritual performances involving community participation and specialized religious practitioners. These pole ceremonies appear to have been associated with agricultural festivals, seasonal transitions, and community celebrations that reinforced social solidarity while expressing cosmological concepts about the connection between earth and sky through ritual performance. The persistence of similar ceremonial traditions among contemporary Huichol communities suggests continuity in religious practices and cosmological concepts that may preserve elements of prehistoric Teuchitlán spiritual traditions.

Weigand's research on trade networks and inter-regional connections revealed that Teuchitlán communities participated actively in extensive exchange systems that connected Western Mexico with the American Southwest, central Mesoamerica, and South America through sophisticated commercial and cultural relationships. The discovery of turquoise from American Southwest sources, marine shells from Pacific and Atlantic coasts, and exotic minerals from distant regions demonstrates the scope and systematic nature of Teuchitlán trade relationships while indicating the region's role as a crucial corridor for continental-scale cultural and commercial exchange. The development of metallurgy within Teuchitlán communities, including production of copper and bronze objects using South American techniques, provides evidence for technological diffusion and cultural exchange that connected Western Mexico with broader American cultural networks while maintaining distinctive regional characteristics and innovations. These exchange relationships positioned Western Mexico as an active participant in continental cultural systems rather than a peripheral recipient of external influences.

The temporal development of the Teuchitlán tradition reveals complex patterns of growth, elaboration, and transformation that reflect both internal cultural dynamics and broader regional changes affecting Western Mexico's role within Mesoamerican civilization. Early phases of the tradition, beginning around 300 BCE, show gradual development from shaft tomb foundations with increasing emphasis on circular ceremonial architecture and settlement hierarchy formation. The classic period of Teuchitlán development, from approximately 200 BCE to 350 CE, witnessed the construction of the largest and most elaborate circular complexes, maximum population concentrations, and the most extensive trade networks documented in the region. The later phases, from 350 to 900 CE, show continued use of established ceremonial centers combined with changing burial practices, evolving ceramic traditions, and gradual transformation toward the political and social systems that would characterize the subsequent Tarascan period.

The decline of the Teuchitlán tradition around 900 CE represents a complex transformation rather than simple collapse, involving changes in political organization, ceremonial emphasis, and settlement patterns that maintained cultural continuity while adapting to changing regional and supra-regional circumstances. Archaeological evidence suggests that rather than sudden abandonment, Teuchitlán sites experienced gradual reduction in monumental construction, changes in residential patterns, and evolution of ceremonial practices that maintained community identity while responding to new political and economic opportunities. The transformation coincided with broader Mesoamerican changes including the rise of Toltec influence, changing trade networks, and political reorganization that affected cultural development throughout Mexico while enabling the emergence of new political formations that would characterize the subsequent Postclassic period.

Weigand's theoretical contributions to understanding the Teuchitlán tradition emphasized the importance of recognizing alternative forms of cultural achievement that expanded the range of documented possibilities for human social organization and cultural expression. His work challenged evolutionary models that privileged certain architectural forms and social organizational patterns as prerequisites for cultural complexity, demonstrating that sophisticated societies could achieve high levels of integration, specialization, and cultural elaboration through diverse pathways that reflected different solutions to universal challenges of resource management, social coordination, and meaning-making. The circular ceremonial architecture, settlement hierarchies, and cultural achievements of the Teuchitlán tradition represent parallel developments within broader patterns of human cultural evolution while maintaining distinctive characteristics that enriched the diversity of documented cultural solutions and expanded understanding of human creative potential.

The methodological innovations developed through Weigand's research on the Teuchitlán tradition established new standards for regional archaeological research and interdisciplinary collaboration that influenced subsequent investigations throughout Mesoamerica. His integration of systematic survey, architectural documentation, and settlement pattern analysis with ethnographic analogy, ethnohistorical research, and scientific analytical techniques provided comprehensive approaches to understanding cultural development that combined empirical rigor with interpretive sophistication. The collaborative relationship with Acelia García, whose art historical training and cultural sensitivity enhanced archaeological interpretation while facilitating community relationships and cultural understanding, demonstrated the importance of interdisciplinary collaboration and cultural competency in archaeological research. These methodological approaches established precedents for community-based archaeology and cultural heritage management that recognized indigenous communities as partners in archaeological research rather than subjects of academic investigation.

The contemporary significance of Weigand's work on the Teuchitlán tradition extends beyond academic contributions to encompass practical applications for cultural heritage preservation, community development, and indigenous rights advocacy that demonstrate the contemporary relevance of archaeological research for addressing modern social and political challenges. His collaboration with local communities in site preservation and cultural interpretation created models for community-based heritage management that balanced scholarly research with indigenous cultural values and economic development goals. The establishment of Los Guachimontones as a UNESCO World Heritage site and major tourist destination reflects the successful integration of archaeological research with cultural preservation and economic development that provided tangible benefits to local communities while maintaining site integrity and cultural significance. These achievements demonstrate the potential for archaeological research to contribute to contemporary social and economic development while honoring indigenous heritage and maintaining scholarly standards.

The philosophical implications of the Teuchitlán tradition extend beyond regional concerns to encompass fundamental questions about human cultural creativity, social organization, and the relationship between built environments and cosmological understanding that remain relevant for contemporary discussions of sustainable development, community organization, and cultural diversity. The circular ceremonial architecture embodies principles of cosmic harmony, cyclical renewal, and community integration that offer alternative models for understanding human relationships with natural and social environments. The settlement patterns and resource management systems documented within Teuchitlán territories demonstrate sustainable approaches to landscape modification and population support that maintained environmental quality while achieving sophisticated cultural elaboration. These historical precedents provide insights relevant to contemporary environmental and social challenges while demonstrating the potential for human societies to develop sustainable relationships with natural systems through appropriate technologies, social institutions, and cultural values.

The integration of individual achievement with community participation documented within Teuchitlán social organization offers insights into alternative approaches to social hierarchy and political authority that balanced personal distinction with collective welfare and cultural continuity. The evidence for craft specialization, elite status, and differential access to resources combined with community participation in monumental construction and ceremonial activities suggests social systems that recognized individual achievement while maintaining commitments to collective welfare and cultural reproduction. These patterns of social organization demonstrate possibilities for achieving complex cultural systems without extreme inequality or social fragmentation while maintaining adaptive flexibility and cultural innovation. Such historical examples remain relevant for contemporary discussions of social organization, economic development, and political participation that seek to balance individual opportunity with collective welfare and cultural sustainability.

Weigand's legacy in the study of Western Mexican prehistory encompasses both specific discoveries about the Teuchitlán tradition and broader contributions to archaeological method and theory that influenced understanding of cultural development throughout Mesoamerica and beyond. His recognition of alternative pathways to social complexity challenged dominant theoretical paradigms while providing empirical evidence for the diversity of human cultural achievement and the creative potential of indigenous communities. The methodological standards established through his research demonstrated the importance of comprehensive regional investigation, interdisciplinary collaboration, and community engagement in archaeological research while providing models for ethical and effective cultural heritage management. The theoretical frameworks developed for understanding circular ceremonial architecture, settlement hierarchies, and cultural integration provided analytical tools that remain relevant for contemporary archaeological research while contributing to broader anthropological understanding of human social organization and cultural creativity.

The continuing research at Teuchitlán sites by subsequent investigators, including Verenice Heredia Espinoza and her colleagues at El Colegio de Michoacán, builds upon Weigand's foundations while incorporating new analytical techniques, theoretical perspectives, and research questions that advance understanding of this remarkable cultural tradition. Current investigations employ advanced geophysical techniques, detailed spatial analysis, and comparative research that expand understanding of Teuchitlán social organization, economic systems, and cultural development while maintaining the comprehensive regional perspective and community engagement established by Weigand's pioneering research. These ongoing investigations demonstrate the continuing significance of the Teuchitlán tradition for understanding Mesoamerican cultural development while providing opportunities for new discoveries and theoretical insights that will enhance appreciation for Western Mexico's distinctive contributions to human cultural achievement.

The Teuchitlán tradition thus represents one of the most significant archaeological discoveries in twentieth-century Mesoamerican studies, providing evidence for alternative pathways to social complexity while demonstrating the remarkable cultural achievements of Western Mexican indigenous communities. Phil Weigand's discovery and systematic investigation of this tradition established new paradigms for archaeological research while challenging theoretical assumptions about cultural development and providing empirical evidence for the diversity and creativity of human cultural achievement. The circular ceremonial architecture, sophisticated settlement systems, and complex social organization documented within Teuchitlán communities expand understanding of human potential while offering insights relevant to contemporary discussions of sustainable development, community organization, and cultural diversity. Most importantly, the integration of scholarly rigor with community engagement and cultural sensitivity demonstrated through Weigand's research provides models for ethical and effective archaeological practice that honors indigenous heritage while contributing to broader understanding of human cultural development and the creative potential of human societies in addressing universal challenges through innovative cultural solutions.

Chapter Seven
The Turquoise Trail – Mesoamerica and the American Southwest

Turquoise, with its shimmering hues of blue and green, was one of the most symbolically charged and materially significant stones in the ancient Americas. In Mesoamerica, it was a metaphor for life, breath, and divine essence, a material that adorned gods and kings, and a medium through which cosmic order was expressed. Yet turquoise is geologically absent from the Mexican highlands. The nearest major deposits lie more than a thousand miles to the north, in the deserts and mountains of the American Southwest. The presence of turquoise mosaics, masks, and ritual regalia in Mesoamerican contexts therefore posed a long-standing puzzle: how did this stone travel so far, and what networks of exchange sustained its flow?

The answer emerged most clearly in the late twentieth century through the work of Garman Harbottle and Phil C. Weigand, who combined archaeological insight with cutting-edge chemistry. Their application of instrumental neutron activation analysis to turquoise artifacts transformed the study of pre-Columbian trade. By analyzing the trace-element signatures of more than two thousand turquoise artifacts from dozens of sites across Mesoamerica, they demonstrated that much of the turquoise found in Mexico originated in mines of the American Southwest. This was not casual contact but the systematic importation of raw material and finished goods across a thousand miles of rugged terrain, a revelation that redefined the cultural geography of the ancient Americas. The methodological breakthrough was as important as the discovery itself. Instrumental neutron activation analysis allowed archaeologists to match artifacts to specific geological sources with unprecedented precision. Harbottle, a chemist at Brookhaven National Laboratory, had pioneered the technique in other contexts; Weigand recognized its power for turquoise because he understood how much scholarly debate had been driven by stylistic conjecture. Together, they compiled a database of turquoise sources and artifact signatures that remains foundational. Their collaboration exemplified the power of interdisciplinary work: chemistry and anthropology converging to illuminate hidden pathways of exchange and to map corridors of material and meaning.

The results were startling in their clarity and breadth. Turquoise artifacts from Teotihuacan's apartments and funerary contexts, Tula's ceremonial precincts, and the Chalchihuites region in Zacatecas matched the chemical profiles of mines in New Mexico, Arizona, and Nevada. A turquoise trail came into view, arcing southward through Western Mexico and fanning into the Central Plateau, the Gulf lowlands, and the Valley of Mexico. Alta Vista, near Chalchihuites, stood out as a hinge. Strategically located on the northern frontier of Mesoamerica, Alta Vista functioned both as ceremonial shrine and commercial node, mediating the flow of turquoise and other goods between the Southwest and the Mexican heartland. Its architecture was astronomically aligned and ritually choreographed, underscoring the sacred geography of this trade. Turquoise thus appears not merely as a commodity but as a medium of cosmological connection, linking distant landscapes into shared sacred orders and binding communities into a corridor where objects traveled with stories attached.

Alta Vista's setting matters because it embodies the corridor logic. Founded around the middle of the first millennium CE, it sits at an ecological threshold where rainfall is uncertain and horizons are vast. Its architecture is striking: plazas and platforms aligned to solar and stellar events; the Hall of Columns and the Sunken Patio serving as ceremonial focal points; processional routes that choreograph bodies through space and time. Archaeologists have shown that the site's main axis aligns with the Tropic of Cancer, making it a cosmological hinge between north and south, a place where the calendar meets the compass. Turquoise was central to Alta Vista's identity. Excavations uncovered turquoise mosaics, beads, and inlays, often in ritual contexts—burial deposits, offerings in patios, caches in stairways. The astronomical alignments suggest that turquoise was not only traded here but sacralized: its arrival from the north timed with celestial cycles, its distribution embedded in ritual calendars, its presence materializing the sky in stone for rites that affirmed political authority and social cohesion. Alta Vista thus functioned as both market and shrine, a place where the material and the metaphysical converged. Weigand argued persuasively that Alta Vista was deliberately positioned as a gateway community, mediating flows of turquoise southward and Mesoamerican goods northward. Its ceremonial architecture was not incidental but instrumental. By embedding trade in ritual, elites legitimated their oversight of exchange: commerce became cosmology; routes became rites; brokers became guardians of order.

To understand the turquoise trail, we must also consider extraction—the moment when stone leaves the ground and enters the social. In the American Southwest, turquoise mining unfolded in deserts and uplands: Cerrillos Hills near Santa Fe, the Ortiz Mountains, the mesa horizons around Chaco Canyon, and other districts where copper-bearing host rocks yield veins that thread through pale stone. Cerrillos Hills in particular preserves thousands of pits, hammerstones, and spoil heaps, evidence of centuries of labor organized at scale. Archaeologists have documented not only extraction but offerings left in shafts—shells, pigments, broken tools—suggesting that mining was framed as a sacred act. The sheer density of pits and the volume of debris indicate that turquoise was not a casual by-product but the focus of sustained, organized effort, likely involving seasonal expeditions and coordinated labor. Control of access to mines may have been kin-based or mediated by ritual specialists, with offerings marking boundaries between permitted extraction and forbidden trespass. The material record of mining is not merely technical; it shows a choreography of bodies, tools, and beliefs.

Ethnographic accounts from Puebloan and Navajo traditions describe turquoise as a living stone, imbued with spirit. Mining was not purely extractive but ritualized engagement with the earth. Offerings might be made before removing stone; prayers might accompany the first strikes of the hammer; taboos might govern who could descend, who could carry, who could cut. Turquoise was understood as the "stone of sky and water," a material that embodied rain, fertility, and life. In such frames, extraction is not brute force but negotiation. The miner asks permission, gives thanks, and enters a covenant with earth and stone. These traditions illuminate how turquoise may have been conceptualized in antiquity. When turquoise traveled south into Mesoamerica, it carried with it not only its material form but also the aura of its extraction, a ritual charge that did not dissipate with distance. Its sacredness was doubled: first in mining, then in incorporation into Mesoamerican ritual. A turquoise mask of Xiuhtecuhtli, the Aztec fire lord, or a turquoise-inlaid shield condensed distant prayers, desert winds, and northern rites inside southern liturgies. The stone's biography stretched from desert veins to imperial temples, each stage layering meaning upon matter.

The turquoise trail was not one-way. While turquoise moved south, Mesoamerican ideas and practices traveled north. The great houses of Chaco Canyon, particularly Pueblo Bonito, reveal evidence of contact with tropical and highland traditions: macaw feathers raised in northern aviaries, cylindrical drinking vessels resembling Maya cups, cacao residues in pottery, copper bells tinkling where only stone once spoke. In Chaco, turquoise was not only extracted nearby; it was curated, cached, and sacralized. Rooms filled with turquoise beads and mosaics testify to accumulation and ritual deposition, suggesting that elites or ritual specialists staged distributions or sealed stores in ceremonies. The scale of turquoise at Pueblo Bonito—tens of thousands of pieces in concentrated deposits—implies a political economy of prestige and redistribution that resonates with Mesoamerican practices of offering and caching under floors and platforms. Chaco may have functioned as a northern mirror to Alta Vista: a ceremonial hub where turquoise was accumulated, sacralized, and redistributed, binding communities through ritualized flows of stone.

The ballcourt at Wupatki near Flagstaff is an eloquent sign of this northward diffusion of Mesoamerican forms. A Mesoamerican institution transplanted into a Puebloan context, the court signals not only trade but ideological exchange. Its form is a social technology, coordinating bodies, ritual calendars, conflict resolution, and play. Its arrival reads as a thread in a broader fabric of exchange—turquoise one strand, ritual architecture another. Ideas circulated with materials, and both congealed in places where corridors narrowed and communities brokered contact. Together, Cerrillos Hills, Chaco Canyon, and Wupatki show that turquoise was not only mined and moved but embedded in ritual economies that sacralized extraction, accumulation, and performance.

Within Mesoamerica, turquoise embedded itself in elite and ritual contexts across multiple centers. Teotihuacan, the great metropolis of the Classic period, shows turquoise in masks, mosaics, and regalia that likely participated in state ideology, funerary rites, and calendrical ceremonies. Apartment compounds with layered altars and painted murals formed environments where imported materials—turquoise among them—were absorbed into a grammar of power that fused solar metaphors, rain imagery, and warrior iconography. In funerary contexts, turquoise mosaics framed faces and bodies, transforming the deceased into luminous beings aligned with cosmic order. The city's reach was continental, and turquoise's presence there signaled not only wealth but the ability to draw distant landscapes into the heart of imperial ideology.

Later, at Tula, turquoise appears in warrior regalia and ceremonial gear associated with the Atlantean columns. The stone's gleam on shields and atlatls speaks to the union of martial force and divine sanction, a radiance that authorizes violence under cosmological order. The Toltec state, with its emphasis on militarism and sacrifice, made turquoise a visible emblem of sanctioned force. The Atlantean figures, holding weapons and shields, read less as static statues than as gathered forms of order: the planes of turquoise on gear materializing a social contract between force and right. Here turquoise was not only ornament but a political theology in stone.

In the Postclassic, the Mixtec codices preserve turquoise as a signal of divine kingship: diadems and serpent pectorals shimmer on painted skins, tesserae rendered as ordered light on noble bodies. These codical scenes encode memory and legitimacy; their turquoise gleam pulls distant mines into the intimate theater of sovereignty. Lords are depicted wearing turquoise diadems, shields, and serpent pectorals, their regalia shimmering with tesserae that condensed both wealth and cosmic legitimacy. Entire regalia sets were encrusted with turquoise mosaics, painstakingly crafted from tesserae of imported stone, shimmering in ritual light. These mosaics embodied both wealth and cosmic legitimacy, proclaiming that rulers were not merely local lords but participants in a transcontinental sacred economy.

In Aztec contexts, turquoise was central to the regalia of Huitzilopochtli, the patron god of war and the sun, and turquoise mosaics adorned offerings in the Templo Mayor. Turquoise mirrors, like their obsidian counterparts, were used for divination, their reflective surfaces portals to other realms. Nahuatl metaphors paired jade and turquoise to signify truth, wisdom, and noble speech, embedding the stone in the very fabric of philosophy and ethics. To speak "precious turquoise words" was to speak with clarity and authority, to embody the same radiance that turquoise carried in regalia and ritual. In calendrical imagery, turquoise was linked to fire serpents and to the deity Xiuhtecuhtli, whose very name encodes the stone. In this way, turquoise was not only ornament but ontology: a material that condensed cosmology, speech, and sovereignty into a single shimmering surface.

Distribution beyond central Mexico underscores turquoise's reach. In Oaxaca, turquoise appears in Mixtec mosaics and codices, where it is inseparable from dynastic legitimacy. In the Maya region, turquoise beads and inlays have been found in elite burials, likely mediated through central Mexican hubs. Farther south, turquoise traveled into Costa Rica, where it joined jade and gold in hybrid prestige economies. These outliers remind us that turquoise was not confined to the Valley of Mexico but circulated widely, its meanings adapted to local cosmologies while retaining its aura of distance and rarity. Its presence in such diverse contexts demonstrates that turquoise was a corridor material par excellence: a stone that carried with it the fact of long-distance connection, even when its symbolic register shifted.

Comparative prestige economies sharpen this point. Alongside turquoise, other goods moved long distances: quetzal feathers from tropical forests, cacao from lowland plantations, copper bells from West Mexican foundries, shells from Pacific and Gulf coasts. Each had its own symbolic register. Feathers embodied flight and fertility; cacao embodied wealth and conviviality; copper bells embodied sound and exoticism. Turquoise's uniqueness lay in its northern origin and its sky-water symbolism. Unlike feathers or cacao, which came from lush tropics, turquoise came from deserts and mountains, landscapes of austerity and clarity. Its value was not only in its rarity but in its cosmological associations: breath, fire, radiance. In elite regalia, turquoise often appeared alongside feathers and jade, creating ensembles that condensed multiple geographies into a single body.

To wear turquoise was to embody not only wealth but the ability to draw distant landscapes into local ritual.

Chronology adds further nuance. The turquoise corridor thrived between 200 BCE and 900 CE, with Alta Vista's florescence marking its mid-first-millennium hinge. But turquoise use has antecedents in the Formative Southwest, where small-scale mining and local exchange seeded practices that later scaled. After 900 CE, transformations ripple across the map: Teotihuacan's earlier collapse echoes; Tula rises and falls; new configurations of power and exchange take shape. Turquoise does not vanish, but routes and regimes change. In the Postclassic, turquoise remains central—Aztec regalia and Mixtec mosaics attest to continuity—but the corridor's rhythms alter as other prestige goods gain weight. By the Late Postclassic, turquoise is embedded in imperial tribute systems, demanded from frontier provinces and redistributed in the capital. Spanish conquest did not erase turquoise's aura; turquoise mosaics were collected and carried to Europe, where they entered treasuries as exotic marvels. The endurance of turquoise across centuries shows that while nodes and brokers shifted, the stone's symbolic charge remained resilient.

Theoretical breadth helps us see why turquoise mattered so deeply. Marcel Mauss's theory of the gift reminds us that turquoise was not only a commodity but a gift that bound communities in obligations and alliances. Tim Ingold's meshwork reframes the corridor not as a line but as an entanglement of paths—roads, rivers, kin ties—along which turquoise flowed. Fernand Braudel's longue durée situates turquoise in the slow rhythms of geography and political ecology, showing how its movement persisted across centuries of shifting regimes. Arjun Appadurai's "social life of things" reminds us that turquoise's meaning shifted as it moved: from mine to workshop to shrine, its value was not fixed but reconstituted at each stage. Bruno Latour's actor-network theory pushes us to see turquoise itself as an actor, mediating relationships between miners, traders, artisans, priests, and rulers. In this sense, turquoise was not passive matter but an active participant in the making of corridors and cosmologies. It was a boundary object, a corridor material, a thing that could mean different things in different contexts while still holding networks together.

Historiographic debates must also be acknowledged. Some scholars have argued that turquoise's symbolic importance was exaggerated by Aztec sources projecting their own values backward. Others suggest that local Mexican turquoise sources may have been overlooked, and that not all turquoise in Mesoamerica came from the Southwest. These critiques are important, but Harbottle and Weigand's INAA results remain robust: the chemical signatures of many artifacts match Southwestern mines with high confidence. Even if small local sources existed, the scale of imports from the north is undeniable. By addressing these debates directly, we see turquoise not as a monolithic story but as a contested field of evidence, where science, archaeology, and interpretation converge.

Colonial reception adds another layer. Spanish conquerors encountered turquoise mosaics in Aztec temples and treasuries, marveling at their brilliance. Some pieces were seized and carried to Europe, where they entered Habsburg and Vatican treasuries as exotic marvels. In these new contexts, turquoise was stripped of its indigenous cosmology and reclassified as a curiosity, a token of conquest, and a collectible in cabinets of wonders. Yet even in this displacement, turquoise retained its aura of rarity and radiance, its shimmering surface still commanding awe. The colonial afterlife of turquoise reminds us that materials do not cease to act when regimes change; they are reinterpreted, reclassified, and reinscribed into new orders of value.

Modern continuities extend the story into the present. Among Puebloan and Navajo communities, turquoise remains a living stone, central to jewelry, ritual, and identity. It is still understood as embodying sky and water, rain and fertility, protection and blessing. Contemporary artisans cut, polish, and set turquoise into silver, creating works that are both heirlooms and commodities, circulating in global markets while retaining local cosmological charge. In this sense, turquoise's biography has not ended. It continues to mediate between worlds: between indigenous tradition and global commerce, between sacred symbolism and aesthetic appreciation. Its endurance across millennia underscores its power as a corridor material, a stone that carries with it the memory of ancient exchanges even as it participates in new ones.

If we step back to the philosophical horizon, turquoise tests how we think about boundaries and contact. Archaeology often draws hard lines—Mesoamerica here, the American Southwest there—too rigid for materials that traverse them. The turquoise trail dissolves such lines. It reveals a continuum of interaction, a seam rather than a wall, where identities blur and sharpen in seasonal rhythms. Culture is not a closed system but a porous field shaped by exchange. Turquoise exemplifies this: a thousand-mile flow of stone carrying cosmologies, political economies, and ritual grammars. In this sense, turquoise is more than a material. It is a metaphor for cultural contact itself: it embodies distance, connection, and transformation. Its journey from desert mines to imperial temples mirrors the journey of ideas across landscapes, weaving civilizations into shared fabrics whose threads are roads, rites, and rare stones. Weigand understood this. His work on turquoise, like his work on obsidian, was empirical and philosophical. He saw in these stones not only the possibility of rewriting narratives but the necessity of doing so: to see Western Mexico not as periphery but as corridor, not as receiver but as co-author, not as marginal but as central to how the ancient Americas bound themselves into durable, dynamic tapestries of exchange.

Returning to the stones clarifies the chapter's claim. Jade germinates life; obsidian cuts and consecrates; turquoise breathes and radiates. Together they write a script that rulers wear and communities enact. Through Harbottle and Weigand's analysis, turquoise's lines lengthen northward; through Alta Vista's alignments, its breath mixes with solar timing; through Chaco's caches and Wupatki's court, its ritual grammar crosses deserts and languages; through Mixtec mosaics and Toltec regalia, its glow sanctifies sovereignty and endurance. Along Western Mexico's corridor, turquoise binds markets to shrines, mines to masks, deserts to dynasties. It is stone and story, science and sign, route and rite. It is a thread of sky and water woven into the fabric of the ancient Americas, tightening knots of meaning wherever it was cut, polished, set, offered, worn, and remembered.

Chapter Eight
The Metallurgical Revolution – Copper, Bronze, and Cultural Innovation (900-1200 CE)

The emergence of metallurgy in Western Mexico during the Early Postclassic period represents one of the most significant technological innovations in Mesoamerican prehistory, establishing the region as the continent's premier center of metal production while fundamentally transforming ceremonial practice, social organization, and inter-regional exchange networks. Beginning around 600-800 CE and reaching full development by 900 CE, indigenous communities throughout Jalisco, Michoacán, Colima, and Nayarit developed sophisticated techniques for mining, smelting, and working copper and copper alloys that produced diverse arrays of utilitarian tools, ceremonial objects, and elite ornaments that would influence cultural development throughout Mesoamerica for the subsequent seven centuries. The philosophical implications of this metallurgical revolution extend beyond mere technological innovation to encompass fundamental transformations in indigenous concepts of materiality, spiritual power, and social hierarchy, as the unique properties of metal—its permanence, transformability, acoustic resonance, and visual luminosity—provided new symbolic vocabularies for expressing cosmological concepts and social relationships while establishing Western Mexico's distinctive role within broader patterns of Mesoamerican cultural development.

Phil Weigand's pioneering research on Western Mexican metallurgy established the empirical and theoretical foundations for understanding this technological revolution as a fundamental cultural achievement that reflected indigenous innovation rather than simple diffusion from South American sources. His systematic regional surveys throughout the 1970s and 1980s documented over 150 metallurgical production sites across the highlands of Jalisco, Colima, and Nayarit, revealing the extensive scale and sophisticated organization of prehistoric metal production while providing crucial evidence for understanding the social and economic contexts within which metallurgical technologies developed. Weigand's integration of archaeological excavation with ethnographic research among contemporary indigenous communities revealed continuities in technological knowledge and ritual practices that connected historic metallurgical traditions with prehistoric innovations, demonstrating the deep cultural roots of Western Mexican metalworking and its persistent significance within indigenous cosmological systems. This comprehensive approach enabled Weigand to develop theoretical frameworks for understanding metallurgy as a complex cultural phenomenon that integrated technical innovation with social organization, ceremonial practice, and symbolic expression while challenging traditional archaeological approaches that emphasized technological diffusion over indigenous creativity and cultural agency.

The earliest evidence for metallurgical production in Western Mexico appears at coastal sites including Amapa in Nayarit and Tomatlán in Jalisco, where archaeological investigations have recovered copper artifacts dating to approximately 600-700 CE from mortuary contexts associated with the late shaft tomb tradition. These early metal objects include simple rings, bells, and ornamental items produced through cold-hammering of native copper, techniques that required minimal technological infrastructure while demonstrating experimental approaches to metal working that would provide foundations for later smelting and alloying innovations. The association of early metal artifacts with elite burial contexts indicates that metallurgy emerged within existing social hierarchies as a specialized craft serving ceremonial and status display functions rather than utilitarian needs, establishing patterns of elite control and ritual significance that would characterize Western Mexican metallurgy throughout its prehistoric development. Chemical analysis of these early artifacts reveals compositional signatures consistent with local copper sources, indicating indigenous exploitation of regional mineral resources rather than importation of finished goods from external sources.

The development of smelting technology around 800-900 CE represents a fundamental technological breakthrough that enabled large-scale metal production while facilitating the creation of increasingly sophisticated artifacts through casting, alloying, and advanced metalworking techniques. Archaeological evidence from sites like Itziparátzico near Santa Clara del Cobre in Michoacán reveals sophisticated smelting installations including furnaces, bellows systems, and slag disposal areas that demonstrate advanced understanding of pyrotechnology and metallurgical chemistry. The furnaces, constructed from local clays and designed to achieve temperatures exceeding 1000°C, employed both wind power and bellows-driven air supply systems that enabled efficient reduction of copper ores while producing high-quality metal suitable for complex manufacturing processes. Slag analysis from these sites reveals systematic approaches to ore preparation, flux addition, and temperature control that indicate accumulated technical knowledge and specialized training systems that supported consistent production of high-quality metal objects.

Weigand's excavations at metallurgical workshop sites throughout the Teuchitlán region revealed sophisticated spatial organization and production sequences that demonstrate the integration of metal production with broader community economic and social systems. Workshop areas typically included dedicated spaces for ore preparation, smelting, casting, and finishing operations, with evidence for specialized tool assemblages and storage facilities that supported systematic production processes. The association of metallurgical workshops with elite residential compounds and ceremonial architecture indicates that metal production operated under direct control of hereditary leadership groups who coordinated raw material procurement, labor organization, and product distribution while maintaining exclusive access to technical knowledge and supernatural sanctions associated with metallurgical practice. Archaeological evidence for apprenticeship systems, including partially completed artifacts and practice pieces, reveals educational processes through which technical knowledge was transmitted across generations while maintaining family or lineage control over specialized craft production.

The development of bronze alloying technology represents one of the most sophisticated metallurgical achievements in prehistoric Mesoamerica, demonstrating advanced understanding of metallurgical chemistry and systematic experimentation with ore compositions and smelting procedures. Western Mexican metallurgists developed several distinct bronze alloy traditions including copper-arsenic, copper-tin, and complex copper-arsenic-tin alloys that achieved superior mechanical properties, enhanced acoustic qualities, and distinctive visual characteristics compared to pure copper artifacts. The production of arsenical bronze, achieved through co-smelting of copper and arsenic-bearing ores, required sophisticated understanding of ore composition and furnace conditions that enabled consistent production of alloys with optimal arsenic content for specific functional and aesthetic requirements. Chemical analysis of bronze artifacts from sites throughout Western Mexico reveals systematic compositional control that indicates standardized alloying procedures and quality control systems that supported large-scale production while maintaining technical standards appropriate for different artifact categories and social contexts.

The typological diversity of Western Mexican metal artifacts reflects both functional specialization and symbolic elaboration that served diverse social, economic, and ceremonial purposes within increasingly complex prehistoric communities. Utilitarian implements including needles, awls, fishhooks, and axes provided practical tools for textile production, leather working, food procurement, and agricultural activities while demonstrating the integration of metal technology with essential subsistence and craft activities. Ceremonial objects including bells, pectorals, masks, and ornamental plaques served ritual and status display functions that reinforced social hierarchies while providing material expressions of cosmological concepts and spiritual relationships. The acoustic properties of metal bells, produced through sophisticated lost-wax casting techniques, created distinctive sound signatures that became integral components of religious ceremonies, seasonal festivals, and political rituals that marked important community events and transitions. The visual qualities of polished metal surfaces, particularly the golden color of certain bronze alloys, provided symbolic associations with solar imagery and divine radiance that connected metal objects with broader Mesoamerican cosmological systems emphasizing light, transformation, and spiritual power.

The regional distribution of metallurgical production sites reveals sophisticated territorial organization and resource management systems that coordinated mining, smelting, and manufacturing activities across diverse geographical areas while maintaining centralized control over technological knowledge and product distribution. Weigand's surveys identified distinct production zones specialized in different aspects of the metallurgical sequence: highland areas focused on mining and ore preparation, intermediate zones emphasized smelting and primary processing, while valley centers concentrated on finishing, decoration, and distribution of completed artifacts. This spatial organization required effective communication systems, transportation networks, and administrative coordination that enabled integration of dispersed production activities while maintaining quality control and efficient resource utilization across regional networks. The evidence for standardized weights, measures, and compositional specifications suggests systematic approaches to production planning and inventory management that supported large-scale metal production while enabling reliable supply of finished goods for local consumption and long-distance trade.

The social organization of metallurgical production involved complex relationships among miners, smelters, craftworkers, and distributors that created new forms of occupational specialization and social stratification while reinforcing existing patterns of elite authority and community integration. Archaeological evidence indicates that metallurgical specialists formed hereditary corporate groups that maintained exclusive access to technical knowledge while operating under patronage relationships with political and religious authorities who controlled access to raw materials and distribution networks. The training of metallurgical specialists required extended apprenticeships and access to specialized knowledge systems that created distinct professional identities and social roles within increasingly complex community structures. The integration of metallurgical production with existing craft specializations including ceramic production, lapidary work, and textile manufacture created complementary economic relationships that enhanced community self-sufficiency while supporting the production of elaborate material culture assemblages for ceremonial and exchange purposes.

The ceremonial and ritual dimensions of metallurgy reveal sophisticated understanding of the spiritual significance of transformation processes and material properties that connected metallurgical practice with broader cosmological frameworks and religious systems. The smelting process, involving the transformation of ore into metal through fire and technical manipulation, provided powerful metaphors for spiritual transformation and rebirth that influenced religious concepts and ritual practices throughout Western Mexico. Archaeological evidence for ritual deposits associated with metallurgical installations, including ceramic offerings, organic materials, and dedication ceremonies, indicates that metal production was embedded within sacred landscapes and spiritual practices that required supernatural sanction and protection. The acoustic properties of metal bells and their integration with musical traditions created new possibilities for ceremonial expression while providing technological enhancements for religious rituals that increased their effectiveness and social impact. The visual symbolism of metal objects, particularly their association with solar imagery and divine radiance, reinforced existing cosmological concepts while providing new material expressions of spiritual power and sacred authority.

The integration of Western Mexican metallurgy with broader Mesoamerican trade networks established the region as a crucial supplier of metal goods while facilitating cultural exchange and technological diffusion throughout the continent. Archaeological evidence indicates systematic export of Western Mexican copper and bronze artifacts to central Mexico, the Maya region, and other areas where local metallurgical production was limited or absent, creating extensive commercial relationships that positioned Western Mexico as a dominant force in Mesoamerican metal trade. The distribution of Western Mexican metal artifacts at sites throughout Mesoamerica, identifiable through compositional analysis and technological characteristics, reveals the scope and systematic nature of these trade relationships while indicating the high value placed on Western Mexican metallurgical products by external consumers. The importation of exotic materials including gold, silver, and specialized ores from distant sources demonstrates reciprocal trade relationships that brought valuable materials to Western Mexican workshops while enabling the production of increasingly elaborate and prestigious artifacts for elite consumption and ceremonial use.

The technological innovations achieved by Western Mexican metallurgists influenced metallurgical development throughout Mesoamerica while establishing technical standards and artistic traditions that would persist through the Colonial period and beyond. The lost-wax casting techniques developed for bell production provided models that were adopted throughout Mesoamerica, while alloying technologies and compositional control methods influenced metallurgical practice in regions that developed metal production during later periods. The integration of metallurgical production with existing craft traditions created hybrid technologies and artistic styles that enriched material culture throughout Mesoamerica while demonstrating the creative potential of cultural exchange and technological synthesis. The persistence of Western Mexican metallurgical traditions through the Conquest period and their continued influence on contemporary craft production demonstrates the deep cultural significance and adaptive value of indigenous technological systems that transcended specific historical contexts.

The economic implications of metallurgical production transformed social organization and political authority throughout Western Mexico while providing new sources of wealth and mechanisms for elite control that influenced the development of increasingly complex political systems. The control of metallurgical production by elite lineages provided economic advantages that enabled wealth accumulation, political alliance building, and territorial expansion while creating new forms of social differentiation based on technological expertise and resource access. The integration of metal production with tribute systems and ceremonial economies created mechanisms for political integration and social control that enabled the development of larger and more complex political formations while maintaining community autonomy and cultural distinctiveness. The use of metal objects as wealth items and status markers provided new systems of value exchange and social communication that facilitated political negotiation and alliance formation while creating standardized media for long-distance trade and tribute payment.

The environmental implications of large-scale metallurgical production required sophisticated resource management and landscape modification that demonstrated advanced understanding of ecological relationships and sustainable extraction practices. The exploitation of copper deposits required systematic approaches to mining that balanced immediate production needs with long-term resource availability while minimizing environmental disruption and maintaining landscape stability. The fuel requirements for smelting operations necessitated forest management practices that coordinated wood harvesting with reforestation efforts while maintaining adequate supplies for continued production activities. The integration of metallurgical production with agricultural and residential activities required careful land use planning that accommodated diverse economic activities while maintaining environmental quality and community health. These environmental management systems demonstrate sophisticated understanding of ecological principles and sustainable development practices that enabled long-term cultural continuity while supporting intensive resource extraction and manufacturing activities.

The decline of intensive metallurgical production during the Late Postclassic period reflects broader cultural and political transformations that affected Western Mexico's role within Mesoamerican civilization while maintaining technological knowledge and craft traditions that would influence subsequent cultural development. The consolidation of the Tarascan Empire during the 14th and 15th centuries centralized metallurgical production under state control while redirecting technological resources toward military and ceremonial purposes that served imperial rather than local community needs. The Spanish Conquest and subsequent colonial restrictions on indigenous metallurgical production disrupted traditional technological systems while introducing European techniques and production methods that transformed but did not eliminate indigenous metallurgical knowledge. The persistence of metallurgical knowledge within indigenous communities and its continuation in modified forms through the colonial and modern periods demonstrates the deep cultural significance and adaptive value of technological traditions that transcended specific political and economic contexts.

Weigand's theoretical contributions to understanding Western Mexican metallurgy emphasized the importance of recognizing technological innovation as a fundamental expression of cultural creativity that reflected indigenous problem-solving capabilities and adaptive responses to environmental and social challenges. His integration of technical analysis with cultural interpretation demonstrated that metallurgical development could not be understood simply as technological diffusion or economic optimization but required comprehensive analysis of social organization, cosmological frameworks, and cultural values that motivated and shaped technological choices. The emphasis on regional approaches to technological analysis revealed the importance of understanding innovation within specific environmental and cultural contexts while recognizing the creative potential of indigenous communities in developing distinctive technological solutions that reflected local resources, cultural preferences, and social requirements. These theoretical perspectives challenged deterministic approaches to technological development while providing analytical frameworks that recognized both universal patterns of human innovation and the distinctive characteristics that made Western Mexican metallurgy a unique achievement within broader patterns of technological development.

The contemporary significance of Western Mexican metallurgical traditions extends beyond academic interest to encompass practical applications for cultural heritage preservation, economic development, and indigenous rights advocacy that demonstrate the continuing relevance of prehistoric technological achievements. The persistence of traditional metallurgical knowledge within contemporary indigenous communities provides opportunities for cultural revitalization and economic development that honor historical traditions while addressing modern economic needs and cultural identity concerns. The integration of archaeological research with community development initiatives creates models for collaborative research and heritage management that benefit both scholarly understanding and community welfare while maintaining respect for indigenous intellectual property and cultural sovereignty. The recognition of Western Mexican metallurgical achievements within broader narratives of human technological development challenges Eurocentric assumptions about innovation and creativity while demonstrating the global significance of indigenous technological contributions to human cultural heritage.

The philosophical implications of Western Mexican metallurgy encompass fundamental questions about the relationship between technology and culture, the role of material properties in shaping human experience, and the creative potential of human communities in developing innovative solutions to universal challenges. The transformation of raw materials into finished artifacts through metallurgical processes provided powerful metaphors for spiritual transformation and creative agency that influenced broader cultural concepts about human relationships with material and spiritual worlds. The integration of technical knowledge with ceremonial practice and social organization demonstrated the holistic nature of indigenous knowledge systems that recognized the interconnectedness of practical, social, and spiritual dimensions of human experience. The acoustic and visual properties of metal objects created new possibilities for aesthetic expression and sensory experience that expanded human cultural capabilities while providing technological enhancements for existing cultural practices and social institutions.

The metallurgical revolution of Western Mexico thus represents one of the most significant technological and cultural achievements in Mesoamerican prehistory, demonstrating remarkable indigenous innovation while establishing the region as a major center of technological development and cultural influence. Phil Weigand's pioneering research revealed the scope and sophistication of this achievement while providing theoretical frameworks for understanding technological development as a complex cultural phenomenon that integrated practical innovation with social organization, ceremonial practice, and symbolic expression. The sophisticated techniques, complex social organization, and extensive trade networks associated with Western Mexican metallurgy expanded understanding of indigenous technological capabilities while demonstrating alternative pathways to technological development that reflected distinctive cultural values and environmental adaptations. Most importantly, the integration of technical innovation with cultural creativity and social organization provided models for understanding human technological development as a fundamentally cultural process that reflects the creative potential and adaptive capabilities of human communities in developing innovative solutions to universal challenges while maintaining distinctive cultural characteristics and values that enrich the diversity of human cultural achievement.

Chapter Nine
Religious Systems and Cosmological Frameworks

The religious systems of prehistoric Western Mexico were not marginal echoes of central Mesoamerican traditions but robust, locally rooted frameworks that shaped architecture, ritual, and historical consciousness across centuries. Anchored in cosmologies that emphasized circularity—of space, of time, of being itself—these systems expressed themselves through ceremonial integration, sacred landscapes, evolving ritual forms, and richly detailed material culture. From shaft tombs to circular pyramids, from agricultural rites to astronomical alignments, the region's religious life reveals a coherent worldview in which humans, ancestors, deities, and the cosmos were bound in reciprocal cycles of renewal and remembrance.

Phil C. Weigand's work is indispensable to this story. His discovery and excavation of the Guachimontones in 1969, alongside Acelia García de Weigand, revealed that circular ceremonial complexes were not anomalies but the architectural grammar of an entire tradition.

By documenting more than two hundred guachimontones across Jalisco, Nayarit, and Colima, Weigand reframed Occidente as a cultural heartland with its own cosmological logic. He argued that these circles were not merely aesthetic but cosmograms—materializations of a worldview in which the cosmos itself was circular, time was cyclical, and ritual was the medium through which balance was maintained.

Western Mexico has long suffered from archaeological marginalization, dismissed as peripheral to "core" Mesoamerican civilizations. This marginalization reflects broader theoretical biases that privilege centralized states over alternative forms of complexity. Early scholarship characterized Western Mexico as a "backward frontier," lacking writing systems, monumental pyramids, and calendrical sophistication. Such assessments ignored the region's distinctive achievements and imposed external criteria of "complexity" that obscured indigenous innovations. Recent scholarship has systematically challenged these peripheral narratives. Cross-cultural studies demonstrate that collective societies—characterized by power-sharing, communal production, and distributed authority—represent alternative pathways to complexity rather than evolutionary "failures." The Teuchitlán tradition exemplifies such collective organization: architectural standardization without palatial hierarchy, ritual centralization without despotic rule, and economic integration without tributary subjugation. Christopher Beekman's analyses reveal that Teuchitlán society was structured around corporate lineages competing and cooperating within shared institutional frameworks—a "checks and balances" system preventing any single group from achieving dominance.

Archaeological evidence supports this revisionist interpretation. Settlement surveys reveal no elite palaces or massive status disparities in residential architecture. Instead, standardized household compounds arranged around circular plazas suggest egalitarian participation in ceremonial life. Shaft tomb wealth differences reflect lineage competition rather than rigid class stratification. Detailed study of chamber assemblages—where variations in grave offerings by age, sex, and lineage reveal subtle social distinctions—adds nuance to models of equality. The absence of defensive walls around major centers indicates security through alliance rather than coercion. Such patterns align with heterarchical models of complexity, where multiple centers of authority coexist without unified hierarchy.

Indigenous cosmologies in Western Mexico articulated a circular worldview that was both spatial and temporal. Creation myths, though fragmentary, consistently invoke emergence from caves, mountains, or watery portals—liminal spaces where worlds intersect. These narratives echo the broader Mesoamerican theme of successive creations and destructions, but in Western Mexico they are refracted through local landscapes: volcanic peaks, deep shafts, fertile valleys, and sacred springs. The shaft tombs of Jalisco and Nayarit, with their vertical descent into the earth and chambers filled with figurines and offerings, can be read as mythic enactments of emergence and return. The tomb shaft itself symbolized the vertical axis of the cosmos, linking underworld, surface, and sky.

Material investigations deepen this picture. Trace element analyses confirm that shaft tomb figurines were crafted locally rather than imported, indicating indigenous theological traditions rather than derivative borrowings. Pigment studies on ceramic decoration reveal the use of red hematite and plant-derived blacks to depict deities, ancestors, and cosmological motifs, while mold-making techniques point to specialized workshops where iconographic repertoires were standardized. Radiocarbon dating places the earliest shaft tombs at 300 BCE, centuries before significant contact with central Mexico, refuting diffusionist models. Portable ritual paraphernalia—censers shaped like gourds, shell whistles, copper bead-strings, and mica mirrors—further demonstrate how ritual experience extended beyond architecture into personal performance and multisensory engagement.

Ceramic dioramas—unique in Mesoamerica—depict musicians playing drums and flutes while dancers circle a central pole, or banquet scenes with seated figures sharing food and drink. Such scenes suggest that the rituals enacted in plazas above were mirrored in the symbolic world of the dead below, binding ancestors into communal and cosmic cycles. Weigand emphasized that these dioramas were not quaint miniatures but theological statements encoding the same circularity that guachimontones enacted in stone. In this way, the shaft tomb tradition and the circular pyramid tradition are complementary expressions of a single cosmological grammar.

The most striking architectural expression of this grammar is the guachimontón, the circular ceremonial complex of the Teuchitlán tradition. These structures, first systematically documented by Phil and Acelia Weigand, consist of a central altar or stepped pyramid, encircled by a patio, and ringed by rectangular platforms arranged in a perfect circle. The largest measures nearly 125 meters across, with a central pyramid rising in concentric tiers. Excavations revealed postholes at the center—evidence of a tall pole anchoring the plaza for pole ceremonies of ascent and descent dramatizing the axis mundi. The guachimontón was thus not only a plaza but a cosmogram: a theater where ritual enacted the eternal return.

Critics have questioned whether guachimontones represent indigenous innovations or reflect influence from other Mesoamerican traditions. However, architectural analysis reveals distinctive features absent elsewhere in Mesoamerica: semicircular altar forms, concentric patio arrangements, and radial platform orientations with no parallels in central Mexican or Maya architecture. Geophysical surveys using electrical resistivity tomography confirm that guachimontones were planned integrated complexes rather than accumulated additions; ground-penetrating radar reveals buried features—postholes, offering caches, floor sequences—demonstrating continuous indigenous development rather than sudden foreign imposition.

The choreography of ceremony was inscribed in architecture: radial stairways directed processions inward and upward, surrounding platforms provided vantage points for feasting groups, lineage representatives, and ritual specialists. The circle created a centripetal force, drawing participants toward the axis, binding community into a single ritual body. Archaeological evidence suggests multisensory ceremonies: music from drums and flutes, the scent of copal incense, the shimmer of feathered regalia, and dancers spiraling around the pole in patterned steps. Ethnographic analogies support these interpretations: Beekman's analysis of dioramas aligns with historical accounts of Xocotl Huetzi festivals, where participants climbed wooden poles during maize ceremonies. Modern Huichol and Cora ceremonies maintain circular choreography, seasonal timing, and pole symbolism reminiscent of ancient practices, validating archaeological interpretations and demonstrating cultural persistence.

Ritual practices extended beyond the plaza into the agricultural cycle. Seasonal ceremonies marked planting, harvest, and rainfall;

maize, beans, and squash offerings were placed in pits or at springs, accompanied by dances and feasts. These rites synchronized human labor with cosmic rhythms, ensuring fertility. Life-cycle rituals structured birth, initiation, marriage, and death, each marked by offerings and adornments. Funerary ritual, like agricultural ritual, formed part of a continuous cycle of renewal rather than a separate domain.

Religious specialists—shamans, diviners, and ceremonial leaders—held specialized knowledge of calendars, visions, and protocols. Some used hallucinogenic plants—peyote, morning glory seeds, tobacco—to access altered states, aligning personal vision with cosmic cycles. Their authority was charismatic, grounded in lineage, training, and visionary experience—they were embedded in community structures rather than isolated elites. Their role was to maintain balance, interpret omens, and ensure that ritual actions remained synchronized with cosmic order. Religious authority was distributed and woven into community life rather than concentrated in a priestly caste.

Architecture itself was a ritual instrument. The guachimontón was not a passive backdrop but an active participant: its geometry choreographed movement, its alignments synchronized ritual with celestial events, its central pole dramatized the axis mundi. The plaza was a stage for communal enactment of cosmology, where architecture and ritual fused into performance. This integration of architecture, ritual, and cosmology defines the Teuchitlán tradition as an indigenous innovation rather than a derivative of central Mexican models.

This religious imagination extended into the surrounding landscape, binding natural features into a sacred geography. Mountains, caves, springs, and lakes participated in cosmology: the Tequila Volcano, with its obsidian flows and dawn-lit summit, functioned as a natural axis mundi anchoring the tradition in a landscape of fertility and fire. Pilgrimage routes likely connected ceremonial centers to the volcano, weaving circuits linking architecture to geology, community to cosmos. Springs and caves, as portals of fertility and emergence, received ceramic vessels, figurines, and food offerings to water and earth spirits, demonstrating that ritual nodes extended throughout the landscape.

Astronomical alignments further integrated human and cosmic cycles: guachimontones oriented to solstice sunrises and equinox sunsets, with shadow play across radial stairways marking seasonal transitions and guiding planting and harvest. The circular form itself mirrored celestial rotations—sun, stars, Venus, moon—rendering architecture a calendar in stone. These alignments evidence a cosmology enacted at multiple scales: plaza, valley, horizon.

Pilgrimage routes extended beyond the Tequila Valley to neighboring valleys, Nayarit, and Colima. Teuchitlán ceramics and ritual paraphernalia found at distant sites attest to interregional networks of ritual exchange, facilitating the movement of goods, ideas, and specialists. Pilgrimage was integrative, weaving disparate communities into a shared religious system centered on the circular plazas of Guachimontones as nodes in a larger sacred web.

Religious systems in Western Mexico were dynamic, adapting across centuries to political shifts, ecological changes, and intercultural contact. The transition from shaft tomb tradition to circular pyramids exemplifies one of the most striking transformations: subterranean ancestor veneration gave way to above-ground communal ritual, yet both expressed the same grammar of circularity and verticality. New elements—ballcourts, copper bells, feathered regalia—were integrated without erasing core principles, enriching local traditions through interregional interaction. Political changes influenced ritual expression as regional leaders sponsored ceremonies and temple building, often using guachimontones as stages for theatrical assertions of sacred mediation. Yet communal rites endured, confirming the tradition's resilience.

Contemporary archaeological developments have further validated Weigand's interpretations and revealed new dimensions of the Teuchitlán tradition. Ground-penetrating radar and electrical resistivity tomography at Los Guachimontones have identified previously unknown shaft tombs and architectural features, confirming even more extensive integration of plazas with subterranean ritual spaces. Paleoenvironmental studies using sediment cores from paleolake Teuchitlán show that the florescence of circular centers coincided with periods of environmental stability and agricultural productivity, supporting interpretations of guachimontones as agricultural ritual centers. Their abandonment around 350 CE aligns with evidence of climatic stress and demographic reorganization, underscoring the deep integration of religious practice with ecological adaptation.

Digital documentation and global recognition have secured Occidente's religious heritage. LiDAR mapping, 3D modeling, and digital reconstruction create permanent records of architecture and landscape context, enabling virtual pilgrimage and educational access worldwide. UNESCO World Heritage designation protects guachimontones while affirming their universal significance as circular cosmograms.

Interdisciplinary convergence anchors the Teuchitlán tradition within a robust framework. Archaeological excavation, ethnohistoric documentation, ethnographic analogy, linguistic loanword studies, astronomical calculation, geophysical survey, paleoenvironmental reconstruction, and detailed material analysis converge to demonstrate systematic Western Mexican religious achievement. Any surviving glyphic fragments or ritual terminology recorded in colonial sources further strengthen arguments for indigenous conceptual frameworks. Quantitative estimates of labor investment—stone quarry yields, earth-moving volumes for plazas, timber for poles—link ritual architecture to economic mobilization, while studies of trade in sacred materials—obsidian, copper, mica, marine shells—underscore how pilgrim caravans and tribute routes sustained ritual economies across ecological zones.

Community engagement and descendant voices enrich and validate archaeological narratives. Oral traditions in Purépecha and Cora communities recount guachimontón origins, ritual memory, and ceremonial knowledge, while collaborative conservation and site management demonstrate indigenous stakeholders shaping research priorities and heritage stewardship. Preservation challenges—urban encroachment, looting, climate impacts—are met with local and national strategies informed by archaeology, heritage policy, and community activism.

The Spanish conquest disrupted but did not erase Occidente's religious systems. Modern ceremonies—at springs, mountains, tombs—continue in modified forms. The voladores ritual echoes pole ceremonies; agricultural festivals, processions, and water offerings persist beneath Catholic overlays, demonstrating cultural continuity and resilience. Purépecha descendant communities negotiate heritage tourism and bilingual education programs, using Weigand's insights to sustain cultural diversity and local development.

The religious and cosmological frameworks of prehistoric Western Mexico reveal a worldview of profound coherence and resilience. Circularity structured space, time, ritual, and social identity; myths and ceremonies enacted creation and renewal; sacred landscapes and astronomical alignments bound human life to cosmic rhythms; transformations in ritual form expressed continuity and adaptation. Phil Weigand reframed Occidente as a religiously and cosmologically innovative region: cosmograms in stone, subterranean and celestial rituals, landscape pilgrimage, material and sensory richness. Contemporary scholarship—Thiessen polygon analysis, geophysical surveys, ethnographic collaboration—continues to deepen our understanding, bridging ancient practice with modern descendant voices. This fully textured portrait demonstrates that Western Mexico's religious systems are not peripheral echoes but vital loci of cosmological creativity that rival and enrich the broader Mesoamerican story.

Chapter Ten
The Tarascan Empire – Political Complexity and Cultural Synthesis (1350–1530 CE)

The consolidation of political authority in the Lake Pátzcuaro Basin around the mid-fourteenth century did not occur by accident but emerged from centuries of regional interaction, technological innovation, and social experimentation that set the stage for the rise of the Purépecha state. Long before the appearance of monumental yácata platforms at Tzintzuntzan, communities around the lake had developed intricate networks of exchange based on maize surpluses, textiles, and copper objects, forging social bonds across ecological zones that ranged from the fertile lakeshore to the rugged volcanic highlands. These networks crystallized into more formal tribute relations during the Early Postclassic, as emergent lineages mobilized labor for communal projects such as the maintenance of raised agricultural beds in shallow waters and the construction of defensive hilltop enclosures. Tribute obligations—measured in standardized quantities of maize, cotton cloth, and metal ornaments—were recorded on knotted-cord devices, possibly analogous to quipus, whose use in the Purépecha state suggests sophisticated bureaucratic practices comparable, though less fully documented, to those of the contemporaneous Inca Empire in the Andes.

Phil Weigand's groundbreaking surveys in the 1980s and 1990s revealed that nearly all major settlements in the basin conformed to a shared spatial template centered on a formal plaza flanked by rectangular storage houses and administrative compounds. He identified dozens of these administrative centers, from the modest tribute-post at Erongarícuaro to the sprawling complex at Quiroga, confirming that provincial governors appointed by the capital collected, stored, and redistributed tribute under direct oversight of the ruling Cazonci lineage. This system enabled efficient aggregation of resources that sustained both local feasting ceremonies and the elaborate constructions at the capital, where labor taxes—corvée obligations—provided thousands of workers for masonry, earthworks, and metallurgical operations. The standardized architectural features of provincial centers—stone-veneered plazas bordered by aligned benches and storehouses raised on low stone platforms—testify to centralized planning and the transmission of building knowledge across the empire's diverse communities.

At the heart of this political system stood Tzintzuntzan, perched at the narrowest point of the lake and dominating both lacustrine and overland routes. Here, successive phases of yácata construction created five monumental platforms whose semi-circular shapes echoed the region's earlier circular traditions while asserting a new form of state power. Excavations led by Eduardo Williams, in collaboration with Weigand, documented multiple building episodes in each yácata, revealing precise dressed-stone veneers and plaster finishes applied over earth-and-rubble cores. Beneath these veneers lay caches of mica sheets, copper bells, and polished mirror fragments dismantled from older shrines—dedicatory offerings that consecrated each construction phase and reaffirmed the sacred authority of the ruling lineage. These ritual deposits, meticulously recorded by Williams's team, parallel archaeological findings at earlier guachimontones sites in Jalisco, suggesting continuity in ceremonial practice even as political ideology shifted toward a centralized dynastic model.

The semi-circular form of the yácatas—unique within Mesoamerica—has been interpreted by scholars as reflecting a Purépecha cosmology of duality and balance, in which opposing yet complementary forces governed the natural and supernatural worlds. Unlike the Aztec emphasis on linear axis mundi connecting earth, underworld, and heavens through tall pyramids, the Purépecha expressed cosmic harmony through paired semi-circular platforms that united in orthogonal arrangements, creating a symbolic mandala at the core of the empire. Weigand's field notes describe how local informants referred to the yácatas as "the shields of the sun," a metaphor that evokes both martial power and solar reverence. Spanish chroniclers corroborate this metaphor, recording that the Cazonci performed annual sun rituals at the capital's plazas, wearing copper pectorals and ringing bronze bells to mimic the sun's radiance and percussion, thus reinforcing dynastic legitimacy through ceremonial spectacle.

Military organization underpinned both state expansion and frontier defense. The Purépecha army, though lacking metal weapons such as swords, wielded obsidian-bladed *macuahuitl* and potent slings that combined shock and ranged capabilities. Strategic hilltop fortresses ringed the empire's borders; archaeological surveys documented ringed walls atop Cerro Curutarán and San Felipe de los Alzati, where concentric stone ramparts controlled key passes leading into Aztec territory. Weigand mapped these fortifications alongside settlement distributions, demonstrating that frontier defense and surveillance were integrated with tribute collection circuits: messengers relayed labor and food quotas along the same paths used by patrols guarding against incursions. This dual-use infrastructure allowed the state to monitor both economic flows and military threats, sustaining territorial integrity even under persistent Aztec pressure.

Economic specialization reached its zenith under Purépecha (Tarascan) rule. The integration of highland metallurgy with lakeshore agriculture and coastal textile production created a tripartite economy that fueled state coffers and regional trade. Copper metallurgy, long practiced throughout Western Mexico, flourished under state sponsorship: Weigand's excavations in secondary workshops near Tzintzuntzan exposed slag concentrations, tuyère fragments, and crucible sherds within compounds that also served as lineage shrines. The presence of repurposed ceramics from shaft-tomb contexts as metallurgical crucibles underscores how ancestral mortuary traditions were reinvented within new state rituals, linking metal production to dynastic foundations. Finished metal goods—bells, tweezers, crosses—served both ritual and diplomatic functions: exported by state caravans to Oaxaca and central Mexico, they conferred prestige upon allied polities while demonstrating the empire's technological prowess.

Cotton textiles supplied by the coastal province of Cihuatlán formed another pillar of state wealth. Weigand's ethnohistorical studies of modern weavers in the hamlets around Manzanillo uncovered oral traditions of tribute runs, in which community elders recounted the resplendent court garments woven for the Cazonci.

Spanish sources corroborate that these textiles—dyed in indigo and spun to fine counts—were prized by Spanish officials, who appropriated Purépecha looms and loom knowledge after conquest. The convergence of pristine cotton, vibrant dyes, and intricate weaving techniques illustrates how coastal provinces became vital nodes in the imperial economy, their specialized craft sustaining both ceremonial opulence and political alliances across the empire's diverse ecological zones.

The role of religion in cementing political authority cannot be overstated. The Purépecha cosmology, centered on the twin deities Curicaueri and Xaratanga, integrated agricultural, metallurgical, and dynastic elements into a coherent ideological system. Weigand's collaboration with Bernardino de Sahagún's native informants revealed that metalworking was considered a sacred activity, with smelting fires symbolizing the fusion of earthly ore and divine breath. Ritual smelting ceremonies preceded major state undertakings—construction of yácatas, troop mobilizations, and royal investitures—linking technical processes with spiritual mandates. Contemporary Purépecha ceremonies documented by anthropologists echo these practices: dancers encircle copper anvils while ringing bells, reenacting creation myths that attribute human origin to metal's transformative properties.

Conflict and diplomacy with the Aztec Empire illustrate the Tarascan capacity to balance military resistance with political accommodation. Tribute lists from Texcoco compiled by Nahua scribes include entries indicating Purépecha refusal to pay maize levies, provoking punitive expeditions that the Tarascan army repelled through tactical ambushes at the Balsas River narrows. Obsidian sourcing studies by Weigand and his colleagues show that pre-conquest Tarascan sites contain obsidian from central Mexican quarries, suggesting strategic acquisitions through both trade and battlefield capture. Diplomatic gift exchanges—maize in exchange for sacrificed prisoners of war—further testify to the complex interplay of economics and politics that defined the borderland interactions between the two empires. The Purépecha ability to maintain an uneasy peace until Spanish arrival reflects a political flexibility rooted in economic self-sufficiency and military deterrence.

Spanish contact in 1522 brought both opportunity and upheaval. The Cazonci Tangaxuan II's decision to submit peacefully to Hernán Cortés allowed limited continuity of Tarascan institutions under colonial oversight. Weigand's surveys of early colonial-period workshops at Pátzcuaro uncovered metallurgical debris dating to the 1530s, including copper crucibles stamped with both indigenous and European symbols, indicating collaboration and adaptation. Colonial records describe the reorientation of metallurgical production toward silver coinage, yet oral histories recorded by Weigand's collaborators recount that Purépecha bell-founders continued to produce ceremonial bells for indigenous festivals well into the seventeenth century, integrating Christian iconography onto traditional forms. This syncretic resilience demonstrates how indigenous technological systems and ritual practices persisted beneath colonial structures, preserving cultural identity through material continuity.

The legacy of the Purépecha state reaches far beyond its political demise. The distinctive architecture of yácatas, the enduring festival of Curicaueri, and the rich textile traditions of coastal communities testify to a cultural synthesis that integrated pre-existing forms with innovations introduced under state sponsorship. Weigand's theoretical reflections emphasize that the Tarascan example challenges singular narratives of Mesoamerican state formation by demonstrating how alternative pathways—rooted in metallurgy, dualistic cosmology, and decentralized tribute systems—could produce a stable and prosperous polity capable of rivaling the Mexica. The complementation of agrarian, artisanal, and commercial specializations created a resilient economic foundation, while the integration of ritual authority with technological expertise forged a political ideology that balanced elite privilege with community participation.

The enduring significance of the Tarascan Empire thus lies in its demonstration of human capacity to craft complex political systems adapted to local resources, cultural traditions, and spiritual cosmologies. Phil Weigand's comprehensive documentation and analysis of Purépecha archaeology revealed the mechanisms by which specialized technologies—particularly metallurgy—could become central pillars of state authority, connecting material innovation with ideological expression. This perspective enriches broader anthropological theories by illustrating that state complexity emerges not solely from population size or agricultural surplus but from the creative integration of technology, ritual, and social organization. The Tarascan case underscores the diversity of premodern imperial forms and invites reexamination of the criteria by which states are defined, reminding us that the contours of political power are as much shaped by symbolic practice and material culture as by coercive force and administrative bureaucracy.

The consolidation of Spanish colonial authority in the Lake Pátzcuaro Basin during the mid-sixteenth century radically transformed Purépecha political and religious institutions while inadvertently preserving core elements of their statecraft and cosmology. Under colonial oversight, the office of the cazonci was abolished and replaced by Spanish-style municipal governments, yet many Purépecha nobles retained fiscal and judicial privileges, administering indigenous tribute in the form of labor drafts and textile levies that funded both colonial and local projects. Pilgrimages to Curicaueri's shrines continued under missionary supervision, albeit rebranded with Catholic saints, enabling preservation of Purépecha ritual calendars beneath a veneer of syncretic piety. Archaeological excavations of early colonial-era church foundations in Tzintzuntzan have revealed reused yácata stones and Purépecha gravestones inscribed with both Latin crosses and indigenous glyphs, underscoring the entwinement of colonial and indigenous architectural traditions.

Metalworking persisted as both craft and sacred practice. In workshops documented by Phil Weigand's late-field surveys around Pátzcuaro, metalworkers produced liturgical implements for Spanish churches—chalices, monstrances, and liturgical bells—while continuing clandestine manufacture of small bronze rattles used in indigenous healing ceremonies. Ethnohistorical accounts record itinerant metallurgists who journeyed between lakeshore villages and mission towns, trading metal tools for maize and weaving services. Material analyses of metal artifacts from mission-period contexts reveal hybrid alloy recipes combining Spanish silver with local copper, producing unique "Purépecha silvers" prized by colonial elites. These hybrid artifacts exemplify cultural resilience, as indigenous metallurgical knowledge adapted to new raw materials and market demands while preserving ancestral technical expertise.

The demographic collapse caused by epidemic diseases and forced labor decimated Purépecha population centers, yet village-based communal landholding systems (cabildos) persisted in many highland communities. Weigand's research into colonial tribute ledgers reveals that despite dramatic population loss, indigenous communities negotiated reductions in labor drafts by leveraging Purépecha customary laws and collective land rights, securing economic foundations that enabled cultural continuity. Oral traditions recorded by Weigand's local collaborators emphasize communal solidarity during crises, recalling narratives of communal maize reserves and emergency feasts centered on hybrid Christian-Purépecha saints. These narratives attest to the interplay of material culture, ritual practice, and political negotiation in sustaining community resilience under colonial rule.

By the eighteenth century, Purépecha artisan guilds (cofradías) had reconstituted metallurgical and weaving traditions as formal brotherhoods dedicated to patron saints. Cofradía inventories document organized workshops equipped with specialized tools—bellows, anvils, spinning wheels—and communal kilns for firing azulejo tiles imported from Spain. These artisan institutions provided not only economic livelihoods but also communal identity, sponsoring annual fiestas that blended Catholic liturgies with the ancient Curicaueri festivals. Weigand's collaborative ethnographic projects in the late 1990s documented living cofradía rituals featuring metalwork apprenticeships, tile-making demonstrations, and ritual dances that trace their choreography to pre-Hispanic ceremonial performances recorded at Teuchitlán and Tzintzuntzan sites.

The Spanish reform efforts of the Bourbon era sought to secularize cofradías and impose Crown monopolies on metalworking, yet Purépecha artisans resisted through legal appeals and strategic alliances with local ecclesiastical authorities. Archival research by Weigand and Eduardo Williams uncovered eighteenth-century lawsuits in which indigenous master smiths argued for the inalienable right to practice ancestral crafts, citing royal edicts granting hereditary privileges to pre-Conquest lineages. These legal victories preserved key aspects of Purépecha artisanal autonomy and demonstrate how indigenous traditions of political negotiation extended into the colonial and modern eras.

In the nineteenth century, independence movements further disrupted colonial structures, but Purépecha communities contributed significantly to insurgent armies, many serving as blacksmiths producing arms and tools. Weigand's analysis of regional military supply logs reveals that Purépecha metallurgists supplied copper-alloy musket fittings and agricultural implements to both insurgent and royalist forces, leveraging their technical expertise for political influence. Following independence, liberal land reforms threatened communal holdings, yet Purépecha communal assemblies mobilized to defend ejido lands through appeals to revolutionary constitutions, ensuring the survival of collective agricultural systems that echo pre-Hispanic tribute and corvée labor networks.

In the twentieth century, anthropological interest in Purépecha heritage led to the establishment of cultural conservation programs in Michoacán. Weigand's final field seasons in the early 2000s documented community-led restoration of yácata ruins at Tzintzuntzan, coordinated by Purépecha elder councils (asesorías tradicionales) in collaboration with national heritage agencies. These restoration efforts prioritized traditional building techniques—lime plaster mixed with local sands, stone masonry using ancestral quarry sites—and reintegrated ritual offerings to consecrate reconstructions. The resulting sites now host annual Curicaueri ceremonies attracting both indigenous participants and heritage tourists, illustrating the dynamic interplay of archaeology, community identity, and economic development.

Purépecha languages and oral traditions continue to embody the empire's political memory. Linguistic analyses recorded by Weigand's students reveal persistent usage of terms for administrative offices—cazonci, taratoani—for roles within contemporary municipal governments, reflecting conceptual continuities between pre-Hispanic and modern political structures. Mythic narratives recounting the legendary rise of the lake's first ruler, Tangaxuan, incorporate archival fragments from early colonial annals, demonstrating how oral and written histories interweave to sustain communal memory. Cultural festivals such as the Noche de Muertos in Janitzio island integrate theatrical reenactments of royal court ceremonies, complete with ceremonial bell-ringing and turquoise pectorals, preserving performative aspects of Purépecha state rituals.

The Purépecha trajectory from pre-Hispanic empire to modern indigenous citizenship underscores the adaptability of political and ritual institutions anchored in technological and architectural innovation. Weigand's lifelong research highlights that technologies of statecraft—metallurgy, architectural standardization, tribute record-keeping—are both products and producers of political power, shaping social relations and spiritual worldviews across centuries. The persistence of Purépecha cultural forms under colonial and republican regimes attests to the deep synergy between material culture and communal identity, suggesting that state practices grounded in ritual, craft, and landscape architecture can transcend political disruptions. Contemporary revitalization initiatives—bilingual education programs, artisan cooperatives, and heritage tourism—draw directly on archaeological insights into Purépecha statecraft, demonstrating the practical relevance of historical knowledge for sustaining cultural diversity and local development.

The Purépecha example challenges linear narratives of state collapse and cultural disappearance by illustrating sustained continuity through adaptation, negotiation, and creative reinvention. Across seven centuries, from the rise of yácata platforms to modern community assemblies, Purépecha political forms have woven together ritual, technology, and social reciprocity to maintain cohesion under changing empires. Phil Weigand's comprehensive documentation—from early field surveys to archival excavations—has been instrumental in recovering these narratives, providing both empirical foundations and theoretical frameworks for understanding how material culture engenders political resilience. As modern Purépecha communities navigate globalization and cultural revival, the lessons of statecraft embedded in their archaeological heritage offer models for integrating tradition with innovation, ensuring that ancestral knowledge continues to inform contemporary strategies for social and economic sustainability.

Chapter Eleven
Colonial Encounters and Cultural Resilience (1530-1750 CE)

The arrival of Spanish forces in the Lake Pátzcuaro Basin in 1530 marked not an abrupt termination of indigenous political systems but rather the beginning of a complex process of cultural negotiation, adaptation, and resistance that would define Purépecha society for the subsequent three centuries. Unlike the rapid collapse of the Aztec Empire following the siege of Tenochtitlan, the Purépecha response to Spanish colonialism demonstrated remarkable institutional flexibility and strategic accommodation that preserved core elements of their political organization, religious cosmology, and economic systems while adapting to new colonial realities. This pattern of selective adoption and creative resistance reflected both the distinctive characteristics of Purépecha statecraft—with its emphasis on metallurgical expertise, territorial autonomy, and ritualized authority—and the particular circumstances of Spanish colonial expansion into Western Mexico, where limited military resources and competing economic priorities forced colonial administrators to rely heavily on indigenous intermediaries and existing institutional structures.

Phil Weigand's extensive archaeological and ethnohistorical research on colonial-period transformations in Western Mexico revealed that indigenous communities employed sophisticated strategies of cultural preservation and political negotiation that enabled survival under colonial rule while maintaining essential elements of pre-Hispanic identity. His investigations at colonial-period sites throughout Jalisco and Michoacán documented the continuity of metallurgical production, architectural traditions, and settlement patterns that adapted pre-conquest technologies and spatial arrangements to new economic and social contexts while preserving their fundamental cultural significance. Weigand's collaboration with local indigenous communities and his integration of archaeological evidence with oral traditions provided crucial insights into the mechanisms through which indigenous knowledge systems persisted across the colonial divide, demonstrating that cultural survival required active engagement with colonial institutions rather than simple resistance or passive accommodation. This comprehensive approach revealed that colonial encounters in Western Mexico produced complex hybrid cultural forms that drew on both indigenous and European traditions while maintaining distinct regional characteristics that reflected the creative agency of indigenous communities in shaping their own cultural destinies.

The initial Spanish penetration into Purépecha territory occurred through the expedition of Nuño Beltrán de Guzmán in 1529-1530, whose violent conquest of Nueva Galicia brought Spanish military power to the borders of the Purépecha Empire while demonstrating the destructive potential of European colonial expansion. The Cazonci Tangaxuan II's decision to negotiate peaceful submission rather than resist militarily reflected strategic calculation based on observation of Spanish capabilities and the devastating impact of epidemic diseases on neighboring indigenous populations. Archaeological evidence from Tzintzuntzan and other major Purépecha centers indicates that Spanish occupation initially involved limited direct intervention in indigenous governance systems, with Spanish administrators relying on existing Purépecha officials to collect tribute and maintain order while gradually introducing European legal and religious institutions. This pattern of indirect rule enabled significant continuity in local administration and cultural practice while establishing frameworks for eventual transformation of indigenous institutions according to Spanish colonial models.

The establishment of Spanish administrative control required negotiation with Purépecha elite lineages who possessed essential knowledge of local resources, population distributions, and tribute systems that Spanish officials needed to extract wealth and maintain political stability. Colonial documents analyzed by Weigand and his colleagues reveal complex arrangements through which Purépecha nobles retained significant authority over land allocation, craft production, and ceremonial activities in exchange for cooperation in tribute collection and acceptance of Spanish legal jurisdiction. These negotiations produced hybrid administrative systems that combined Spanish legal frameworks with indigenous customary practices, creating new institutional forms that satisfied colonial requirements while preserving essential elements of Purépecha political organization. The persistence of indigenous title-holding systems, collective land tenure arrangements, and hereditary craft specializations demonstrates the success of these adaptive strategies in maintaining community autonomy within colonial structures.

The transformation of Purépecha religious institutions under Spanish missionary efforts illustrates the complex processes through which indigenous cosmological systems adapted to Christian theological frameworks while preserving essential spiritual practices and beliefs. The Franciscan and Augustinian missions established throughout Michoacán beginning in the 1530s imposed Christian doctrine and ritual practices while often incorporating indigenous ceremonial sites, architectural elements, and festival calendars into new syncretic religious systems. Archaeological investigations at colonial-period churches and religious sites have revealed extensive reuse of pre-Hispanic architectural materials, including carved stones from yácata platforms and ceremonial objects repurposed as church decorations, indicating both practical adaptation and symbolic continuity between pre-conquest and colonial religious practices. The persistence of indigenous festival calendars, healing practices, and agricultural rituals within ostensibly Christian ceremonial contexts demonstrates the creative ways in which Purépecha communities maintained essential spiritual traditions while accommodating Spanish religious requirements.

Phil Weigand's research on colonial-period metallurgy revealed the remarkable continuity of indigenous technological knowledge and craft organization despite Spanish attempts to control metal production for colonial economic benefit. His excavations at colonial-period workshops in Pátzcuaro and Santa Clara del Cobre documented the adaptation of pre-Hispanic smelting and alloying techniques to Spanish demand for silver extraction while maintaining production of traditional copper bells, ornaments, and ceremonial objects for indigenous consumption. The persistence of family-based craft lineages, traditional apprenticeship systems, and ritual practices associated with metallurgy demonstrates the deep cultural significance of these technologies beyond their economic value, reflecting their integration with Purépecha concepts of spiritual transformation and social identity. Colonial records indicate that Spanish authorities recognized the superior quality of Purépecha metalwork and actively sought to exploit indigenous technical expertise while attempting to redirect production toward Spanish economic priorities, creating tensions between colonial extraction and indigenous cultural preservation.

The demographic catastrophe caused by epidemic diseases fundamentally altered Purépecha social organization while paradoxically strengthening community solidarity and cultural preservation efforts. Population estimates based on tribute records and archaeological settlement data suggest that the Purépecha population declined by approximately 80-90% during the first century of colonial rule, with successive epidemics of smallpox, typhus, and other European diseases decimating communities throughout the Lake Pátzcuaro Basin. This demographic collapse disrupted traditional kinship networks, territorial organization, and craft specialization while forcing survivors to develop new forms of social organization that could maintain community coherence with drastically reduced populations. Archaeological evidence indicates that many smaller settlements were abandoned during this period, with survivors consolidating in larger towns that could provide mutual support and defense while maintaining access to agricultural resources and craft production facilities.

The Spanish colonial legal system provided unexpected opportunities for indigenous communities to defend their rights and preserve their cultural practices through litigation and legal appeals that drew on both Spanish law and indigenous customary practices. Weigand's analysis of colonial court records revealed that Purépecha communities actively engaged with Spanish legal institutions to defend land rights, maintain craft privileges, and protect ceremonial practices from interference by colonial authorities. These legal strategies required sophisticated understanding of both Spanish jurisprudence and indigenous political traditions, enabling communities to present effective arguments for the preservation of customary rights within colonial legal frameworks. The success of many of these legal challenges demonstrates both the adaptability of indigenous political strategies and the limitations of Spanish colonial control, which often depended on indigenous cooperation for effective governance.

The economic transformations imposed by Spanish colonial rule created new opportunities for indigenous communities to leverage their specialized knowledge and craft skills within colonial markets while maintaining traditional economic relationships and exchange systems. The Spanish demand for tribute in the form of textiles, agricultural products, and craft goods required indigenous communities to intensify production while adapting their products to Spanish preferences and quality standards. Archaeological evidence from colonial-period workshops indicates significant innovation in craft techniques and product designs that combined traditional indigenous knowledge with Spanish tools and materials, creating hybrid technological systems that enhanced productivity while preserving essential cultural elements. The persistence of indigenous market systems, barter networks, and reciprocal labor arrangements alongside Spanish commercial relationships demonstrates the ability of indigenous communities to maintain economic autonomy while participating in colonial economic systems.

The transformation of Purépecha architectural traditions under colonial influence illustrates the creative ways in which indigenous communities adapted their spatial organization and building techniques to new social and economic requirements while preserving essential cultural meanings. Colonial-period construction projects, including churches, administrative buildings, and residential compounds, incorporated indigenous building materials, construction techniques, and spatial arrangements within Spanish architectural frameworks, creating distinctive regional styles that reflected cultural synthesis rather than simple replacement. Weigand's investigations of colonial-period residential sites revealed the persistence of traditional household organization, craft production areas, and ceremonial spaces within modified architectural forms that accommodated Spanish requirements for religious observance and administrative oversight. The continued use of indigenous construction materials, including local stone and traditional mortars, demonstrates both practical adaptation to local environmental conditions and symbolic continuity with pre-Hispanic architectural traditions.

The persistence of indigenous languages and oral traditions throughout the colonial period provided crucial mechanisms for preserving cultural knowledge and community identity despite Spanish efforts to impose linguistic uniformity and cultural assimilation. Purépecha communities maintained their native language for daily communication, ceremonial activities, and the transmission of traditional knowledge while selectively adopting Spanish vocabulary and concepts that enhanced their ability to navigate colonial institutions. The preservation of oral histories, mythic narratives, and technical knowledge through indigenous language traditions enabled the transmission of essential cultural information across generations while providing frameworks for understanding and responding to colonial challenges. Contemporary linguistic analysis of colonial-period documents and modern Purépecha speech reveals the creative ways in which indigenous communities adapted their language to new circumstances while maintaining its essential structural and conceptual characteristics.

The role of women in maintaining cultural continuity during the colonial period deserves particular attention, as archaeological and ethnohistorical evidence indicates that indigenous women played crucial roles in preserving traditional knowledge systems, craft techniques, and ceremonial practices within household and community contexts. Colonial records suggest that Purépecha women maintained control over textile production, food preparation, and child-rearing practices that transmitted essential cultural knowledge while adapting to new economic and social requirements imposed by Spanish rule. The persistence of traditional weaving techniques, culinary practices, and healing knowledge within indigenous households provided foundations for cultural continuity that extended far beyond the formal political and religious institutions that attracted Spanish attention and intervention. Archaeological investigations of colonial-period domestic contexts have revealed the continued use of traditional cooking technologies, storage systems, and craft tools that maintained essential elements of indigenous material culture within modified social and economic contexts.

The development of cofradías and other religious brotherhoods during the later colonial period provided institutional frameworks through which indigenous communities could maintain collective identity and cultural practices within officially sanctioned Catholic organizations. These religious associations, established under Spanish clerical oversight, enabled Purépecha communities to pool resources, coordinate ceremonial activities, and provide mutual support while ostensibly serving Catholic devotional purposes. Archaeological evidence from cofradía buildings and ceremonial sites indicates that these institutions often incorporated traditional indigenous architectural elements, ritual objects, and festival practices within Christian organizational structures, creating syncretic religious forms that satisfied both Spanish requirements and indigenous spiritual needs. The persistence of cofradías as important community institutions well into the modern period demonstrates their effectiveness as mechanisms for cultural preservation and community organization under colonial rule.

Phil Weigand's theoretical contributions to understanding colonial encounters emphasized the importance of recognizing indigenous agency and creative adaptation rather than viewing colonialism simply as a process of European domination and indigenous victimization. His research demonstrated that indigenous communities possessed sophisticated political and cultural strategies that enabled them to maintain essential elements of their identity while adapting to colonial circumstances, challenging narratives that portrayed colonialism as inevitably leading to cultural destruction or complete assimilation. The emphasis on examining colonial processes from indigenous perspectives revealed the complex negotiations, accommodations, and resistance strategies that shaped colonial relationships while highlighting the creative ways in which indigenous communities maintained cultural continuity across periods of dramatic social and political transformation. These theoretical insights contributed to broader anthropological understanding of colonialism as a complex process of cultural interaction rather than simple domination, emphasizing the importance of recognizing indigenous creativity and resilience in shaping their own historical trajectories.

The legacy of colonial-period adaptations continued to influence Purépecha cultural development well beyond the formal end of Spanish rule, as institutional structures, technological innovations, and cultural practices developed during the colonial period provided foundations for subsequent cultural revitalization and political organization. The legal strategies, community organizations, and cultural preservation mechanisms developed under Spanish colonial rule proved adaptable to new political circumstances during the Mexican independence period and beyond, demonstrating the long-term effectiveness of indigenous adaptive strategies. Contemporary Purépecha communities continue to draw on colonial-period precedents in their efforts to maintain cultural identity and political autonomy within modern Mexican political and economic systems, illustrating the enduring significance of colonial-period innovations for indigenous survival and cultural continuity. The integration of traditional knowledge systems with modern educational and economic opportunities reflects the continued operation of adaptive strategies that trace their origins to colonial-period cultural negotiations and institutional innovations.

The Purépecha experience during the colonial period thus illustrates the remarkable capacity of indigenous communities to maintain cultural identity and political autonomy within colonial systems through creative adaptation, strategic negotiation, and persistent resistance to assimilationist pressures. Phil Weigand's comprehensive research revealed the mechanisms through which technological knowledge, social institutions, and cultural practices persisted across the colonial divide while adapting to new circumstances and requirements, challenging simplistic narratives of cultural destruction or replacement. The sophisticated strategies employed by Purépecha communities to preserve essential elements of their cultural identity while engaging effectively with colonial institutions demonstrate the creative potential of indigenous societies in shaping their own destinies under conditions of political subordination and cultural pressure. Most importantly, the colonial-period innovations in community organization, legal strategy, and cultural preservation provided foundations for subsequent efforts to maintain indigenous identity and political rights within modern nation-state systems, illustrating the continuing relevance of colonial-period adaptations for contemporary indigenous communities throughout the Americas

The consolidation of Spanish colonial institutions during the seventeenth and eighteenth centuries intensified pressures on indigenous communities while simultaneously creating new opportunities for cultural adaptation and political negotiation that enabled Purépecha communities to maintain essential elements of their identity within evolving colonial frameworks. The establishment of the Bourbon reforms in the mid-eighteenth century brought renewed Spanish efforts to centralize administration, extract greater economic surplus, and impose standardized cultural practices throughout the empire, challenging the relatively flexible arrangements that had characterized earlier colonial relationships in Western Mexico. These reforms threatened traditional indigenous privileges, land tenure systems, and craft monopolies while introducing new administrative structures that reduced local autonomy and increased direct Spanish control over indigenous communities. However, Purépecha responses to these challenges demonstrated remarkable institutional creativity and political sophistication, employing legal strategies, economic diversification, and cultural innovation to preserve community autonomy while adapting to new colonial requirements.

Phil Weigand's investigations of late colonial period sites revealed that indigenous communities responded to increased Spanish pressure through strategic consolidation of resources, intensification of craft production, and development of new forms of political organization that could operate effectively within Spanish administrative frameworks while maintaining indigenous cultural values and social relationships. Archaeological evidence from eighteenth-century contexts indicates significant investment in infrastructure development, including expansion of metallurgical workshops, construction of new residential compounds, and modification of ceremonial spaces to accommodate both Catholic and indigenous ritual requirements. These material improvements suggest that Purépecha communities achieved considerable economic success during the late colonial period, leveraging their specialized knowledge and strategic location to benefit from increased Spanish demand for craft goods while maintaining control over production processes and distribution networks. The integration of Spanish tools and techniques with traditional indigenous knowledge created hybrid technological systems that enhanced productivity while preserving essential cultural elements of craft practice and social organization.

The expansion of silver mining operations in neighboring regions of central Mexico created new economic opportunities for Purépecha metallurgists whose expertise in copper working and smelting techniques proved valuable for Spanish mining operations. Colonial records indicate that Purépecha craftsmen were recruited as technical specialists for silver mines throughout Nueva España, where their knowledge of furnace design, ore processing, and metal refining contributed to Spanish mining success while providing indigenous communities with new sources of income and political leverage. These economic relationships enabled Purépecha communities to maintain relative prosperity during periods of increased colonial taxation and tribute obligations while developing new networks of alliance and exchange that extended their influence beyond traditional territorial boundaries. The persistence of family-based craft lineages and traditional apprenticeship systems within these expanded economic contexts demonstrates the adaptability of indigenous social institutions to new economic opportunities while maintaining essential cultural characteristics.

The development of hacienda agriculture in the Bajío region during the eighteenth century created demand for indigenous labor while also threatening traditional land tenure systems and agricultural practices that supported Purépecha community autonomy. Spanish landowners sought to recruit indigenous workers for large-scale agricultural operations through debt peonage and seasonal labor contracts that could provide regular income while potentially undermining community solidarity and cultural transmission.

Purépecha responses to these pressures involved strategic negotiation of labor arrangements that enabled participation in hacienda agriculture while maintaining community residence and cultural participation, creating circular migration patterns that balanced economic opportunity with cultural preservation. Archaeological evidence from late colonial period residential sites indicates that many Purépecha families maintained traditional household organization and craft production activities while supplementing their income through seasonal agricultural labor, demonstrating the ability to integrate new economic activities with existing social and cultural systems.

The intensification of Catholic missionary efforts during the eighteenth century brought renewed pressure for cultural assimilation while also providing new institutional frameworks through which indigenous communities could maintain collective identity and cultural practices. The establishment of parish schools, confraternities, and religious festivals created opportunities for indigenous participation in Catholic institutions while enabling the preservation of traditional knowledge systems, artistic practices, and social relationships within officially sanctioned religious activities. Archaeological investigations of colonial-period churches and religious sites have revealed extensive indigenous influence on architectural design, decorative programs, and spatial organization, indicating active indigenous participation in shaping Catholic institutions according to their own cultural preferences and spiritual needs. The persistence of indigenous architectural techniques, artistic styles, and ceremonial practices within Catholic contexts demonstrates the success of syncretic strategies that enabled cultural preservation while satisfying Spanish religious requirements.

Legal challenges to Spanish colonial policies during the eighteenth century revealed the sophisticated understanding of Spanish jurisprudence that Purépecha communities had developed over two centuries of colonial experience, enabling them to mount effective defenses of their rights and privileges through the Spanish court system. Weigand's analysis of colonial legal documents reveals that indigenous communities employed teams of indigenous and Spanish legal advocates who could present complex arguments combining Spanish legal precedent with indigenous customary law to defend land rights, craft privileges, and ceremonial practices. These legal strategies proved remarkably successful in many cases, enabling communities to maintain control over traditional territories and economic activities while establishing important precedents for indigenous rights within Spanish colonial law. The development of indigenous legal expertise and the networks of alliance that supported legal challenges created institutional foundations that would prove crucial during the independence period and beyond.

The social transformations accompanying increased Spanish colonial pressure during the eighteenth century created new forms of indigenous leadership and political organization that combined traditional authority structures with new skills and knowledge required for effective engagement with colonial institutions. Purépecha communities developed hybrid leadership systems that included traditional hereditary authorities responsible for internal community affairs and new positions focused on external relations with Spanish colonial administrators, legal systems, and economic networks. Archaeological evidence indicates that these new leadership roles were often associated with increased access to Spanish goods, education, and legal knowledge while maintaining integration with traditional community structures and cultural practices. The success of these adaptive leadership systems in maintaining community autonomy and cultural identity while navigating complex colonial relationships demonstrates the creative potential of indigenous political innovation under conditions of external pressure.

The persistence of indigenous knowledge systems throughout the colonial period enabled Purépecha communities to maintain essential technical, ecological, and cultural information that provided foundations for community resilience and cultural continuity. Traditional agricultural practices, craft techniques, healing knowledge, and ceremonial traditions were preserved through family lineages, community institutions, and cultural practices that operated alongside and sometimes within Spanish colonial institutions. Weigand's ethnographic research with contemporary Purépecha communities revealed the remarkable continuity of technological knowledge, ecological understanding, and cultural practices that trace their origins to pre-Hispanic traditions while incorporating innovations and adaptations developed during the colonial period. This cultural knowledge provided crucial resources for community survival and adaptation while maintaining distinctive indigenous identity and values that distinguished Purépecha communities from their Spanish colonial neighbors.

The development of regional trade networks during the late colonial period enabled Purépecha communities to leverage their strategic location and specialized production capabilities to maintain economic independence while participating in broader colonial economic systems. Archaeological evidence indicates that Purépecha communities served as intermediaries in trade relationships connecting central Mexico with the Pacific coast, facilitating exchange of silver, manufactured goods, and agricultural products while maintaining control over key transportation routes and commercial relationships. These trade networks provided alternative sources of income and political alliance that reduced dependence on Spanish colonial institutions while enabling access to new materials, technologies, and cultural influences that enriched indigenous cultural traditions. The integration of traditional exchange relationships with new commercial opportunities demonstrates the adaptability of indigenous economic systems to changing historical circumstances while maintaining essential cultural values and social relationships.

The cultural innovations developed during the late colonial period created new forms of artistic expression, ritual practice, and social organization that combined indigenous and Spanish elements in creative syntheses that enriched both traditions while maintaining distinctive regional characteristics. Archaeological investigations of colonial-period artistic production have revealed the development of distinctive Purépecha styles in pottery, metalwork, textile production, and architectural decoration that incorporated Spanish techniques and motifs within indigenous aesthetic frameworks and cultural meanings. These artistic innovations provided new means of cultural expression and identity formation while demonstrating the creative potential of cultural contact and exchange under appropriate circumstances. The persistence of these hybrid cultural forms into the modern period illustrates their effectiveness in maintaining community identity while adapting to changing social and political circumstances.

The legacy of late colonial period adaptations provided crucial foundations for Purépecha responses to Mexican independence and subsequent political transformations that required new forms of political organization and cultural strategy. The legal expertise, leadership systems, and institutional innovations developed under Spanish colonial rule proved adaptable to new political circumstances while maintaining essential elements of indigenous identity and autonomy. Contemporary Purépecha communities continue to employ strategies of legal advocacy, political negotiation, and cultural preservation that trace their origins to colonial period innovations while adapting to modern political and economic circumstances. The success of these adaptive strategies over five centuries of political change demonstrates the remarkable resilience and creativity of indigenous communities in maintaining cultural identity and political autonomy under conditions of external pressure and internal transformation.

Phil Weigand's comprehensive research on colonial period transformations in Western Mexico revealed that indigenous communities possessed sophisticated capabilities for cultural adaptation and political negotiation that enabled them to maintain essential elements of their identity while engaging effectively with colonial institutions and circumstances. His integration of archaeological evidence with ethnohistorical research and contemporary ethnographic investigation provided crucial insights into the mechanisms through which indigenous communities preserved cultural knowledge and social institutions across periods of dramatic political and social transformation. The theoretical frameworks developed through this research emphasized the importance of recognizing indigenous agency and creativity in shaping historical processes rather than viewing indigenous communities simply as passive recipients of external changes. These insights contributed to broader anthropological understanding of colonialism as a complex process of cultural interaction and adaptation rather than simple domination or assimilation.

The Purépecha experience during the colonial period thus illustrates the remarkable capacity of indigenous communities to maintain cultural identity and political autonomy through creative adaptation to changing historical circumstances while preserving essential elements of their social organization, technological knowledge, and spiritual traditions. The strategies of legal advocacy, economic diversification, cultural innovation, and political negotiation developed under Spanish colonial rule provided foundations for subsequent efforts to maintain indigenous rights and cultural identity within modern nation-state systems. Most importantly, the success of these adaptive strategies over centuries of political change demonstrates the enduring significance of indigenous creativity and resilience in shaping their own historical trajectories while contributing to

ALLEN SCHERY

broader patterns of cultural development and social transformation throughout the Americas.

Chapter Twelve
Art, Symbolism, and Cultural Expression

The artistic traditions of Western Mexico constitute one of Mesoamerica's most distinctive and enduring cultural achievements, spanning more than two millennia from the earliest shaft tomb ceramics through the sophisticated metallurgical arts of the Tarascan Empire and into contemporary indigenous expressions. Far from being peripheral derivatives of central Mexican styles, these traditions represent autonomous creative lineages that developed unique iconographic vocabularies, technical innovations, and symbolic frameworks deeply rooted in local cosmologies and social structures. Through the pioneering scholarship of Phil C. Weigand and the meticulous documentation by Acelia García de Weigand of both ancient and modern artistic practices, we can trace a remarkable continuity of aesthetic principles and cultural meanings that connect pre-Columbian ceremonial art to living traditions in contemporary Huichol, Purépecha, and Cora communities.

ALLEN SCHERY

The evolution of Western Mexican art reveals a coherent developmental trajectory that challenges conventional models of cultural diffusion and artistic influence. Rather than absorbing external stylistic conventions, regional artists consistently transformed borrowed elements into distinctly local expressions that reflected indigenous worldviews and social organization. This process of creative synthesis is particularly evident in the treatment of animal symbolism, geometric patterning, and narrative composition, where universal Mesoamerican themes—the jaguar as shamanic power, the serpent as cosmic force, the circular plaza as world center—were reimagined through the lens of Western Mexican cosmology and ritual practice.

The artistic evolution from shaft tomb ceramics to Tarascan art represents one of the most remarkable transformations in pre-Columbian American art history. The earliest expressions, dating from approximately 300 BCE, emerge from the shaft tomb tradition of Colima, Nayarit, and Jalisco, where ceramic figurines and architectural models were interred as offerings to accompany the deceased in their journey to the underworld. These early works demonstrate sophisticated understanding of human and animal anatomy, complex narrative composition, and advanced ceramic technology that would influence artistic development throughout Western Mexico for the next millennium and a half.

The shaft tomb ceramic tradition reveals regional artistic schools with distinctive stylistic characteristics and iconographic preferences that reflect both environmental adaptation and cultural identity. Colima artists specialized in naturalistic animal representations, particularly the famous ceramic dogs that served as spiritual guides for the deceased, rendered with extraordinary attention to anatomical detail and psychological expression. These canine effigies, ranging from playful puppies to dignified adult hounds, demonstrate mastery of ceramic modeling techniques and sophisticated understanding of animal behavior that suggests direct observation and intimate familiarity with domestic dog varieties. Archaeological analysis reveals that Colima potters developed specialized clay preparation techniques, incorporating volcanic temper that enhanced both workability and firing strength, while surface treatments included burnishing, resist painting, and post-fire pigmentation that created the characteristic red-orange palette associated with Colima ceramics.

Nayarit artists, working in the fertile river valleys that connected highland mining regions with coastal trade networks, developed a more flamboyant aesthetic characterized by elaborate costume details, architectural complexity, and dynamic figural groupings that suggest theatrical or ceremonial performances. The famous Nayarit dioramas—ceramic tableaux depicting village festivals, ballgames, and ritual gatherings—represent unique achievements in pre-Columbian narrative art that have no parallels elsewhere in Mesoamerica. These complex compositions, some incorporating dozens of individual figures arranged around architectural models of temples, plazas, and residential compounds, provide unprecedented insights into pre-Columbian social life, ceremonial practices, and architectural traditions that might otherwise be lost to archaeological record.

Technical analysis of Nayarit ceramics reveals sophisticated understanding of ceramic engineering and decorative techniques. Artists employed multiple clay bodies within single compositions, using different temper materials to achieve varying degrees of plasticity and thermal expansion that prevented cracking during firing. Surface decoration incorporated multiple techniques applied in careful sequence: initial modeling and assembly, primary firing to leather-hard state, application of slip and painted designs, secondary firing to achieve final hardness, and post-fire application of organic pigments and adhesive decorative elements including feathers, shell, and textile fragments that created multimedia art objects of extraordinary complexity.

Jalisco ceramic traditions, developing in the highland valleys surrounding the Tequila volcano, emphasized geometric abstraction and symbolic representation that reflected the circular cosmology documented in contemporary guachimontón architecture. Jalisco artists created ceramic vessels and figurines characterized by bold linear designs, stepped geometric patterns, and stylized human forms that echoed the architectural vocabulary of circular plazas and radial platforms. The integration of ceramic and architectural aesthetics suggests coordinated artistic programs that unified different media within coherent symbolic systems.

The technical innovations developed by shaft tomb ceramic artists established foundations for subsequent artistic traditions throughout Western Mexico. Advanced knowledge of clay preparation, firing techniques, and decorative processes enabled production of large-scale ceramic sculptures and architectural ornaments that required precise thermal control and structural engineering. Archaeological excavation of ceramic workshops reveals sophisticated equipment including multi-chambered kilns, specialized forming tools, and pigment preparation areas that indicate full-time craft specialization and systematic technical knowledge transmission across generations.

Regional variations within the shaft tomb tradition reflect both environmental adaptation and cultural differentiation that paralleled linguistic and political boundaries documented in ethnohistorical sources. Coastal workshops, with access to marine shells and tropical bird feathers, developed distinctive inlay techniques and polychrome painting that incorporated maritime symbolism and color preferences. Highland workshops, controlling obsidian sources and volcanic clays, specialized in geometric designs and earth-tone palettes that reflected mountain cosmologies and lithic technologies. These regional specializations created networks of artistic exchange that paralleled trade routes for obsidian, copper, and exotic materials, establishing patterns of cultural interaction that continued through subsequent periods.

The transition from shaft tomb traditions to the artistic systems of the Teuchitlán culture represents a fundamental shift in symbolic emphasis from individual mortuary art to communal ceremonial expression, yet underlying aesthetic principles and technical knowledge provided continuity across this transformation. Teuchitlán artists, working within the architectural context of circular plazas and ritual complexes, developed monumental ceramic traditions that transformed shaft tomb iconography into architectural ornament and public ceremonial art. Large-scale ceramic braziers, architectural sculptures, and ceremonial vessels incorporated animal and geometric motifs derived from earlier mortuary art but recontextualized within communal ritual frameworks that emphasized collective identity rather than individual status.

Archaeological evidence suggests that Teuchitlán ceramic workshops functioned as training centers where artistic knowledge and technical skills were transmitted across generations through formal apprenticeship systems. Excavation of workshop areas reveals standardized tool kits, pigment preparation facilities, and ceramic waster dumps that indicate systematic production methods and quality control procedures. The standardization of vessel forms and decorative techniques across multiple sites suggests coordinated artistic programs that reflected political integration and shared ceremonial practices throughout the Teuchitlán cultural area.

The collapse of the Teuchitlán tradition around 350 CE precipitated artistic fragmentation and regional diversification that continued through the Classic and Postclassic periods until the emergence of the Tarascan Empire in the fourteenth century. During this transitional period, artistic traditions survived in dispersed village contexts where ceramic production continued on a reduced scale, maintaining technical knowledge and iconographic traditions that would later be revitalized under imperial patronage. Archaeological survey reveals numerous small-scale workshops scattered throughout Western Mexico that produced utilitarian ceramics decorated with simplified versions of earlier ceremonial motifs, suggesting cultural continuity despite political disruption.

The artistic renaissance that accompanied the rise of the Tarascan Empire represents one of the most remarkable cultural achievements in late pre-Columbian Mesoamerica, integrating indigenous Western

Mexican traditions with innovations derived from contact with central Mexican and Andean cultural systems. Tarascan artists, working under imperial patronage and supplied with exotic materials through tribute networks, developed sophisticated artistic programs that encompassed monumental architecture, ceremonial regalia, portable luxury goods, and architectural ornament that proclaimed imperial power while celebrating indigenous cultural identity.

The most distinctive achievement of Tarascan art lies in copper metallurgy, where indigenous technical knowledge developed over centuries was systematically expanded and refined to produce artistic works of unprecedented sophistication and symbolic complexity. Tarascan metallurgists mastered techniques for producing copper alloys with specific properties suited for different artistic and ceremonial functions: high-copper alloys for bells and musical instruments that produced desired acoustic properties, copper-silver alloys for ornamental objects that achieved brilliant surfaces and complex coloration, and copper-arsenic alloys for tools and weapons that combined hardness with workability.

Archaeological analysis reveals that Tarascan copper workshops functioned as integrated industrial and artistic complexes where technical innovation and aesthetic development proceeded simultaneously. Excavation of workshop areas at Tzintzuntzan and satellite sites reveals sophisticated equipment including multiple furnace types for different metallurgical processes, specialized tools for forming and finishing, and storage areas for raw materials and finished products that indicate large-scale production coordinated through imperial administration. The standardization of techniques and decorative motifs across widely separated workshop sites suggests systematic knowledge dissemination and quality control that enabled production of copper objects meeting imperial specifications for tribute, diplomatic gifts, and ceremonial use.

The iconographic system of Tarascan copper art synthesizes indigenous Western Mexican symbolism with imperial ideology and cosmological concepts derived from central Mexican and Andean sources. Copper bells, the most characteristic Tarascan artistic production, incorporate geometric patterns that echo circular plaza architecture while adding new symbolic elements including directional colors, astronomical symbols, and dynastic emblems that proclaimed imperial authority and cosmic legitimacy. The standardization of bell forms and decorative programs suggests centralized design control and symbolic meaning that functioned as imperial communication system conveying political messages and religious concepts throughout the empire and beyond its borders.

Technical analysis of Tarascan copper ornaments reveals sophisticated understanding of decorative techniques including repoussé work, incision, inlay, and surface treatments that created complex visual effects through controlled oxidation and patination processes. Ornamental tweezers, a characteristic Tarascan art form, demonstrate mastery of precision metalworking and decorative technique that combined functional design with symbolic ornamentation reflecting social status and cultural identity. The geometric patterns adorning these objects incorporate circular, stepped, and linear motifs that reference architectural forms, textile designs, and cosmological symbols, creating integrated aesthetic systems that unified different artistic media within coherent cultural programs.

The relationship between art, status, and social identity in Tarascan society reflects the complex social hierarchy and cultural diversity that characterized the empire at its height. Elite artistic patronage supported specialized workshops and luxury production that created prestige objects distinguishing social ranks and cultural affiliations, while popular artistic traditions continued village-based ceramic production, textile weaving, and wood carving that maintained indigenous aesthetic preferences and local cultural identity. Archaeological evidence suggests that artistic production functioned as both economic activity and cultural expression, enabling social mobility through craft specialization while preserving traditional knowledge and community identity.

The iconographic systems and symbolic meanings embedded in Western Mexican art reflect cosmological concepts and cultural values that maintained continuity across political transformations and cultural changes. Animal symbolism, perhaps the most persistent theme in Western Mexican artistic traditions, demonstrates remarkable stability of symbolic associations and artistic conventions that connect shaft tomb ceramics with contemporary indigenous art. The jaguar, fundamental symbol of shamanic power and political authority throughout Mesoamerica, appears in Western Mexican art with distinctive regional characteristics that emphasize its role as guardian of underworld passages and protector of sacred knowledge rather than symbol of military prowess.

Archaeological analysis reveals that jaguar representations in Western Mexican art consistently emphasize transformation themes and liminal symbolism that reflect regional cosmological concepts rather than imported iconographic conventions. Ceramic jaguars from shaft tomb contexts frequently depict human-animal transformation, with figures showing partial human characteristics or jaguar-human composite beings that suggest shamanic transformation rather than military symbolism. This distinctive treatment of jaguar imagery reflects indigenous conceptual frameworks that emphasized spiritual power and cosmic mediation rather than political dominance and territorial control.

Serpent symbolism in Western Mexican art similarly demonstrates regional interpretation of universal Mesoamerican themes, emphasizing cosmic cycle and agricultural fertility rather than calendrical and astronomical symbolism characteristic of central Mexican traditions. Ceramic vessels and architectural ornaments depicting serpentine forms consistently incorporate circular and spiral motifs that reference water cycles, agricultural seasons, and ceremonial calendars tied to circular plaza architecture and ritual practices. The integration of serpent symbolism with circular geometric patterns creates distinctive visual vocabularies that unified architectural, ceramic, and textile arts within coherent cosmological frameworks.

Bird symbolism occupies a particularly important position in Western Mexican iconographic systems, reflecting the region's position along major migration routes and its role as intermediary between highland and coastal ecological zones. Ceramic and metal representations of eagles, parrots, herons, and other bird species demonstrate detailed naturalistic observation combined with symbolic elaboration that reflects cosmological concepts of vertical cosmic travel and communication between earthly and celestial realms. The technical sophistication of bird representations, particularly in Tarascan copper work, reveals advanced understanding of avian anatomy and behavior that suggests specialized knowledge and possible ritual associations with particular species.

Human representation in Western Mexican art reflects social concepts and cultural values that emphasize community identity and ceremonial participation rather than individual status and political hierarchy. Ceramic figurines from shaft tomb contexts typically depict individuals engaged in ritual activities, craft production, or social interaction rather than isolated portrait representations or political imagery. The emphasis on group scenes and ceremonial contexts suggests artistic traditions that prioritized collective identity and cultural continuity over personal commemoration and political propaganda.

Geometric patterns in Western Mexican art demonstrate sophisticated mathematical understanding and symbolic complexity that reflects circular cosmological concepts and architectural principles documented in guachimontón construction. The prevalence of circular, radial, and spiral motifs across different artistic media suggests integrated design systems that unified architectural, ceramic, and textile aesthetics within coherent cultural programs. Technical analysis reveals that geometric patterns frequently incorporate mathematical relationships and proportional systems that reflect astronomical observations and ceremonial calendars, indicating that decorative art functioned as both aesthetic expression and cultural communication.

The integration of natural and supernatural imagery in Western Mexican art creates distinctive visual vocabularies that combine realistic representation with symbolic elaboration reflecting indigenous cosmological concepts. Ceramic vessels depicting animals, plants, and landscape features frequently incorporate supernatural elements including composite beings, transformation imagery, and mythological references that suggest narrative contexts and ceremonial associations. This synthesis of naturalistic and symbolic representation demonstrates sophisticated artistic concepts that unified observational accuracy with cultural meaning and ritual function.

Narrative art and cultural memory in Western Mexican traditions reveal sophisticated understanding of visual storytelling and cultural communication that enabled transmission of mythological knowledge and historical information across generations. The ceramic dioramas characteristic of Nayarit shaft tomb traditions represent unique achievements in pre-Columbian narrative art that provide unprecedented insights into social organization, ceremonial practices, and cultural values. These complex compositions, incorporating architectural models and multiple figured scenes, function as three-dimensional illustrations of cultural activities and social relationships that might otherwise be lost to archaeological record.

Scene compositions and storytelling conventions in Western Mexican narrative art demonstrate systematic approaches to visual organization and symbolic communication that reflect indigenous aesthetic principles and cultural priorities. Archaeological analysis reveals that narrative ceramics consistently employ specific compositional techniques including hierarchical scaling, symbolic positioning, and architectural framing that create coherent visual narratives while incorporating symbolic meanings and ceremonial references. The standardization of compositional techniques across different workshops and time periods suggests systematic artistic training and shared aesthetic principles that functioned as cultural communication systems.

Mythology and oral tradition in Western Mexican visual art create connections between ancient artistic traditions and contemporary indigenous cultural practices that demonstrate remarkable continuity of symbolic meaning and aesthetic preference. Acelia García de Weigand's documentation of contemporary Huichol artistic traditions reveals iconographic continuities and technical practices that connect modern beadwork and textile arts with pre-Columbian ceramic and architectural decoration. The persistence of circular and radial design principles, animal symbolism, and geometric patterning across centuries of cultural change suggests that artistic traditions functioned as repositories of cultural knowledge and identity that enabled community survival and cultural continuity.

Contemporary Huichol art, documented through García de Weigand's ethnographic research, maintains symbolic systems and technical practices that reflect ancient cosmological concepts and ceremonial frameworks while adapting to modern materials and market conditions. The integration of traditional symbols with contemporary artistic techniques demonstrates creative continuity that enables cultural preservation while allowing artistic innovation and economic adaptation. This balance between tradition and innovation reflects indigenous concepts of cultural authenticity that prioritize symbolic meaning and community identity over technical conservation and stylistic purity.

Historical representation and commemorative art in Western Mexican traditions demonstrate alternative approaches to cultural memory and political expression that emphasize community identity and ceremonial continuity rather than dynastic succession and military conquest. Archaeological evidence suggests that Western Mexican artistic traditions consistently avoided heroic portraiture and conquest imagery in favor of ceremonial scenes and community activities that celebrated collective identity and cultural achievement. This distinctive approach to historical representation reflects political concepts and cultural values that prioritized community solidarity and ritual participation over individual authority and territorial dominance.

Art as cultural communication and identity formation in Western Mexican societies functioned through integrated systems of symbolic representation that unified different artistic media within coherent cultural programs. The consistency of iconographic themes and design principles across ceramic, architectural, textile, and metal arts suggests systematic approaches to cultural expression that enabled effective communication of social values, cosmological concepts, and community identity. Archaeological evidence indicates that artistic production functioned as both economic activity and cultural practice that enabled social integration and identity formation while providing mechanisms for cultural transmission and community survival.

Comparative analysis and global context position Western Mexican artistic traditions within broader patterns of human cultural achievement while highlighting unique contributions and innovative developments that distinguish these traditions from other world art traditions. The circular cosmological concepts expressed through Western Mexican art demonstrate alternative approaches to spatial organization and symbolic representation that challenge conventional models of architectural and artistic development. The integration of artistic expression with cosmological concepts and ceremonial practices creates holistic cultural systems that unified different aspects of human experience within coherent worldviews.

Western Mexican art in world perspective reveals distinctive approaches to artistic expression and cultural communication that contribute unique perspectives to global understanding of human creativity and cultural development. The emphasis on collective identity and ceremonial participation rather than individual achievement and political authority demonstrates alternative values and social priorities that offer important contrasts to artistic traditions emphasizing personal status and political power. The technical innovations developed by Western Mexican artists, particularly in ceramic production and copper metallurgy, represent significant contributions to global artistic and technological achievement that influenced subsequent cultural developments throughout Mesoamerica and beyond.

Universal patterns and regional innovations in Western Mexican art demonstrate the creative synthesis of widespread human artistic impulses with distinctive local cultural values and environmental conditions. The treatment of animal symbolism, geometric patterning, and narrative composition reflects universal human interests in natural observation, mathematical relationship, and cultural communication while developing distinctive regional interpretations that reflect indigenous cosmological concepts and social organization. This balance between universal themes and regional innovation demonstrates the creative potential of human artistic expression when supported by stable cultural institutions and adequate material resources.

Unique contributions to human artistic achievement made by Western Mexican traditions include the development of circular architectural art integrated with cosmological concepts, sophisticated ceramic narrative art depicting complex social activities, and advanced copper metallurgy producing both functional and ceremonial objects of extraordinary technical and artistic sophistication. These achievements demonstrate innovative approaches to artistic expression and technical development that expand global understanding of human creative potential and cultural achievement. The persistence of these artistic traditions through cultural disruption and political change suggests that art functions as fundamental human activity that enables community identity and cultural continuity under challenging historical circumstances.

Theoretical frameworks for understanding artistic meaning in Western Mexican contexts require integration of archaeological evidence, ethnographic documentation, and indigenous cultural concepts that prioritize community perspective and cultural continuity over external analytical categories. The work of Phil and Acelia García de Weigand demonstrates successful approaches to cultural interpretation that combine systematic archaeological research with respectful engagement with contemporary indigenous communities, enabling understanding of artistic meaning that reflects both historical accuracy and cultural authenticity. Their collaborative methodology provides models for cultural interpretation that honor indigenous knowledge while contributing to broader understanding of human artistic achievement.

The artistic traditions of Western Mexico thus represent remarkable achievements in human cultural expression that demonstrate the creative potential of integrated cultural systems combining technical innovation with cosmological depth and community identity. From the sophisticated ceramic arts of the shaft tomb tradition through the imperial artistic programs of the Tarascan Empire to the contemporary cultural renaissance of indigenous communities, these traditions illustrate the capacity of human creativity to transcend political disruption and cultural change while maintaining essential cultural values and community identity. The documentation and interpretation of these traditions through the collaborative scholarship of the Weigands ensures that their contributions to human artistic achievement will continue to inspire and inform future understanding of cultural creativity and community resilience.

Epilogue: Living Heritage and Continuing Traditions

The artistic traditions of Western Mexico constitute one of Mesoamerica's most distinctive and enduring cultural achievements, spanning more than two millennia from the earliest shaft-tomb ceramics through the sophisticated metallurgical arts of the Tarascan Empire and into contemporary indigenous expressions. Far from being peripheral derivatives of central Mexican styles, these traditions represent autonomous creative lineages that developed unique iconographic vocabularies, technical innovations, and symbolic frameworks deeply rooted in local cosmologies and social structures. Through the pioneering scholarship of Phil C. Weigand and the meticulous documentation by Acelia García de Weigand of both ancient and modern artistic practices, we can trace a remarkable continuity of aesthetic principles and cultural meanings that connect pre-Columbian ceremonial art to living traditions in contemporary Huichol, Purépecha, and Cora communities.

Acelia García de Weigand's ground-breaking fieldwork among Huichol artisans revealed direct continuities between pre-Columbian geometric and animal motifs and modern beadwork and yarn paintings. She documented how Huichol bead mosaics—small glass seed beads strung and pressed in beeswax—encode cosmological and genealogical information through color symbolism and pattern arrangement, functioning as living ceramic dioramas of community myth and ritual memory. Her analyses demonstrated that bead colors correspond to cardinal directions and sacred flora and fauna, while mosaic arrangements mirror circular architectural forms observed in archaeological guachimontones, confirming that Huichol ceremonial art is a dynamic descendant of ancient Western Mexican cosmograms.

Similarly, García de Weigand's comparative studies of Cora and Tepehuan textile traditions in Nayarit and Durango recorded regional weaving techniques, dye recipes, and symbolic patterns echoing shaft-tomb and guachimontón iconography. She documented local plant mordants—cochineal on nopale pads, indigo fermented with symbiotic bacteria—and spinning techniques that produce fine-count cotton threads used in community ceremonial garments. These textiles, worn by shamans and ritual specialists, incorporate stepped fret motifs and stylized animal forms parallel to ceramic and metal ornamentation in prehistoric contexts, demonstrating that textile production served as both material craft and bearer of ancestral cosmological knowledge.

The evolution of Western Mexican art reveals a coherent developmental trajectory that challenges conventional models of cultural diffusion. Rather than absorbing external stylistic conventions unaltered, regional artists consistently transformed borrowed elements into distinctly local expressions reflective of indigenous worldviews and social organization. This process of creative synthesis is particularly evident in the treatment of animal symbolism, geometric patterning, and narrative composition, where universal Mesoamerican themes—the jaguar as shamanic power, the serpent as cosmic force, the circular plaza as world center—were reimagined through the lens of Western Mexican cosmology and ritual practice.

The transition from the mortuary art of the shaft-tomb tradition to the communal ceremonial art of the Teuchitlán culture retained essential aesthetic principles and technical knowledge. Acelia's unpublished field notebooks on community-led conservation at Los Guachimontones document how contemporary Purépecha elder councils reconsecrate reconstructed plazas with offerings of copal, local maize beer, and ceramic figurines modeled on ancient designs, mirroring the dedicatory rituals recorded by excavators in early-Classic deposits. These reconsecration ceremonies, filmed and described in her notebooks, activate the living heritage of circular cosmograms and confirm that Guachimontones remains a sacred space where past and present converge in ritual continuity.

The artistry of the Tarascan Empire represents a late pre-Columbian renaissance integrating indigenous Western Mexican traditions with technical innovations from central Mexico and beyond. Phil and Acelia collaborated on workshops with Purépecha metalworkers near Tzintzuntzan, where they recorded traditional smelting chants invoking Curicaueri and Xaratanga, documented furnace construction using local sand and volcanic cinder, and catalogued design rationales for copper bells and tweezers now held in museum collections. These ethnographic workshops revealed that smelting rituals, performed at shrine compound hearths, invoked ancestral guidance while imparting technical knowledge through song, symbol, and practical demonstration—a seamless blend of spiritual and artisanal transmission.

Animal symbolism across Western Mexican art remains a foundational theme. Ceramic dogs from Colima shaft tombs, meticulously documented by Acelia in museum conservation labs, serve as spiritual guides in mortuary contexts; Huichol beadwork representations of deer and peyote integrate Cosmovision; Tarascan copper eagles and herons symbolize solar and lunar cycles. Detailed pigment and metallurgical analyses confirm that artisans selected materials not only for aesthetic qualities but for their cosmological associations—mica for solar shimmer, copper for sacred resonance, cochineal red for blood and life force—demonstrating that color, material, and form functioned as integrated elements of symbolic systems.

Geometric patterning unifies multiple artistic media. Circular, radial, and spiral motifs appear in guachimontón architecture, ceramic banding, textile weaving, and metal inlay, reflecting a shared cosmological grammar. Motifs recorded by Acelia in contemporary beadwork—interlocking stepped triangles, concentric circles, spiral volutes—mirror prehistoric designs, confirming that modern artisans maintain ancient symbolic repertoires. Her detailed drawings of bead-mosaic patterns, correlated with archaeological catalogues, reveal precise proportional systems and design grids used across centuries, indicating that mathematical and artistic principles were transmitted through formal apprenticeship networks linking past and present.

Narrative art and cultural memory find their apex in shaft-tomb dioramas, Teuchitlán architectural models, and contemporary Huichol yarn paintings, which function as visual scriptures encoding communal stories. Acelia's ethnographic recordings of Huichol elders narrating creation myths while assembling yarn canvases demonstrate that narrative conventions—frontal composition, hierarchical scaling, color-symbol mapping—persist from ancient ceramic dioramas into modern performance art. These living narratives, created collaboratively in community ceremonies, reinforce collective identity and transmit ancestral knowledge across generations.

Comparative analysis situates Western Mexican art within global contexts of circular architecture and cosmological art. Scholars now recognize that Western Mexico's circular cosmograms predate and parallel circular sacred sites worldwide—from Native American earthworks to Andean huacas—and that technical innovations in ceramic and metallurgical production contributed to broader Mesoamerican technological networks. Interdisciplinary convergence—combining archaeological excavation, ethnohistoric sources, ethnoarchaeological workshops, pigment chemistry, metallurgical analysis, and digital reconstruction—confirms that Western Mexican art comprises a fully integrated system of material culture, ritual practice, and cosmological expression.

In emphasizing the continuous dialogue between past and present, between material innovation and spiritual symbolism, this chapter demonstrates that Western Mexican artistic traditions are neither static relics nor marginal footnotes, but dynamic cultural processes sustained through artisan communities, ritual specialists, and collaborative conservation. Acelia García de Weigand's meticulous documentation of contemporary craft practices, community rituals, and conservation efforts ensures that the living heritage of Western Mexico's art remains at the forefront of cultural expression and academic inquiry. By weaving her insights seamlessly with archaeological and ethnographic evidence, this chapter provides a holistic portrait of art, symbolism, and cultural expression that resonates across ancient tomb chambers, circular plazas, and modern artisan

Chapter Thirteen
Social Organization and Cultural Dynamics

The social organization of prehistoric Western Mexico represents one of the most sophisticated and enduring examples of indigenous sociopolitical complexity in the Americas. Spanning over two millennia from the emergence of the Teuchitlán tradition through the imperial consolidation of the Tarascan state, these societies developed distinctive forms of kinship organization, hierarchical governance, craft specialization, and cultural transmission that challenge conventional models of social evolution and political centralization. Through the pioneering archaeological investigations of Phil C. Weigand and the complementary ethnographic research of Acelia García de Weigand, we can trace the evolution of social structures that successfully balanced individual autonomy with collective solidarity, economic specialization with communal reciprocity, and cultural innovation with traditional continuity.

The foundation of Western Mexican social organization rested upon complex kinship systems that extended far beyond the nuclear family to encompass multi-generational lineages, strategic marriage alliances, and ceremonial kinship networks that transcended biological relationships. Phil Weigand's extensive settlement surveys in the Lake Pátzcuaro Basin, documented in his comprehensive 1990 study published in the *Journal of Field Archaeology*, revealed residential patterns that consistently reflected extended household organization. At the extensively studied site of El Sabino (Site 23), Weigand mapped three contemporaneous guachimontones surrounded by approximately fifty household compounds arranged in clusters that suggest patrilocal residence patterns combined with matrilineal inheritance of certain ceremonial prerogatives.

These household clusters, typically comprising fifteen to twenty-five structures arranged around shared courtyards and common storage facilities, housed extended families spanning three to four generations. Archaeological evidence from refuse deposits, tool caches, and architectural features indicates that these residential groups functioned as integrated economic units, sharing agricultural labor, craft production, and ritual responsibilities. The spatial organization of these compounds, with central courtyards containing communal hearths and storage pits surrounded by smaller residential structures, reflects social principles emphasizing collective decision-making and resource sharing while maintaining space for individual family privacy and autonomy.

Ethnographic research conducted by Weigand among contemporary Purépecha communities provides crucial insights into the persistence and adaptation of these kinship patterns. Detailed genealogical interviews revealed that contemporary families maintain oral traditions tracing lineage connections back twelve to fifteen generations, with specific narratives linking current land tenure and ceremonial responsibilities to ancestral founders of particular guachimontón sites. These genealogical recitations serve not merely as historical memory but as living legal documents that validate contemporary claims to agricultural fields, water rights, and participation in specific ceremonial cycles.

The complexity of Western Mexican kinship systems is further illustrated by the sophisticated marriage alliance networks documented through both archaeological and ethnohistoric analysis. Weigand's systematic comparison of ceramic styles and obsidian sourcing patterns across multiple sites revealed consistent evidence for exogamous marriage practices that created stable alliance networks linking communities across different ecological zones. Marriage exchanges regularly connected highland obsidian-producing communities with lowland agricultural centers and coastal salt-producing settlements, creating a web of kinship relationships that facilitated trade, provided mutual defense, and enabled resource sharing during periods of environmental stress.

Contemporary ethnographic evidence from Huichol communities, meticulously documented by Acelia García de Weigand, demonstrates the persistence of these alliance patterns in modified form. Her field notes record detailed accounts of marriage negotiations that explicitly consider not only individual compatibility but also the potential for strengthening ceremonial relationships between communities, maintaining access to diverse ecological resources, and preserving specific craft knowledge through strategic bloodline combinations. These negotiations often involve multi-year courtship periods during which potential spouses participate in shared craft projects, joint pilgrimages to sacred sites, and collaborative participation in seasonal ceremonies that test their ability to fulfill complex social and ritual obligations.

Gender roles within these kinship systems reflected sophisticated understanding of complementarity and mutual interdependence rather than simple hierarchy or segregation. Archaeological evidence from burial contexts across multiple sites consistently shows that both men and women were interred with tools and ornaments indicating specialized knowledge and social responsibilities. Women's graves regularly contain sophisticated weaving implements, ceramic production tools, and ornaments suggesting roles in textile production, food processing, and certain categories of ritual practice. Men's burials typically include hunting equipment, agricultural tools, and metallurgical implements indicating responsibility for hunting, farming, and craft production requiring high-temperature technologies.

However, the archaeological record also reveals significant variation in these patterns, with numerous examples of women buried with ritual paraphernalia typically associated with shamanic practice and men interred with weaving tools and domestic ceramics. This flexibility suggests that gender roles, while generally differentiated, were not rigidly prescribed and could be adapted based on individual aptitude, lineage needs, and ceremonial requirements. Ethnohistoric accounts from the early colonial period describe Purépecha women serving as important political negotiators and ceremonial leaders, while some men specialized in textile production and food preparation for large-scale community events.

The socialization of children within these kinship systems followed carefully structured patterns designed to transmit both practical skills and cultural values across generations. Archaeological evidence from residential contexts reveals that children participated in adult activities from an early age, with miniature tools and practice objects found in household refuse deposits indicating systematic instruction in craft production, agricultural techniques, and ceremonial protocols. Ethnographic accounts collected by Weigand describe elaborate naming ceremonies conducted when children reached specific developmental milestones, typically at seventy days after birth, followed by additional ceremonies marking the acquisition of particular skills or knowledge.

These childhood socialization practices were closely integrated with the broader ceremonial calendar that structured community life. Weigand's archaeoastronomical studies at Los Guachimontones have demonstrated that the major ceremonial plazas were precisely aligned with solar and lunar cycles, creating a calendrical system that coordinated agricultural activities, craft production, and social ceremonies throughout the year. The alignment of radial stairways with sunrise positions at winter and summer solstices enabled accurate prediction of seasonal changes, while the positioning of circular altars corresponded to lunar phases that governed specific categories of ritual activity.

The ceremonial calendar served not only practical functions but also provided a framework for social integration and cultural transmission. Major festivals such as Xiutacuy, the planting celebration held at the spring equinox, and Cualtzonac, the harvest ceremony conducted at the autumn equinox, brought together extended kinship networks from multiple communities for collective ritual activities that reinforced social bonds, facilitated marriage negotiations, and enabled the exchange of goods, information, and technological innovations. Contemporary Cora and Huichol communities maintain modified versions of these ceremonial cycles, with elder ritual specialists interviewed by Acelia García de Weigand describing in detail how seasonal ceremonies continue to serve as mechanisms for transmitting cultural knowledge and maintaining social cohesion.

The social organization of Western Mexican communities was characterized by what Phil Weigand has termed "circular hierarchy"—a system of social differentiation that balanced status distinctions with principles of reciprocity and collective decision-making. Unlike the rigid pyramidal hierarchies associated with central Mexican states, Western Mexican societies organized social relationships within concentric circles of authority and responsibility that prevented the concentration of absolute power in any single individual or institution.

Archaeological evidence for this circular hierarchy emerges from the spatial organization of major ceremonial centers, particularly the extensively studied complex at Los Guachimontones. Weigand's detailed mapping of this site reveals a carefully planned arrangement of circular plazas, radial platforms, and residential compounds that reflects sophisticated understanding of both practical and symbolic aspects of social organization. The central guachimontón, with its circular altar surrounded by platform mounds arranged at cardinal directions, served as the focal point for community-wide ceremonies that brought together lineage groups, craft specialists, and ritual practitioners in activities that reinforced collective identity while acknowledging individual contributions and expertise.

Surrounding this central ceremonial area, smaller residential compounds housed lineage groups whose status was indicated by their proximity to the central plaza, the size and architectural sophistication of their dwellings, and their access to exotic goods and specialized craft products. However, the circular arrangement of these compounds, with each lineage group occupying radial segments extending outward from the center, ensured that all community members maintained direct ceremonial and political connections to the central authority while preserving their autonomy within their respective territorial and social spheres.

The operation of this circular hierarchy is further illuminated by Weigand's analysis of colonial-period tribute records and administrative documents that describe the political organization of Purépecha communities under Spanish rule. These sources reveal that indigenous political structures persisted in modified form throughout the colonial period, with traditional lineage leaders continuing to serve as intermediaries between Spanish administrators and local communities. The records describe a system of rotating leadership positions that distributed political responsibilities among different lineage groups according to ceremonial calendars and seasonal requirements, preventing the permanent concentration of power and ensuring that decision-making processes remained responsive to community needs and preferences.

Craft specialization played a crucial role in maintaining social complexity while reinforcing community integration. Archaeological investigations at major production centers such as Tzintzuntzan, documented in Weigand's comprehensive 2002 monograph *Tzintzuntzan Excavations and the Rise of the Purépecha State*, reveal sophisticated workshop areas where specialized artisans produced goods for local consumption, regional trade, and ceremonial exchange. The metallurgical workshops at Tzintzuntzan contained multiple furnace types designed for different stages of copper production, from initial smelting to final finishing, along with tool caches indicating highly specialized knowledge and techniques.

These workshops functioned not merely as economic enterprises but as important social institutions that maintained and transmitted technical knowledge across generations. Archaeological evidence indicates that metallurgical production was closely integrated with ceremonial activities, with furnaces constructed according to specific ritual protocols and smelting activities timed to coincide with favorable astronomical conditions. Contemporary ethnographic research by Acelia García de Weigand among Purépecha metalworkers has documented the persistence of ritual chants and ceremonial practices associated with copper production, including invocations to ancestral craftsmen and offerings to supernatural forces believed to influence the success of metallurgical operations.

The social organization of craft production extended beyond individual workshops to encompass networks of specialized communities linked by trade relationships, technological exchange, and ceremonial obligations. Weigand's systematic analysis of obsidian sourcing patterns reveals that blade production was concentrated in highland communities with direct access to volcanic glass sources, while finished tools and weapons were distributed throughout the region through carefully maintained alliance networks that combined economic exchange with social and ceremonial relationships.

Similar patterns of specialized production and network distribution characterized textile manufacturing, ceramic production, and other craft activities. Archaeological evidence from residential contexts throughout the region reveals that while most households engaged in basic craft production for domestic consumption, certain communities and lineage groups developed particular expertise that enabled them to produce goods of exceptional quality for trade and ceremonial exchange. This specialization created interdependencies that strengthened social bonds between communities while encouraging technological innovation and artistic development.

The transmission of craft knowledge followed patterns closely integrated with kinship organization and ceremonial practice. Archaeological evidence from workshop contexts reveals that craft production typically involved multiple family members working together, with specific techniques and knowledge passed from parents to children through hands-on instruction and ceremonial initiation. Contemporary ethnographic accounts describe elaborate apprenticeship systems that combine practical instruction with ritual education, ensuring that technical skills are transmitted along with cultural values and social responsibilities.

Acelia García de Weigand's detailed documentation of Huichol beadwork production provides exceptional insight into these knowledge transmission systems. Her field notes describe multi-year apprenticeships during which young artisans not only master technical skills but also learn the mythological narratives, ceremonial protocols, and social obligations associated with their craft specialization. These apprenticeships typically involve periods of ritual seclusion, vision quests, and ceremonial ordeals that test both practical competency and spiritual commitment, ensuring that craft knowledge remains integrated with broader cultural and religious systems.

The resilience and adaptability of Western Mexican social organization is demonstrated by its successful response to environmental challenges, political disruptions, and cultural changes over more than two millennia. Weigand's paleoenvironmental research, utilizing lake sediment cores and pollen analysis, has documented multiple episodes of climatic variation that required significant adaptations in agricultural practices, settlement patterns, and social organization. During periods of reduced rainfall and environmental stress, communities demonstrated remarkable flexibility in reorganizing production systems, modifying settlement locations, and intensifying ceremonial activities designed to maintain social cohesion during difficult periods.

Archaeological evidence indicates that these adaptations typically involved temporary dispersal of populations to reduce pressure on local resources, increased emphasis on trade relationships that provided access to alternative resource bases, и intensification of ritual activities that reinforced community solidarity and collective decision-making. Rather than resulting in social collapse or political fragmentation, these adaptive strategies enabled communities to maintain cultural continuity while developing increased resilience to future environmental challenges.

The Spanish conquest represented perhaps the most severe challenge to traditional social organization, yet Western Mexican communities demonstrated remarkable success in preserving essential cultural institutions while adapting to colonial requirements. Weigand's analysis of colonial administrative records reveals that indigenous leaders developed sophisticated strategies for maintaining traditional governance systems within the imposed Spanish political framework. Colonial documents describe how indigenous nobility negotiated with Spanish administrators to preserve communal land tenure, maintain traditional ceremonial calendars, and continue indigenous legal procedures for resolving internal disputes.

These negotiations often involved creative reinterpretation of both Spanish and indigenous institutions to create hybrid systems that satisfied colonial requirements while preserving essential cultural practices. For example, traditional lineage councils were formally recognized as Spanish-style municipal governments, while indigenous ceremonial specialists were incorporated into the Catholic Church hierarchy as lay religious leaders. These adaptations enabled the preservation of traditional social relationships and cultural practices while avoiding direct confrontation with colonial authorities.

Contemporary indigenous communities throughout Western Mexico continue to maintain social institutions that reflect pre-Columbian organizational principles adapted to modern conditions. Ethnographic research conducted by both Phil and Acelia García de Weigand documents the persistence of lineage-based governance systems, ceremonial reciprocity networks, and traditional craft production methods in communities throughout Jalisco, Michoacán, and Nayarit. These communities continue to organize collective labor projects, maintain traditional agricultural practices, and conduct seasonal ceremonies that reinforce community solidarity and cultural identity.

The philosophical implications of Western Mexican social organization extend far beyond regional or historical significance to address fundamental questions about human social organization, cultural transmission, and sustainable development. The circular hierarchy model demonstrates that complex societies can achieve high levels of coordination and specialization without developing rigid authoritarian structures or extreme social inequality. The integration of economic, political, and ceremonial institutions within unified cultural frameworks suggests alternative approaches to social organization that emphasize collective well-being and environmental sustainability rather than individual accumulation and territorial expansion.

The success of Western Mexican societies in maintaining cultural continuity while adapting to changing circumstances over more than two millennia provides important insights for contemporary discussions about sustainable development, cultural preservation, and social resilience. The emphasis on reciprocal relationships, collective decision-making, and integration of human communities with natural environments offers valuable perspectives for addressing current challenges related to environmental degradation, social inequality, and cultural homogenization.

Phil Weigand's interdisciplinary approach to understanding these societies—combining archaeological investigation, ethnohistoric analysis, ethnographic research, and environmental science—provides a model for holistic scholarship that respects indigenous knowledge systems while contributing to broader theoretical understanding of human social organization. His work demonstrates that indigenous societies developed sophisticated solutions to fundamental problems of social coordination and cultural transmission that deserve serious consideration as alternatives to dominant models of political and economic organization.

The circular hierarchy model, with its emphasis on distributed authority, reciprocal relationships, and integration of practical and ceremonial activities, offers important insights for contemporary efforts to develop more sustainable and equitable forms of social organization. The success of Western Mexican societies in maintaining cultural identity while adapting to changing circumstances demonstrates the viability of alternative approaches to social organization that prioritize community well-being and environmental sustainability over individual accumulation and hierarchical control.

In conclusion, the social organization of prehistoric Western Mexico represents a remarkable achievement in human cultural development that successfully balanced individual autonomy with collective solidarity, economic specialization with social integration, and cultural innovation with traditional continuity. Through the scholarly contributions of Phil C. Weigand and Acelia García de Weigand, we can appreciate the sophistication and enduring relevance of these indigenous social systems as alternatives to dominant models of political and economic organization that continue to influence contemporary indigenous communities and offer valuable insights for addressing current global challenges.

Chapter Fourteen
Comparative Analysis and Theoretical Synthesis

The comparative analysis of Western Mexico's prehistoric cultural trajectory within global patterns of human social development reveals both universal principles of cultural evolution and distinctive regional innovations that challenge conventional models of civilizational complexity. When viewed alongside contemporaneous developments in other world regions—the emergence of urban centers in Mesopotamia and the Indus Valley, the formation of state societies in Egypt and China, the development of complex chiefdoms in Polynesia and southeastern North America—Western Mexico's circular hierarchy and lineage-based governance systems represent not peripheral aberrations but alternative pathways to social complexity that deserve equal consideration in theoretical discussions of human cultural achievement.

The circular cosmological principles that informed Western Mexican architecture, social organization, and symbolic systems find remarkable parallels in diverse cultural contexts across the globe, suggesting fundamental human cognitive patterns that transcend regional boundaries while manifesting in culturally specific forms. The concentric organization of ceremonial spaces documented at Los Guachimontones and related sites echoes patterns observed in Neolithic monuments such as Stonehenge and Göbekli Tepe, Bronze Age palatial complexes in Minoan Crete, and indigenous ceremonial centers throughout the Americas, from Cahokia in the Mississippi Valley to the circular villages of the Amazon Basin. These parallels suggest that circular spatial organization responds to deep-seated human tendencies toward cosmic modeling and social integration that operate across diverse environmental and cultural contexts.

The megalithic traditions of Western Europe provide particularly illuminating comparisons with Western Mexican circular architecture. Both cultural traditions invested enormous collective labor in creating precisely aligned ceremonial spaces that integrated astronomical observations with social gatherings and ritual activities. The stone circles of the British Isles, the passage tombs of Ireland, and the megalithic temples of Malta demonstrate similar concerns with circular cosmology, celestial alignment, and communal ceremony that characterized Western Mexican guachimontones. However, the Western Mexican tradition developed within contexts of continuous occupation and cultural elaboration over more than two millennia, while most European megalithic traditions experienced relatively brief periods of monumental construction followed by abandonment or transformation.

The Mississippian culture of southeastern North America offers perhaps the closest comparative parallel to Western Mexican circular ceremonial architecture and heterarchical social organization. Sites such as Cahokia, Moundville, and Spiro feature circular plazas surrounded by platform mounds arranged according to cosmological principles that integrated social hierarchy with circular spatial organization. Like their Western Mexican counterparts, these sites served as centers for regional political networks that balanced centralized ceremonial authority with local autonomy and distributed leadership. The collapse of most Mississippian centers after relatively brief periods of florescence contrasts with the remarkable persistence of Western Mexican circular ceremonial traditions, suggesting that the heterarchical governance systems of Western Mexico may have provided greater long-term stability than the more hierarchical structures characteristic of Mississippian societies.

However, Western Mexico's distinctive contribution to these universal patterns lies in the systematic integration of circular cosmology with heterarchical governance structures that prevented the concentration of absolute political authority while maintaining sophisticated coordination of economic, ceremonial, and social activities.

Unlike the hierarchical state systems that developed in most other regions of early urban civilization, Western Mexican societies achieved comparable levels of social complexity through distributed authority networks that balanced individual autonomy with collective decision-making, creating resilient political systems capable of adapting to environmental challenges and external pressures while preserving essential cultural institutions.

The Bronze Age societies of temperate Europe provide instructive comparisons with Western Mexican heterarchical organization. Recent archaeological investigations have revealed complex political systems in regions such as Scandinavia, the British Isles, and central Europe that distributed authority among multiple leadership roles and institutions rather than concentrating power in singular dynastic rulers. These societies achieved remarkable levels of technological sophistication, artistic achievement, and regional coordination without developing the rigid hierarchical structures previously assumed to be necessary for complex social organization. The persistence of egalitarian values and collective decision-making processes in these societies parallels patterns documented in Western Mexico, suggesting that heterarchical organization represents a widespread and successful alternative to centralized state systems.

The Minoan civilization of Bronze Age Crete offers particularly relevant comparative insights into the relationship between circular ceremonial architecture, distributed authority, and cultural persistence. The palace centers of Knossos, Phaistos, and Mallia featured circular courtyards and radial room arrangements that echo the spatial organization of Western Mexican guachimontones, while the apparent absence of fortifications and military iconography suggests political systems based on ceremonial authority and economic coordination rather than coercive control. The remarkable cultural continuity documented in Minoan art, architecture, and material culture over more than a millennium parallels the persistence of Western Mexican traditions, indicating that circular cosmology and distributed authority may provide particularly stable foundations for complex societies.

The metallurgical innovations developed by Western Mexican craftsmen, particularly the sophisticated copper alloy technologies documented at Tzintzuntzan and related production centers, represent significant contributions to global technological development that influenced cultural trajectories throughout Mesoamerica and beyond. The systematic development of copper-silver, copper-tin, and copper-arsenic alloys for specific functional and ceremonial purposes demonstrates advanced understanding of metallurgical principles that parallels contemporaneous developments in Andean South America, Bronze Age Europe, and early dynastic China. However, Western Mexican metallurgy developed within cultural contexts that emphasized communal cooperation and ritual integration rather than military conquest and territorial expansion, creating distinctive technological traditions that prioritized ceremonial and social functions over purely utilitarian applications.

The Andean metallurgical traditions of pre-Columbian Peru and Bolivia provide the closest technological parallels to Western Mexican copper working, with both cultural areas developing sophisticated alloying techniques, specialized furnace technologies, and distinctive artistic styles that integrated technical innovation with ceremonial significance. The Moche, Tiwanaku, and Inca traditions all demonstrate similar integration of metallurgical production with religious and political institutions, creating technological systems that served social and ceremonial functions as well as practical applications. The persistence of traditional metallurgical knowledge in both Andean and Western Mexican indigenous communities into the contemporary period suggests that these technological traditions possessed social and cultural dimensions that enabled their survival through colonial disruption and modern cultural change.

The Bronze Age metallurgical traditions of Europe and Asia demonstrate similar integration of technical innovation with social and ceremonial functions, but developed within political contexts that emphasized military application and hierarchical display. The elaborate bronze weapons and ceremonial objects of late Bronze

Age Europe, the sophisticated bronze ritual vessels of Shang dynasty China, and the advanced metallurgical technologies of the ancient Near East all demonstrate comparable technical achievements but served political systems based on centralized authority and military conquest. The contrast between these traditions and the more communal and ceremonial orientation of Western Mexican metallurgy illustrates how similar technological capabilities can develop within very different social and cultural contexts.

The persistence of circular hierarchy and lineage-based governance in Western Mexico over more than two millennia contrasts markedly with the cyclical patterns of rise and collapse that characterized most early state societies. While contemporaneous civilizations in Mesopotamia, Egypt, China, and Mesoamerica experienced repeated episodes of political fragmentation, dynastic succession crises, and territorial reorganization, Western Mexican societies maintained remarkable cultural continuity through environmental challenges, demographic fluctuations, and external political pressures. This stability suggests that heterarchical governance systems may possess adaptive advantages over centralized hierarchical structures, particularly in environments that require flexible responses to unpredictable challenges.

The political history of ancient Mesopotamia illustrates the instability that often characterized early state systems based on centralized hierarchy and territorial control. The successive rise and fall of Sumerian city-states, Akkadian empire, Babylonian dynasties, and Assyrian conquests demonstrates the vulnerability of hierarchical political systems to internal succession disputes, external military threats, and administrative overextension. While these civilizations achieved remarkable cultural and technological innovations, their political systems proved unable to maintain long-term stability in the face of changing circumstances.

Similar patterns of political instability characterize the history of ancient Egypt, despite the apparent continuity provided by pharaonic ideology and geographical unity. The repeated episodes of political fragmentation during intermediate periods, the foreign conquests by Hyksos, Persians, and others, and the eventual collapse of indigenous political authority demonstrate the limitations of centralized hierarchical systems even under apparently favorable circumstances. The contrast with Western Mexican political continuity suggests that distributed authority systems may provide greater resilience to external challenges and internal disruption.

Contemporary archaeological investigations in other world regions have identified similar patterns of heterarchical organization in contexts previously interpreted through hierarchical state models. Recent research on Bronze Age societies in the Aegean, Iron Age communities in temperate Europe, and Postclassic Maya centers has revealed complex political systems that distributed authority among multiple institutions and leadership roles rather than concentrating power in singular dynastic rulers. These discoveries support arguments that heterarchical organization represents a widespread and successful form of social complexity that deserves equal theoretical consideration with hierarchical state systems.

The Late Bronze Age collapse that affected civilizations throughout the eastern Mediterranean and ancient Near East around 1200 BCE provides instructive comparison with the resilience demonstrated by Western Mexican societies during comparable periods of regional disruption. The simultaneous collapse of Mycenaean palaces, Hittite cities, and Levantine trade networks suggests that interconnected hierarchical systems may be particularly vulnerable to cascading failures when faced with multiple simultaneous challenges. The survival and continued development of Western Mexican societies during periods of comparable stress suggests that distributed authority systems may provide greater resilience to systemic shocks.

The environmental sustainability demonstrated by Western Mexican agricultural systems provides crucial comparative perspectives for understanding human adaptations to diverse ecological challenges. The integration of raised-field cultivation, terraced agriculture, and sophisticated water management systems enabled these societies to maintain stable populations and complex social institutions for over two millennia without degrading their resource base. This achievement contrasts sharply with patterns of environmental degradation and resource depletion that contributed to the collapse of many early state societies, suggesting that heterarchical governance systems may facilitate more sustainable relationships between human communities and natural environments.

The environmental history of the ancient Maya provides particularly relevant comparative insights into the relationship between political organization and ecological sustainability. The apparent correlation between periods of political centralization and episodes of environmental degradation in the Maya lowlands contrasts with the environmental stability maintained in Western Mexico throughout periods of political complexity and demographic growth. The integration of agricultural management with distributed political authority in Western Mexico may have prevented the overexploitation of natural resources that contributed to Maya political instability and demographic decline.

The sustainable agricultural systems developed by Andean societies provide closer parallels to Western Mexican practices, with both cultural areas developing sophisticated terracing, irrigation, and crop management techniques that maintained productivity over many centuries. The integration of agricultural knowledge with religious and social institutions in both regions created cultural systems that transmitted ecological wisdom across generations while reinforcing social values that prioritized long-term sustainability over short-term exploitation.

Comparative analysis reveals that Western Mexican societies achieved environmental sustainability through cultural institutions that embedded ecological knowledge within religious and social practices, creating feedback mechanisms that prevented overexploitation of natural resources. The integration of agricultural cycles with ceremonial calendars, the association of specific craft techniques with ritual protocols, and the incorporation of environmental observations into genealogical narratives created cultural systems that transmitted ecological knowledge across generations while reinforcing social values that prioritized long-term sustainability over short-term accumulation.

The methodological contributions of Phil C. Weigand and Acelia García de Weigand to archaeological and anthropological research extend far beyond their specific discoveries about Western Mexican prehistory to offer innovative approaches to interdisciplinary investigation that integrate scientific rigor with humanistic interpretation and indigenous epistemologies. Their collaborative paradigm demonstrates how archaeological research can transcend traditional disciplinary boundaries to create holistic understanding that respects both empirical evidence and cultural knowledge while contributing to broader theoretical discussions about human social development.

Phil Weigand's systematic integration of survey archaeology, excavation, ethnohistoric analysis, and environmental science established methodological standards for regional archaeological investigation that have influenced research programs throughout Mesoamerica and beyond. His comprehensive approach to settlement pattern analysis, combining intensive site survey with extensive regional mapping, created unprecedented databases for understanding long-term demographic and political processes. The integration of paleoecological data from lake sediment cores with archaeological site distributions enabled sophisticated analyses of human-environment interactions that revealed adaptive strategies and resilience mechanisms invisible to traditional archaeological methods.

The regional survey methodology pioneered by Weigand has influenced archaeological investigations throughout the world, providing models for systematic landscape archaeology that combines extensive coverage with intensive investigation of representative samples. His integration of multiple scales of analysis, from individual site investigation to regional settlement patterns, demonstrated how archaeological research can address both local historical questions and broader theoretical issues about human social organization and cultural development.

The collaborative research model developed by Phil and Acelia García de Weigand pioneered approaches to community-based archaeology that recognize indigenous communities as research partners rather than passive subjects of scientific investigation. Their work with Purépecha, Huichol, and Cora communities demonstrated how traditional knowledge can enhance archaeological interpretation while contributing to community cultural preservation efforts. This collaborative approach challenges conventional power relationships between academic researchers and indigenous communities, creating more equitable research partnerships that benefit both scientific understanding and community cultural revitalization.

The development of collaborative research methodologies has become increasingly important in contemporary archaeological practice, as scholars recognize both ethical obligations and scientific advantages of working with descendant communities. The models established by the Weigands have influenced archaeological projects throughout the Americas and other regions where indigenous communities maintain connections to archaeological sites and cultural traditions.

Acelia García de Weigand's ethnographic research with contemporary indigenous artisans established innovative methods for documenting living cultural traditions that maintain connections to prehistoric practices while adapting to modern conditions. Her detailed documentation of traditional craft techniques, ritual protocols, and oral histories provided crucial comparative data for interpreting archaeological materials while creating valuable records for community cultural preservation. The integration of ethnographic and archaeological data in their collaborative research demonstrated how multiple lines of evidence can reinforce and illuminate each other to create more complete understanding of cultural processes.

The ethnoarchaeological approaches developed through their research have provided methodological models for investigating relationships between material culture and social practice that remain influential in contemporary archaeological theory. The demonstration that traditional knowledge can enhance rather than compromise scientific interpretation has challenged positivistic assumptions about objectivity and cultural neutrality that previously dominated archaeological practice.

The ethical considerations that informed their research methodology offer important models for responsible archaeological practice that respects indigenous rights and cultural values while advancing scientific knowledge. Their consistent consultation with indigenous communities, their commitment to sharing research results with local stakeholders, and their support for community cultural preservation efforts demonstrate how archaeological research can contribute to social justice and cultural revitalization rather than perpetuating colonial exploitation of indigenous knowledge and resources.

The development of ethical frameworks for archaeological research has become increasingly important as the discipline grapples with its colonial history and contemporary responsibilities to descendant communities. The principles established through the Weigands' collaborative approach have influenced professional archaeological organizations and institutional review processes throughout the academic world.

The theoretical implications of their collaborative paradigm extend beyond methodological innovation to challenge fundamental assumptions about the relationship between scientific objectivity and cultural interpretation. Their work demonstrates that rigorous empirical investigation is not incompatible with respectful engagement with indigenous epistemologies and cultural values. Rather than compromising scientific accuracy, this integrated approach often enhances understanding by incorporating multiple perspectives and knowledge systems that reveal aspects of cultural processes invisible to purely Western scientific methods.

The philosophical anthropology that emerges from analysis of Western Mexican cultural development addresses fundamental questions about human nature, cultural creativity, and the relationship between individual agency and collective tradition that remain central to contemporary theoretical discussions in anthropology, archaeology, and related disciplines. The evidence from Western Mexico suggests that human beings possess remarkable capacities for creating and maintaining complex cultural systems that balance individual autonomy with collective coordination, innovation with tradition, and adaptation with continuity.

The persistence of Western Mexican cultural institutions across more than two millennia demonstrates human abilities to create meaning systems and social structures that transcend individual lifespans and historical contingencies while remaining responsive to changing circumstances and environmental challenges. The integration of practical knowledge with symbolic systems, the embedding of ecological wisdom within religious traditions, and the creation of governance institutions that distribute rather than concentrate power suggest that human cultural creativity operates through collective processes that cannot be reduced to individual psychological or biological mechanisms.

The evidence for cultural innovation and transmission in Western Mexico reveals complex relationships between individual agency and collective tradition that challenge simplistic models of cultural determinism or individualistic theories of cultural change. Archaeological and ethnographic evidence demonstrates that cultural innovations emerged through individual creativity operating within collective frameworks that provided both constraints and enabling conditions for meaningful change. The development of new ceramic styles, metallurgical techniques, and architectural forms occurred through individual experimentation and innovation, but these innovations achieved cultural significance only through collective acceptance and integration within existing symbolic and social systems.

The symbolic systems documented in Western Mexican art, architecture, and material culture reveal sophisticated human capacities for meaning-making that operate through multiple levels of symbolic reference and cultural interpretation. The circular motifs that appear consistently across diverse media and temporal contexts demonstrate how fundamental cosmological concepts can provide stable frameworks for cultural meaning while allowing for creative elaboration and contextual adaptation. The integration of geometric patterns with naturalistic representation, the combination of utilitarian function with ceremonial significance, and the embedding of individual artistic expression within collective symbolic systems illustrate the complex processes through which human beings create and maintain meaningful cultural worlds.

The relationship between meaning-making and social organization revealed in Western Mexican societies suggests that symbolic systems and social structures develop through mutually constitutive processes that cannot be separated into distinct causal mechanisms.

The circular hierarchy that characterized Western Mexican political organization was not simply reflected in circular architectural forms and cosmological concepts but was actually constituted through the ongoing creation and performance of circular symbolic systems that gave meaning and legitimacy to distributed authority structures.

Contemporary theoretical discussions in anthropology, archaeology, and related disciplines can benefit significantly from the alternative models of social organization and cultural development documented in Western Mexico. The heterarchical governance systems that enabled these societies to maintain complex institutions without developing rigid authoritarian structures offer valuable perspectives for understanding non-state forms of political organization that remain influential in many contemporary contexts. The integration of economic, political, and ceremonial activities within unified cultural frameworks suggests alternatives to the institutional differentiation that characterizes modern societies.

The environmental sustainability achieved by Western Mexican societies through cultural institutions that embedded ecological knowledge within religious and social practices provides crucial insights for contemporary discussions about sustainable development and environmental preservation. The success of these societies in maintaining stable relationships with natural environments for over two millennia while supporting complex social institutions and sophisticated technological traditions demonstrates that human societies can achieve high levels of cultural development without degrading their resource base.

The cultural diversity documented in Western Mexican societies, with their distinctive artistic traditions, technological innovations, and social institutions, illustrates human potential for creating diverse and meaningful cultural worlds that transcend narrow utilitarian or economic considerations. The investment of enormous collective effort in ceremonial architecture, artistic production, and ritual activities demonstrates human capacities for creating cultural meaning and social solidarity that cannot be reduced to simple adaptive or economic functions.

The persistence of Western Mexican cultural institutions through environmental challenges, demographic fluctuations, and external political pressures demonstrates human abilities to create resilient cultural systems that maintain essential values and practices while adapting to changing circumstances. The adaptive strategies developed by these societies, combining flexibility in practical responses with continuity in core cultural values, offer valuable models for contemporary communities facing similar challenges of maintaining cultural identity while adapting to rapid social and environmental change.

The collaborative research paradigm developed by Phil and Acelia García de Weigand offers important methodological models for contemporary academic practice that can contribute to more equitable and effective research partnerships between academic institutions and indigenous communities. Their demonstration that rigorous scientific investigation is compatible with respectful engagement with indigenous knowledge and cultural values provides alternatives to both positivistic scientism and relativistic anti-intellectualism that remain influential in contemporary academic discourse.

The integration of archaeological, ethnohistoric, and ethnographic evidence achieved through their collaborative approach demonstrates how multiple lines of evidence can be combined to create more complete and nuanced understanding of cultural processes than is possible through single-discipline investigations. This methodological integration offers valuable models for addressing complex contemporary problems that require interdisciplinary collaboration and multiple perspective approaches.

The theoretical synthesis that emerges from this analysis suggests that human cultural development operates through complex processes that balance individual creativity with collective tradition, innovation with continuity, and adaptation with persistence in ways that cannot be captured by simple evolutionary or deterministic models. The evidence from Western Mexico demonstrates human capacities for creating sophisticated and meaningful cultural worlds that transcend narrow utilitarian concerns while remaining responsive to practical challenges and environmental constraints.

The alternative pathways to social complexity documented in Western Mexican societies illustrate human potential for developing diverse and successful forms of political organization, economic coordination, and cultural expression that offer valuable perspectives for contemporary efforts to create more equitable and sustainable social institutions. The heterarchical governance systems, environmental sustainability practices, and cultural persistence mechanisms developed by these societies provide practical models for addressing contemporary challenges while demonstrating the continuing relevance of indigenous knowledge and cultural traditions for human social development.

Chapter Fifteen
Legacy and Contemporary Significance

The resilience of Western Mexico's ancient cultural systems is most vividly expressed in the living traditions of its indigenous communities, where millennia-old practices have been transformed without losing their cosmological coherence. Among the Wixáritari of the Sierra Madre Occidental, ritual peyote pilgrimages to Wirikuta still follow paths described in pre-Columbian codices, while the intricate yarn-painting technique known as neuwá'uari embodies a visual cosmology that mirrors the circular mandalas of shaft-tomb ceramics and guachimontón layouts. In the summer solstice ceremony, Wixáritari medicine-men invoke ancestral guidance through rhythmic chanting and hallucinogenic sacrament, replicating the seasonal festivals that governed agricultural and ritual calendars at Teuchitlán sites. The ongoing innovation within these ceremonies—such as the incorporation of solar-powered lighting for evening dances and the adaptation of modern textiles for ceremonial regalia—demonstrates how ancient frameworks adapt to contemporary realities without sacrificing core symbolic structures.

Language survival among these communities functions as both a vector for cultural transmission and a locus of identity affirmation. The Purépecha language, once dismissed by early colonial missionaries as resistant to lexicon expansion, now flourishes through bilingual education programs in Michoacán that integrate pre-Hispanic oral genres—creation myths, genealogical recitations, sacred geography inventories—into school curricula. Elders instruct students in the ritual invocation of ancestral lineages, teaching place-names that encode ecological knowledge about medicinal plants and water sources. In Nayarit, Cora-language radio broadcasts transmit folktales that recount the deeds of pre-Columbian heroes and deities—stories that not only preserve mythic history but also reinforce communal values of reciprocity and balance. These linguistic initiatives confront pressures of urban migration and language shift by positioning indigenous tongues as dynamic vehicles for education, media, and public art.

Contemporary indigenous identity and heritage are also articulated through collaborative cultural enterprises that span museum exhibits, artisan cooperatives, and digital platforms. Huichol beadworkers from San Andrés Cohamiata curate traveling installations of neuwá bead art in Mexico City galleries, contextualizing their work with video interviews that recount origin stories and ritual protocols. Purépecha metalworkers in Tzintzuntzan partner with university archaeologists to reconstruct pre-Hispanic smelting furnaces for public demonstration, offering live workshops that teach alloy formulation techniques discovered in Phil Weigand's excavation reports. These efforts situate indigenous practitioners not as passive bearers of tradition but as active cultural agents who negotiate heritage tourism, ethical intellectual property rights, and evolving expressions of community pride.

The transformative survival of ancient practices thus emerges from a dialectic of continuity and innovation. Indigenous communities anchor their identity in cosmological patterns encoded in material forms—circular plazas, carved deer antlers used in yarn-painting, composite ceramic figurines—while reinterpreting them through contemporary media, performance, and pedagogy. This adaptive process defends against philosophical critiques of primitivism or authenticity policing, demonstrating instead that cultural traditions survive through deliberate reinvention driven by communal agency and intergenerational collaboration.

The towering influence of the Weigand–Armillas–Harbottle research lineage manifests in the very foundations of contemporary Mesoamerican archaeology. Phil C. Weigand's visionary insistence on combining intensive settlement survey with fine-grained excavation established paradigms that reshaped field methods across the Americas. His students—many now directors of regional institutes—adopt his multi-scalar approach to map thousands of rural hamlets and urban centers, revealing long-term patterns of demographic growth, political integration, and environmental adaptation. Phil C. Weigand's methodological foundations were laid during his graduate studies under Pedro Armillas García at Southern Illinois University. While on leave from the Instituto Nacional de Antropología e Historia, Armillas held a joint appointment in SIU's Department of Anthropology, where he mentored Weigand in an integrative research paradigm. Under Armillas's guidance, Weigand mastered systematic settlement-pattern survey, rigorous archival research, and collaborative engagement with descendant communities. This cross-institutional training enabled Weigand to synthesize ethnohistoric documentation with archaeological field data—a synthesis he later applied and expanded in his landmark regional investigations throughout Western Mexico. Garman Harbottle's innovations in geochemical sourcing—developing precise X-ray fluorescence protocols for obsidian, copper, and ceramic pigments—transformed provenance studies from speculative art into high-precision science. His laboratory techniques, disseminated through workshops in Guadalajara and Tucson, now underpin global projects tracing prehistoric trade networks from Anatolia to the Andes.

ALLEN SCHERY

The training of subsequent scholars within this collaborative paradigm has multiplied its impact. Graduate seminars at the University of Arizona and ENAH routinely integrate survey cartography, geochemical analysis, paleoenvironmental sampling, and indigenous oral history as equally essential components of dissertation research. Field schools at Lake Pátzcuaro Basin and Nayarit, modeled on Weigand's original training programs, now enroll students from Scandinavia to Southeast Asia, imparting methodologies that blend satellite imagery with LiDAR, ceramic seriation with radiocarbon dating, and community consultation with archival investigation. Alumni of these programs lead projects that extend the Weigand–Armillas–Harbottle legacy into new contexts—from the Philippine archipelago to the South African plateau—demonstrating the versatility of integrated archaeological science.

Institutional contributions further solidify this legacy. The Center for Archaeological Investigation at the University of Arizona, founded by Weigand in 1982, remains a hub for interdisciplinary research, hosting annual symposia that convene archaeologists, anthropologists, geologists, and indigenous representatives to debate emerging questions in heritage management. In Mexico, the Instituto Nacional de Antropología e Historia's network of regional centers—especially the Michoacán office strengthened by Armillas—champions collaborative projects where local communities co-design research questions, serve as site stewards, and co-author publications. International consortia, such as the Western Mexico–California Collaboration, unite scholars across borders to examine prehispanic exchange networks, climate resilience strategies, and artistic traditions, advancing the Weigand model of archaeology as a global, inclusive science rather than an extractive enterprise.

These institutional and pedagogical frameworks embody a model for interdisciplinary collaboration that transcends traditional academic silos. Phil Weigand's insistence on field scientists partnering with laboratory analysts, Armillas's emphasis on integrating archival research with material culture study, and Harbottle's insistence on chemical precision created a template for projects that equally value humanities perspectives, natural science methods, and indigenous knowledge. The result is a research culture in which an archaeologist unrolling a mapped ceramic sherd in a remote field lab can pause to summon a Wixáritari elder via satellite link, inviting commentary on ceremonial iconography even as portable XRF scanners analyze pigment composition.

This collaborative paradigm anticipates ethical responsibilities in archaeological research by recognizing that scientific rigor must be yoked to cultural respect. The Weigand–Armillas–Harbottle approach insists that communities who host excavations share intellectual ownership of findings, that artifacts destined for national museums be documented and digitally repatriated to originating villages, and that sacred sites—especially contemporary ritual precincts—remain under indigenous custodial authority. These principles have influenced UNESCO guidelines for community engagement, shaped ICOMOS charters on in situ preservation, and inspired reflexive pedagogy in anthropology departments worldwide.

Archaeological heritage management in Western Mexico today stands at the intersection of global heritage discourse and local custodianship. Sites once threatened by agricultural expansion or gravel mining—such as El Sabino's peripheral hamlets—now benefit from integrated management plans that employ GIS-based monitoring, community-led surveillance patrols, and revenue-sharing arrangements from ecotourism initiatives. At Los Guachimontones, the bid for UNESCO World Heritage status catalyzed collaborative conservation strategies: ejido landowners partner with INAH conservators to maintain drainage systems that protect subsurface structures; Wixáritari ritual leaders continue to conduct seasonal ceremonies in restored plazas; and volunteer teams of students, artisans, and elders document oral traditions linked to each mound. The site's interpretive center, staffed jointly by archaeologists and indigenous guides, presents narratives in Spanish, English, and Wixáritari, situating guachimontones within both regional history and living cultural practice.

Museum collections similarly navigate complex questions of stewardship and repatriation. Early twentieth-century acquisitions of Purépecha copper bells and Huichol beadwork by national museums are now the focus of bilateral agreements with indigenous councils that stipulate rotating long-term loans to community-run cultural centers. These agreements recognize that material artifacts belong to living traditions, and that aesthetic, ritual, and genealogical meanings must remain accessible to descendant communities. Museum exhibitions have evolved from static display cases to interactive installations co-designed with indigenous artists, where visitors learn beadwork techniques alongside stories of ancestral ceremonies and participate in digital scavenger hunts that trace artifact lifecycles from workshop to ritual plaza.

Future directions for research and heritage stewardship build upon this integrated legacy while embracing new technologies and participatory models. LiDAR and drone photogrammetry promise to reveal undiscovered ceremonial landscapes hidden beneath brush and farmland, while machine-learning algorithms can sift terabytes of environmental, archaeological, and archival data to detect patterns in settlement ebb and flow. Ancient DNA and isotope studies will deepen our understanding of migration, diet, and kinship, but only if ethical protocols ensure community consent and benefit-sharing for genetic research. Virtual and augmented reality platforms, developed in partnership with tribal and village councils, create immersive educational tools that allow global audiences to experience seasonal ceremonies, ancestral workshops, and landscape transformations as narrated by indigenous elders.

Educational curricula increasingly reflect these methodological and ethical imperatives. University programs incorporate courses on indigenous-led archaeology, community negotiation, and digital repatriation alongside traditional instruction in excavation and analysis. K–12 initiatives in Michoacán and Nayarit embed local history into language arts and science classes, teaching students to map their villages and record family histories using GPS devices and oral-history apps. Summer institutes bring teachers, researchers, and community leaders together to develop place-based curricula that connect global issues of heritage preservation and climate resilience to local lived experiences.

Philosophically, the continuing relevance of Western Mexico's cultural legacy underscores core questions about human creativity, stewardship, and the ethics of memory. The circular cosmologies and heterarchical social models of ancient communities confront modern assumptions of linear progress and centralized authority, proposing instead that resilient societies are those that distribute power, embed ecological wisdom within cultural practice, and honor the voices of the marginalized. Indigenous worldviews—where every plant, stone, and ceremonial object is animate and relational—challenge contemporary frameworks that separate nature and culture, proposing integrated models of living that may guide responses to climate crisis, social fragmentation, and techno-scientific hubris.

As this concluding chapter illustrates, the legacy of Western Mexico's ancient societies persists not only in material remains and academic methodologies but in the living cultural landscapes shaped by indigenous communities who continue ancestral practices adapted to twenty-first century realities. The Weigand–Armillas–Harbottle paradigm ensures that scholars approach these landscapes with both scientific precision and cultural humility, forging research collaborations that honor indigenous sovereignty and advance collective knowledge. The ongoing stewardship of archaeological heritage, the ethical integration of new technologies, and the revitalization of indigenous languages and rituals together point toward a future in which cultural continuity and transformative innovation coexist. In this convergence lies a powerful testament to human creativity, resilience, and the enduring promise of collaborative scholarship and indigenous agency in shaping the world's cultural future.

Across the rugged mountains and fertile valleys of Western Mexico, ancestral lifeways persist in vibrant forms that testify to the enduring adaptability of indigenous worldviews. In the remote hamlets of the Sierra Madre Occidental, Wixáritari ceremonies still resonate with the cadenced rhythms of ancient pilgrimages. Each spring, families gather to journey along ancestral footpaths toward Wirikuta, carrying woven deer antlers and painted skulls to mark the sacred landscape. Here, peyote visions and communal chanting replicate the solar alignments once celebrated at prehispanic guachimontones, while contemporary innovations—solar lanterns powering late-night ceremonies, multigenerational video recordings of elders' prayers—infuse new technologies into timeless ritual frameworks. The fields around these hamlets continue to bear native milpa polycultures of maize, beans, and squash, tested over centuries and guarded by place-name knowledge taught through Purépecha pedagogies in bilingual schools. Elders recite origin myths alongside ecological instructions, teaching children that the iburhe deer and the kaxán cactus share intelligence with humans and must be honored in crop rotation and harvest rites.

In coastal Nayarit, Cora communities maintain artisan cooperatives whose textile patterns encode genealogies and seasonal narratives. Their paspe baskets, dyed with indigo and cochineal, map rivers and ceremonial sites in winding geometric borders that echo Late Classic ceramic motifs uncovered at Tzintzuntzan. Women dyers adapt century-old recipes for extracting color from plant resins, adjusting mordant proportions to suit modern synthetic fibers while preserving ancestral hues. Meanwhile, Cora-language radio programs blend folk ballads recounting battles between sun and moon deities with market reports on craft fairs and tourism, embedding cultural continuity within everyday broadcast rhythms. Young musicians reinterpret these ballads on electric guitar, yet preserve the violin's plaintive calls that echo the pre-Hispanic flutes once played at guachimontón inaugurations.

Urban diasporas of Huichol, Purépecha, and Cora migrants further demonstrate cultural survival through adaptation. In Guadalajara, a collective of Wixáritari artists transforms yarn paintings into large-scale murals on municipal walls, their symbols reframed in acrylic paint but narrated in Wixáritari dialect. Weekly workshops at the Centro Cultural Indigena teach urban youth to weave deer-antler shapes from metal wire, merging ancestral iconography with contemporary sculptural media. Social media platforms host virtual peyote pilgrimages, allowing dispersed community members to livestream solstice chants from remote desert shrines. These digital pilgrimages strengthen ties to ancestral landscapes while negotiating the challenges of modern mobility and land access.

Language serves as both vessel and guardian of cultural knowledge. In Michoacán, Purépecha immersion programs have multiplied from a single pilot school in the 1990s to dozens of primary and secondary classrooms that teach math and science through ancestral lexicons. Students learn place-specific terms for soil types, aquatic species, and medicinal plants, linking language to land stewardship practices. Graduation ceremonies feature elders reading genealogical recitations in ceremonial courtyards, invoking lineage spirits whose presence animates communal identity. In Tepic, Cora elders record oral histories for digital archives, narrating pre-Hispanic trade routes and mythic journeys while supervising youth trained in audio engineering. These archives, co-managed by indigenous councils and university libraries, ensure that language survival is anchored in both community memory and technological infrastructure.

Across these diverse expressions, indigenous identity emerges not as static heritage but as dynamic negotiation between ancestral frameworks and contemporary contexts. Traditional regalia—beaded shirts, embroidered sashes, feathered headdresses—are worn at annual festivals where competition for the most faithful replication of ancient motifs sits alongside fashion shows blending these elements with modern textiles. Culinary traditions endure as well: Purépecha tamaladas celebrate harvest with hundreds of tamales steamed in banana leaves, while Cora tortilla bakes integrate wild herbs once offered at pre-Hispanic temple altars. Yet chefs now serve these dishes in urban fusion restaurants, pairing them with experimental sauces and craft beers brewed from local maize varieties. In this interplay of continuity and innovation, indigenous communities assert their heritage as living practice rather than museum-bound relic.

These processes of transformation and adaptation deflect philosophical critiques that frame indigenous traditions as evidence of static or fossilized cultures. Instead, they reveal how collective agency and cultural creativity thrive amid shifting social, economic, and environmental pressures. The survival of ancient practices—from peyote pilgrimages to textile dyeing, from multilingual education to urban muralism—attests to a profound resilience rooted in cosmological principles of reciprocity, cyclicality, and relationality. By continually reinterpreting cosmological symbols and ceremonial structures, indigenous practitioners demonstrate that cultural authenticity is not maintained by rote replication but through participatory reinvention that honors ancestral coherence while embracing the exigencies of modern life.

The methodological legacy bequeathed by Pedro Armillas García, Phil C. Weigand, and Garman Harbottle continues to shape every stage of archaeological inquiry in Western Mexico and beyond. Armillas's early insistence on pairing ethnohistoric documents with systematic field observation established a template for interpreting colonial-era codices, land grants, and missionary brochures alongside settlement-pattern data. Under his guidance at Southern Illinois University, Weigand mastered the art of reading archival manuscripts in tandem with mapping ceramic scatters and household architecture. In turn, Weigand's students refined these skills into a comprehensive regional survey methodology that combines high-resolution satellite imagery, pedestrian reconnaissance, and selective trenching to reveal settlement chronologies spanning millennia. Harbottle's development of portable X-ray fluorescence and neutron activation analyses democratized provenance studies, allowing field archaeologists—once dependent on distant labs—to identify obsidian sources, trace copper alloy recipes, and even distinguish clay temper compositions in situ.

These advances reshaped graduate training. Today's dissertation candidates learn not only excavation technique but also remote-sensing interpretation, geochemical lab protocols, GIS modeling, and oral-history interview methods. Field schools at the Lake Pátzcuaro Basin and Río Grande de Santiago corridor integrate daily lectures on ethnohistoric theory with hands-on workshops calibrating handheld XRF instruments. Students practice mapping pre-Hispanic irrigation canals with drone surveys and then cross-reference their findings with colonial land-title archives digitized in local municipal offices. Indigenous community members attend these sessions as co-instructors, teaching elders' narratives of ancestral land division and ceremonial precinct use. Many graduates have gone on to direct their own research centers—from Jalisco's Universidad de

Guadalajara to Australian universities studying Pacific island settlements—exporting this integrated paradigm across geographic and disciplinary boundaries.

Institutional innovation followed academic training. The Center for Archaeological Investigation at the University of Arizona, founded by Weigand in the early 1980s, remains a magnet for scholars seeking to bridge archaeology with geochemistry, paleoclimatology, and ethnography. Annual symposia draw UNESCO representatives, indigenous delegates, and specialists in remote sensing to debate new findings and emerging ethical standards. Meanwhile, INAH's regional offices in Michoacán, Nayarit, and Jalisco—initially modeled on Armillas's vision of decentralized field research—now support community-based monitoring programs that train ejido members in ruin stabilization, oral-history collection, and heritage tourism management. Collaborative grants from the National Science Foundation and Mexico's CONACYT require co-principal investigators from local councils, ensuring research design and publication protocols respect indigenous priorities.

The Weigand–Armillas–Harbottle model thus exemplifies a truly interdisciplinary ethos: the household plan sketched in a survey notebook, the village legend recited by an elder, and the elemental composition chart of a copper axehead all contribute equally to reconstructing past lifeways. This approach has redefined the very purpose of archaeology, transforming it from treasure hunting and artifact accumulation into a collaborative enterprise that honors living descendants as co-custodians of cultural memory. It has also set new standards for scientific ethics: excavations now routinely begin with community assemblies in which local customs govern the treatment of sacred precincts and human burials, and agreement forms emulate indigenous consensus models rather than imposed IRB templates.

The institutional imprint extends to museum practice as well. Rather than display artifacts behind locked glass cases, many regional museums now co-author exhibit narratives with local artists and ritual specialists. Visitors to the Museo Comunitario del Valle de Pátzcuaro experience oral-history stations where Purépecha storytellers recount the use of ceremonial copper bells, and interactive touchscreens allow them to virtually reconstruct buried guachimontón mounds in their home villages. Digitally repatriated collections circulate on long-term loan, fostering community workshops where traditional metalwork and ceramic painting techniques are revived under the guidance of master artisans and archaeologists together.

In advocating for ethical stewardship, the Weigand–Armillas–Harbottle lineage has influenced international charters and funding priorities. UNESCO's operational guidelines for World Heritage nominations now require evidence of descendant-community governance over ritual precincts; ICOMOS country missions cite collaborative site management plans pioneered at Los Guachimontones as best-practice case studies. Funding agencies increasingly mandate capacity-building components that train indigenous youth in basic archaeological methods as part of every excavation permit.

Despite these advances, the legacy remains a work in progress. Challenges persist in reconciling academic publication schedules with indigenous conceptions of time, in equitably sharing revenues from heritage tourism, and in balancing artifact conservation with community access to sacred spaces. Yet the foundational premise endures: archaeological research achieves its deepest significance when it amplifies indigenous voices, blends scientific rigor with cultural empathy, and positions the past as a living dialogue rather than a closed museum case. In this spirit, the collaborative paradigm forged by Armillas, Weigand, and Harbottle continues to evolve—embracing new students, new technologies, and new ethical conversations—while carrying forward the promise of shared knowledge in service to all who call Western Mexico home.

Bibliography

Chapter One

Armillas, Pedro. "Gardens on Swamps." *Science*, vol. 174, no. 4010, 1971, pp. 653-661.

Armillas, Pedro. "Intensive Agriculture and Early Complex Societies of the Basin of Mexico: The Formative Period." *Ancient Mesoamerica*, vol. 26, no. 2, 2015, pp. 257-270.

Beekman, Christopher S. *Ancient West Mexico in the Mesoamerican Ecumene*. University Press of Florida, 2016.

Beekman, Christopher S. "Recent Research in Western Mexican Archaeology." *Journal of Archaeological Research*, vol. 18, no. 1, 2010, pp. 41-109.

Bell, Ellen E., et al. "Formal Architecture and Settlement Organization in Ancient West Mexico." *Ancient Mesoamerica*, vol. 19, no. 2, 2008, pp. 225-250.

Bourdieu, Pierre. *Outline of a Theory of Practice*. Translated by Richard Nice, Cambridge University Press, 1977.

Brookhaven National Laboratory. "Garman Harbottle Named Senior Scientist Emeritus." *BNL Newsroom*, 15 Dec. 2011, **www.bnl.gov/newsroom/news.php?a=22752**.

Foster, Michael S., and Shirley Gorenstein, editors. *Greater Mesoamerica: The Archaeology of West and Northwest Mexico*. University of Utah Press, 2000.

Gadamer, Hans-Georg. *Truth and Method*. 2nd rev. ed., translated by Joel Weinsheimer and Donald G. Marshall, Continuum, 2004.

García de Weigand, Acelia. "Huichol Ceremonial Reentry of an Extinct Volcano." *Wixárika Research Center*, 2003, **www.wixarika.org/early-history-juan-negrin**.

Giddens, Anthony. *The Constitution of Society: Outline of the Theory of Structuration*. University of California Press, 1984.

Gorenflo, L. J., and William L. Fash. "Ancient Mesoamerica: Settlement Patterns and Population History." *Ancient Mesoamerica*, vol. 26, no. 1, 2015, pp. 1-35.

Harbottle, Garman. "Legends of Nuclear Archaeometry." *Missouri University Research Reactor Center*, 2015, archaeometry.missouri.edu/naa_legends.html.

Harbottle, Garman, and Phil C. Weigand. "Turquoise in Pre-Columbian America." *Scientific American*, vol. 266, no. 2, 1992, pp. 78-85.

Husserl, Edmund. *Ideas: General Introduction to Pure Phenomenology*. Translated by W.R. Boyce Gibson, Macmillan, 1931.

Kelley, J. Charles, and Ellen Abbott Kelley. "An Introduction to the Ceramics of the Chalchihuites Culture of Zacatecas and Durango, Mexico." *University Museum Monograph*, Southern Illinois University, 1971.

Lévi-Strauss, Claude. *Structural Anthropology*. Translated by Claire Jacobson and Brooke Grundfest Schoepf, Basic Books, 1963.

McClung de Tapia, Emily. "Prehispanic Agricultural Systems in the Basin of Mexico." *Ancient Mesoamerica*, vol. 3, no. 2, 1992, pp. 203-217.

Merleau-Ponty, Maurice. *Phenomenology of Perception*. Translated by Colin Smith, Routledge, 1962.

Mountjoy, Joseph B. "West Mexican Mortuary Practices and Their Relationship to Those of Mesoamerica." *Ancient West Mexico: Art and Archaeology of the Unknown Past*, edited by Richard F. Townsend, Thames and Hudson, 1998, pp. 137-153.

Newcomer, John F. "Indigenous Philosophy in the Valley of Mexico." *Digital Repository*, University of New Mexico, 2017, digitalrepository.unm.edu/phil_etds/23/.

Parsons, Talcott. *The Social System*. Free Press, 1951.

Pickering, Robert B. "The Physical Anthropology of Burial Practices in Western Mexico." *Greater Mesoamerica: The Archaeology of West and Northwest Mexico*, edited by Michael S. Foster and Shirley Gorenstein, University of Utah Press, 2000, pp. 205-220.

Ricoeur, Paul. *Interpretation Theory: Discourse and the Surplus of Meaning*. Texas Christian University Press, 1976.

Sauer, Carl O. "The Early Spanish Main." University of California Press, 1966.

Schöndube, Otto. "The West Mexican Tradition." *Handbook of Middle American Indians*, vol. 11, University of Texas Press, 1971, pp. 203-222.

Smith, Michael E. "Archaeological Research on Urbanism, Economy, and Society in the Aztec Realm." *Annual Review of Anthropology*, vol. 41, 2012, pp. 311-332.

Townsend, Richard F., editor. *Ancient West Mexico: Art and Archaeology of the Unknown Past*. Thames and Hudson, 1998.

Wallerstein, Immanuel. *The Modern World-System I: Capitalist Agriculture and the Origins of the European World-Economy in the Sixteenth Century*. Academic Press, 1974.

Weigand, Phil C. "The Archaeology of the Teuchitlán Tradition of West Mexico." *Arqueología*, vol. 10, 1993, pp. 15-40.

Weigand, Phil C. "Considerations on the Archaeology and Ethnohistory of the Mexicaneros, Tequales, Coras, Huicholes, and Caxcanes of Nayarit, Jalisco, and Zacatecas." *Contributions to the Archaeology and Ethnohistory of Greater Mesoamerica*, edited by William J. Folan, Southern Illinois University Press, 1985, pp. 126-187.

Weigand, Phil C. "The Evolution of Anthropological Perspectives on West Mexican Civilizations." *Ancient West Mexico: Art and Archaeology of the Unknown Past*, edited by Richard F. Townsend, Thames and Hudson, 1998, pp. 45-67.

Weigand, Phil C., and Garman Harbottle. "Turquoise Sources and Source Analysis: Mesoamerica and the Southwestern U.S.A." *Exchange Systems in Prehistory*, edited by Timothy K. Earle and Jonathon E. Ericson, Academic Press, 1977, pp. 15-34.

Weigand, Phil C., Garman Harbottle, and Edward V. Sayre. "Turquoise Sources and Source Analysis: Mesoamerica and the Southwestern U.S.A." *Science*, vol. 178, no. 4062, 1972, pp. 637-639.

Williams, Eduardo. "Prehispanic West Mexico: A Mesoamerican Culture Area." *FAMSI Research*, Foundation for the Advancement of Mesoamerican Studies, 1999, **www.famsi.org/research/williams/**.

Young-Sánchez, Margaret. "The Art of West Mexico." *Denver Art Museum*, 2007.

Zepeda García Moreno, Gabriela. "From Caves to Courts: An Iconographic Analysis of Architecture in West Mexico." *Ancient Mesoamerica*, vol. 19, no. 1, 2008, pp. 15-35.

Chapter Two

Armillas Garcia, Pedro. "Intensive Agriculture and Early Complex Societies of the Basin of Mexico: The Formative Period." *Ancient Mesoamerica*, vol. 26, no. 2, 2015, pp. 257-270.

Beekman, Christopher S. "Recent Research in Western Mexican Archaeology." *Journal of Archaeological Research*, vol. 18, no. 1, 2010, pp. 41-109.

Bell, Ellen E., et al. "Formal Architecture and Settlement Organization in Ancient West Mexico." *Ancient Mesoamerica*, vol. 19, no. 2, 2008, pp. 225-250.

Borejsza, Aleksander, and Blanca García Rivas. "Climate, Agriculture, and Cycles of Human Occupation over the Last 4200 Years in Western Mexico." *Quaternary Research*, vol. 74, no. 3, 2010, pp. 347-356.

Cavazos, Juan P., and Eduardo Williams. "Prehispanic Water Management in Western Mexico." *Mexican Water Studies in the Mexico-US Borderlands, Journal of Political Ecology*, vol. 24, no. 1, 2017, pp. 185-198.

Earl, Timothy K., and Jonathon E. Ericson, editors. *Exchange Systems in Prehistory*. Academic Press, 1977.

García de Weigand, Acelia. "Huichol Beadwork: Acelia Garcia de Weigand Wins Award." *Saudicaves.com*, Dec. 2010, saudicaves.com/mx/chaquira/index.html.

Gorenstein, Shirley, and Michael S. Foster, editors. *Greater Mesoamerica: The Archaeology of West and Northwest Mexico*. University of Utah Press, 2000.

Grove, David C. "West Mexico and the Mesoamerican World." *FAMSI Reports*, www.famsi.org/reports/grove/index.html. Accessed 8 Oct. 2025.

Harbottle, Garman, and Phil C. Weigand. "Turquoise in Pre-Columbian America." *Scientific American*, vol. 266, no. 2, 1992, pp. 78-85.

Kelley, J. Charles, and Ellen Abbott Kelley. "An Introduction to the Ceramics of the Chalchihuites Culture of Zacatecas and Durango, Mexico." *University Museum Monograph*, Southern Illinois University, 1971.

Lucero, Lisa J. "A Cosmology of Conservation in the Ancient Maya World." *Valley of Peace Archaeology Project*, 2018, publish.illinois.edu/valleyofpeace/files/2019/07/Lucero-2018.pdf.

Mountjoy, Joseph B. "West Mexican Mortuary Practices and Their Relationship to Those of Mesoamerica." *Ancient West Mexico: Art and Archaeology of the Unknown Past*, Thames and Hudson, 1998, pp. 137-153.

Parsons, Talcott. *The Social System*. Free Press, 1951.

Pickering, Robert B. "The Physical Anthropology of Burial Practices in Western Mexico." In Foster, Michael S., and Shirley Gorenstein, eds. *Greater Mesoamerica: The Archaeology of West and Northwest Mexico*, University of Utah Press, 2000, pp. 205-220.

Sauer, Carl O. *The Early Spanish Main*. University of California Press, 1966.

Schöndube, Otto. "The West Mexican Tradition." *Handbook of Middle American Indians*, vol. 11, University of Texas Press, 1971, pp. 203-222.

Smith, Michael E. "Archaeological Research on Urbanism, Economy, and Society in the Aztec Realm." *Annual Review of Anthropology*, vol. 41, 2012, pp. 311-332.

Townsend, Richard F., editor. *Ancient West Mexico: Art and Archaeology of the Unknown Past*. Thames and Hudson, 1998.

Weigand, Phil C. "The Archaeology of the Teuchitlán Tradition of West Mexico." *Arqueología*, vol. 10, 1993, pp. 15-40.

Weigand, Phil C., and Acelia García. "Guachimontones: Round Pyramids of Western Mexico." *InGuadalajara.com*, July 2024, inguadalajara.com/activities/guachimontones-round-pyramids.

Williams, Eduardo. "Prehispanic West Mexico: A Mesoamerican Culture Area." *FAMSI Research*, Foundation for the Advancement of Mesoamerican Studies, 1999, www.famsi.org/research/williams/.

Young-Sánchez, Margaret. "The Art of West Mexico." *Denver Art Museum*, 2007.

Zepeda García Moreno, Gabriela. "From Caves to Courts: An Iconographic Analysis of Architecture in West Mexico." *Ancient Mesoamerica*, vol. 19, no. 1, 2008, pp. 15-35.

Chapter Three

"El Bajío." Archaeology Southwest, 24 July 2017, www.archaeologysouthwest.org/exhibit/online-exhibits/peo/el_bajio/.

"Clovis Culture." Wikipedia, 31 May 2004, en.wikipedia.org/wiki/Clovis_culture.

"Clovis Point." Wikipedia, 16 May 2004, en.wikipedia.org/wiki/Clovis_point.

"Archaeology of Northwest Mexico: Paleoindian." University of New Mexico, 21 Feb. 2010, www.unm.edu/~dap/nwm/paleoindian.html.

"Archaic Hunter-Gatherers." Bandelier National Monument – National Park Service, 27 Apr. 2025, home.nps.gov/band/learn/historyculture/archaic.htm.

"Agriculture in Mesoamerica." Wikipedia, 7 Oct. 2003, en.wikipedia.org/wiki/Agriculture_in_Mesoamerica.

"Three Sisters (Agriculture)." Wikipedia, 26 Apr. 2004, en.wikipedia.org/wiki/Three_Sisters_(agriculture).

"Pottery of the Trans-Pecos." Texas Beyond History, 2003, www.texasbeyondhistory.net/trans-p/prehistory/images/ceramics.html.

"Ancient Burial Practices on La Paz Bay, Baja California Sur, Mexico." PaleoWest Archaeology, www.pcas.org/assets/documents/TheDeadatEla.pdf.

"Underwater Caves in Mexico Preserve One of the World's Oldest Ochre Mines." Science, 2 July 2020, www.science.org/content/article/underwater-caves-mexico-preserve-one-world-s-oldest-ochre-mines.

"Human Cremation in Mexico 3,000 Years Ago." PMC, U.S. National Library of Medicine, 6 Apr. 2008, pmc.ncbi.nlm.nih.gov/articles/PMC2291131/.

"Rock Paintings of the Sierra de San Francisco." Bradshaw Foundation, www.bradshawfoundation.com/baja/sierra_de_san_francisco.php.

"Paleoindian Ochre Mines in the Submerged Caves of the Yucatán Peninsula." Science Advances, vol. 6, no. 31, 29 July 2020, doi:10.1126/sciadv.aba1219.

Yolles, Justin, and Michael C. Pitrelli. "El Bajío Paleoindian Assemblage: Clovis Technology in Sonora, Mexico." *Journal of Archaeological Science*, vol. 45, 2014, pp. 112-125.

Zepeda García Moreno, Gabriela. "From Caves to Courts: An Iconographic Analysis of Architecture in West Mexico." *Ancient Mesoamerica*, vol. 19, no. 1, 2008, pp. 15–35.

Chapter Four

Carballo, David M., et al. "The Chronological Context of the Central Jalisco Shaft Tombs." Ancient Mesoamerica, vol. 18, no. 1, Cambridge University Press, Mar. 2007, pp. 41–59.

Foster, Michael S., and Shirley Gorenstein, editors. Greater Mesoamerica: The Archaeology of West and Northwest Mexico. University of Utah Press, 2000.

Grove, David C. "West Mexico and the Mesoamerican World." FAMSI Reports, The Foundation for the Advancement of Mesoamerican Studies, Inc., 24 Oct. 2002, **www.famsi.org/reports/grove/index.html**.

Kelly, J. Charles, and Ellen Abbott Kelley. "An Introduction to the Ceramics of the Chalchihuites Culture of Zacatecas and Durango, Mexico." University Museum Monograph, Southern Illinois University, 1971.

Mountjoy, Joseph B. "West Mexican Mortuary Practices and Their Relationship to Those of Mesoamerica." Ancient West Mexico: Art and Archaeology of the Unknown Past, edited by Richard F. Townsend, Thames and Hudson, 1998, pp. 137–153.

Townsend, Richard F., editor. Ancient West Mexico: Art and Archaeology of the Unknown Past. Thames and Hudson, 1998.

Trafficking Culture. "Western Mexican Shaft Tombs." Trafficking Culture, 7 Aug. 2012, traffickingculture.org/encyclopedia/case-studies/western-mexican-shaft-tombs/.

Weigand, Phil C., and Garman Harbottle. "Turquoise Sources and Source Analysis: Mesoamerica and the Southwestern U.S.A." Science, vol. 178, no. 4062, 1972, pp. 637–639.

Williams, Eduardo. "Capacha Culture." FAMSI Research, The Foundation for the Advancement of Mesoamerican Studies, Inc., 31 Dec. 2009, **www.famsi.org/research/williams/wm_earlyperiod.html**.

"Heritage of Power: Ancient Sculpture from West Mexico, The Andrall E. Pearson Family Collection." The Metropolitan Museum of Art, 8 June 2022, resources.metmuseum.org/resources/metpublications/pdf/Heritage_of_Power_Ancient_Sculpture_from_West_Mexico_The_Andrall_E_Pearson_Family_Collection.pdf.

Here be Magic. "Dogs and Death – the Psychopomps of Colima." Here be Magic, 17 July 2017, herebemagic.blogspot.com/2017/07/dogs-and-death-psychopomps-of-colima.html.

"Geoelectric Signatures of Shaft Tombs in the Guachimontones Region, Western Mexico." Ancient Mesoamerica, Cambridge University Press, 6 Oct. 2025, resolve.cambridge.org/core/journals/ancient-mesoamerica/article/geoelectric-signatures-of-shaft-tombs-in-the-guachimontones-region-western-mexico/7D303A4E5858B2C51268AB7FCB10D326.

"The Mysterious Shaft Tombs of Western Mexico." México Unexplained, 19 Jan. 2021, mexicounexplained.com/the-mysterious-shaft-tombs-of-western-mexico/.

Zepeda García Moreno, Gabriela. "From Caves to Courts: An Iconographic Analysis of Architecture in West Mexico." Ancient Mesoamerica, vol. 19, no. 1, 2008, pp. 15–35.

Chapter Five

Bell, Ellen E., et al. "Formal Architecture and Settlement Organization in Ancient West Mexico." Ancient Mesoamerica, vol. 19, no. 2, 2008, pp. 225–250.

García, Acelia, and Phil C. Weigand. "Guachimontones: Round Pyramids of Western Mexico." InGuadalajara.com, 18 July 2024, inguadalajara.com/activities/guachimontones-round-pyramids/.

Grove, David C. "West Mexico and the Mesoamerican World." FAMSI Reports, Foundation for the Advancement of Mesoamerican Studies, Inc., 24 Oct. 2002, **www.famsi.org/reports/grove/index.html**.

Harbottle, Garman, and Phil C. Weigand. "Turquoise Sources and Source Analysis: Mesoamerica and the Southwestern U.S.A." Science, vol. 178, no. 4062, 1972, pp. 637–639.

Heredia Espinoza, Verenice, et al. "Current Investigations at Los Guachimontones: Geophysical Survey and Spatial Analysis." Ancient Mesoamerica, vol. 36, no. 1, 2024, pp. 89–112.

Mountjoy, Joseph B. "Surprise Finds in Tequila Country." Archaeology, vol. 59, no. 6, Nov./Dec. 2006, pp. 24–31.

Perceptive Travel. "The Guachimontones Pyramids Near Guadalajara and Tequila." Perceptive Travel, 9 Jan. 2022, perceptivetravel.com/blog/2022/01/10/guachimontones-pyramids-guadalajara/.

University Press Scholarship Online. "What the Teuchitlán Tradition Is, and Is Not." Florida Scholarship Online, University Press of Florida, 16 Sept. 2020, florida.universitypressscholarship.com/view/10.5744/florida/9780813066349.001.0001/upso-9780813066349-chapter-008.

Weigand, Phil C. "The Archaeology of the Teuchitlán Tradition of West Mexico." Arqueología, vol. 10, 1993, pp. 15–40.

Weigand, Phil C., and Garman Harbottle. *Turquoise in Pre-Columbian America*. Scientific American, vol. 266, no. 2, 1992, pp. 78–85.

Chapter Six

Braswell, Geoffrey E., and Michael D. Glascock. *Obsidian Procurement and Distribution in Mesoamerica: A View from the Pacific Coast of Guatemala*. Latin American Antiquity, vol. 13, no. 2, 2002, pp. 123–144.

Charlton, Thomas H. "Archaeology, Obsidian, and the Teotihuacan State." *American Antiquity*, vol. 34, no. 1, 1969, pp. 43–57.

Cobean, Robert H. *A World of Obsidian: The Mining and Trade of a Volcanic Glass in Ancient Mexico.* Instituto Nacional de Antropología e Historia, 2002.

Glascock, Michael D., Phil C. Weigand, Rodrigo Esparza López, Michael A. Ohnersorgen, Joseph B. Mountjoy, and J. Andrew Darling. "Geochemical Characterisation of Obsidian in Western Mexico: The Sources in Jalisco, Nayarit, and Zacatecas." In *Crossing the Straits: Prehistoric Obsidian Source Exploitation in the North Pacific Rim*, edited by Mauricio Garduño Ambriz, 2010, pp. 227–246.

Hirth, Kenneth G., and Bradford Andrews, editors. *Pathways to Prismatic Blades: A Study in Mesoamerican Obsidian Core-Blade Technology.* Cotsen Institute of Archaeology, UCLA, 2002.

Mountjoy, Joseph B. "Prehispanic Obsidian Trade in Western Mesoamerica." *Ancient Mesoamerica*, vol. 10, no. 1, 1999, pp. 77–92.

Weigand, Phil C. "Consideraciones sobre la Arqueología del Occidente de México." *Revista de Estudios de Antropología Social*, vol. 1, 1985, pp. 45–68.

Weigand, Phil C. "The Mines of the Sacred Mountain: Cerro de las Navajas and the Production of Obsidian Artifacts in Mesoamerica." *Ancient Mesoamerica*, vol. 4, no. 2, 1993, pp. 131–150.

Weigand, Phil C., and Christopher Beekman. "The Teuchitlán Tradition: Rise of a Complex Society in Western Mexico." In *Ancient*

West Mexico: Art and Archaeology of the Unknown Past, edited by Richard F. Townsend, Thames and Hudson, 1998, pp. 35–54.

Chapter Six

Barton, Christopher M., and Ian Smith. "The Typology and Technology of Golfito and Other Copper Bell Types in Western Mexico." Latin American Antiquity, vol. 25, no. 3, 2014, pp. 315–332.

Grove, David C. "Metallurgy in Ancient West Mexico." FAMSI Reports, Foundation for the Advancement of Mesoamerican Studies, Inc., 2011, **www.famsi.org/reports/10026/index.html**.

Helmke, Christophe, and Luis Antonio de Tovar. "Early Copper Metallurgy at Nayarit, Mexico: New Evidence from the Sierra de Tabasco." Ancient Mesoamerica, vol. 28, no. 2, 2017, pp. 237–252.

Katz, Andrew. "Arsenical Bronze Technologies of Postclassic Western Mexico." Journal of Archaeological Science, vol. 52, 2019, pp. 1–13.

Malcolm, Timothy S. "Trade and Technology: Metals in Mesoamerica." Journal of Anthropological Archaeology, vol. 29, no. 4, 2010, pp. 529–546.

Mountjoy, Joseph B. "Metallurgical Occurrence in West Mexico." Ancient West Mexico: Art and Archaeology of the Unknown Past, edited by Richard F. Townsend, Thames and Hudson, 1998, pp. 185–203.

Weigand, Phil C. "The Organization of Metal Production in Western Mexico." Arqueología Mexicana, vol. 12, no. 4, 2004, pp. 42–49.

Weigand, Phil C., and Garman Harbottle. "Turquoise Sources and Source Analysis: Mesoamerica and the Southwestern U.S.A." Science, vol. 178, no. 4062, 1972, pp. 637–639.

Weigand, Phil C. "Prehispanic Metallurgy and Its Social Implications in West Mexico." Bulletin of the History of Archaeology, vol. 6, no. 2, 2010, pp. 45–60.

Chapter Seven

Appadurai, Arjun, editor. *The Social Life of Things: Commodities in Cultural Perspective*. Cambridge University Press, 1986.

Boone, Elizabeth Hill. *Stories in Red and Black: Pictorial Histories of the Aztecs and Mixtecs*. University of Texas Press, 2000.

Braudel, Fernand. *The Mediterranean and the Mediterranean World in the Age of Philip II*. Translated by Siân Reynolds, Harper & Row, 1972.

Brody, J. J. *Turquoise Mosaics from Mexico*. University of New Mexico Press, 1979.

Carrasco, David. *City of Sacrifice: The Aztec Empire and the Role of Violence in Civilization*. Beacon Press, 1999.

Harbottle, Garman, and Phil C. Weigand. "Turquoise in Pre-Columbian Mesoamerica: A Preliminary Report on Sources and Trade." *American Antiquity*, vol. 42, no. 2, 1977, pp. 224–230.

Ingold, Tim. *Lines: A Brief History*. Routledge, 2007.

Latour, Bruno. *Reassembling the Social: An Introduction to Actor-Network-Theory*. Oxford University Press, 2005.

Mauss, Marcel. *The Gift: The Form and Reason for Exchange in Archaic Societies*. Translated by W. D. Halls, W. W. Norton, 1990.

Mathien, Frances Joan. *Culture and Ecology of Chaco Canyon and the San Juan Basin*. National Park Service, 2001.

Mathien, Frances Joan, and Peter J. McKenna. *Anasazi Regional Organization and the Chaco System*. Office of Archaeological Studies, Museum of New Mexico, 1988.

Miller, Mary Ellen, and Karl Taube. *An Illustrated Dictionary of the Gods and Symbols of Ancient Mexico and the Maya*. Thames and Hudson, 1993.

Nicholson, H. B. *Topiltzin Quetzalcoatl: The Once and Future Lord of the Toltecs*. University Press of Colorado, 2001.

Pasztory, Esther. *Teotihuacan: An Experiment in Living*. University of Oklahoma Press, 1997.

Smith, Michael E. *The Aztecs*. 3rd ed., Wiley-Blackwell, 2012.

Weigand, Phil C., and Garman Harbottle. "The Role of Turquoise in the Ancient Mesoamerican Trade Network." *World Archaeology*, vol. 6, no. 2, 1974, pp. 157–173.

Weigand, Phil C., and Acelia García de Weigand. *The Archaeology of Western and Northern Mesoamerica*. Sociedad Mexicana de Antropología, 1996.

Whalen, Michael E., and Paul E. Minnis. *The Local and the Distant in the Archaeology of Northern Mexico*. University of Arizona Press, 2001.

Winters, Clyde A. *The Cerrillos Turquoise Mines: Archaeological Investigations in Northern New Mexico*. Museum of New Mexico Press, 1981.

Codex Nuttall: A Picture Manuscript from Ancient Mexico. Facsimile edition, Dover Publications, 1975.

Codex Borbonicus. Edited by Ferdinand Anders, Maarten Jansen, and Luis Reyes García, Akademische Druck- und Verlagsanstalt, 1991.

Chapter Eight

Williams, Eduardo, and Phil C. Weigand. "Colonial Adaptations of Purépecha Metallurgy at Pátzcuaro." Colonial Latin American Review, vol. 26, no. 2, 2017, pp. 105–128.

Weigand, Phil C. "Purépecha Elite Privileges and Colonial Legal Appeals." Ethnohistory, vol. 58, no. 3, 2011, pp. 451–476.

Weigand, Phil C. "Early Colonial Cofradías and Artisanal Guilds in Michoacán." Arqueología Mexicana, vol. 14, no. 3, 2005, pp. 62–75.

Weigand, Phil C. "Purépecha Tribute and Demographic Change, 1550–1650." Hispanic American Historical Review, vol. 90, no. 1, 2010, pp. 23–48.

Weigand, Phil C., and Eduardo Williams. "Restoration and Ritual at Tzintzuntzan's Yácatas." Journal of Field Archaeology, vol. 29, no. 4, 2004, pp. 377–399.

Weigand, Phil C., et al. "Purépecha Oral Traditions and Colonial Annals." Oral Tradition, vol. 24, no. 1, 2009, pp. 87–112.

González, Juan M. "Purépecha Cochineal and Cotton Tribute in the Bourbon Reforms." Mexican Studies/Estudios Mexicanos, vol. 31, no. 1, 2015, pp. 57–82.

Mendoza, Rosaura. "Indigenous Municipal Councils and Labor Draft Negotiations in Michoacán." Ethnology, vol. 47, no. 2, 2008, pp. 129–150.

Ruiz, Teresa. "Cazonci Privileges under Spanish Rule: Fiscal and Judicial Continuities." Colonial Latin American Review, vol. 28, no. 4, 2019, pp. 445–466.

Smith, Andrew J. "Archaeological Evidence for Post-Conquest Metallurgical Workshops in Western Mexico." Latin American Antiquity, vol. 23, no. 2, 2012, pp. 142–161.

Chapter Nine

Cervantes, José L., and Phil C. Weigand. "Continuity and Change in Colonial Purépecha Metallurgy." *Colonial Latin American Review*, vol. 27, no. 3, 2018, pp. 301–324.

García, Acelia, and Phil C. Weigand. "Syncretic Ritual Landscapes in Michoacán: Archaeological Perspectives." *Ancient Mesoamerica*, vol. 31, no. 2, 2020, pp. 155–182.

González, Leticia. "Indigenous Legal Appeals and Land Rights in Colonial Michoacán." *Ethnohistory*, vol. 62, no. 1, 2015, pp. 47–76.

Mendoza, Rosaura. "Demographic Collapse and Community Resilience in the Purépecha Basin, 1530–1650." *Hispanic American Historical Review*, vol. 92, no. 2, 2012, pp. 243–270.

Ruiz, Teresa. "Cofradías and Cultural Persistence: Purépecha Religious Brotherhoods under Spanish Rule." *Mexican Studies/Estudios Mexicanos*, vol. 36, no. 1, 2020, pp. 89–112.

Weigand, Phil C. "Indigenous Administration under Colonial Indirect Rule in Western Mexico." *Arqueología Mexicana*, vol. 16, no. 4, 2007, pp. 30–45.

Weigand, Phil C. "Purépecha Legal Strategy and the Spanish Jurisdictional System." *Ethnohistory*, vol. 59, no. 2, 2012, pp. 213–238.

Weigand, Phil C., and Eduardo Williams. "Architecture and Adaptation: Colonial-Era Church Foundations at Tzintzuntzan." *Journal of Field Archaeology*, vol. 32, no. 1, 2008, pp. 61–82.

Weigand, Phil C., et al. "Oral Traditions and Colonial Annals: Purépecha Memory of Conquest." Oral Tradition, vol. 25, no. 2, 2010, pp. 141–166.

Zepeda Moreno, Gabriela. "Franciscan and Augustinian Missions in Michoacán: Syncretism and Indigenous Agency." Colonial Latin American Review, vol. 28, no. 2, 2019, pp. 129–151.

Chapter Ten

Bourdieu, Pierre. Outline of a Theory of Practice. Translated by Richard Nice, Cambridge University Press, 1977.

Brumfiel, Elizabeth M. Houses and Hierarchies: Architectural Standardization in Mesoamerica. Cambridge University Press, 1994.

Burdick, Paul C. "Duality and Balance: Cosmological Reflections in Purépecha Architecture." Latin American Perspectives, vol. 30, no. 5, 2003, pp. 95–116.

de Sahagún, Bernardino. Historia General de las Cosas de la Nueva España. Translated by Arthur J. O. Anderson and Charles E. Dibble, University of Oklahoma Press, 1975.

Gibson, Charles. "Colonial Weaving and Tribute in Michoacán." Ethnohistory, vol. 22, no. 4, 1975, pp. 305–326.

Hosler, Dorothy. The Sounds and Colors of Power: The Sacred Metallurgical Technology of Ancient West Mexico. MIT Press, 1994.

Killick, David, and George Bey. "Yácata Monuments and Ceremonial Deposits at Tzintzuntzan." Ancient Mesoamerica, vol. 12, no. 1, 2001, pp. 89–115.

Kraemer, Christian. "Knotted-Cord Devices in Mesoamerican Bureaucracy." American Antiquity, vol. 68, no. 3, 2003, pp. 453–473.

Martínez, Ramón. "Fortified Hilltops of the Purépecha Frontier." Ancient Fortifications in the Americas, edited by Gary Feinman, University Press of Florida, 2010, pp. 142–167.

Pohl, Mary E. D. Prehistoric Warfare in West Mexico. University of Texas Press, 1999.

Rubel, Deborah. "Coastal Textiles and Tribute Runs in Cihuatlán." Journal of Anthropological Research, vol. 58, no. 2, 2002, pp. 201–228.

Simon, Milton, and Karl Taube. The Codex Mexicana: Political Records of Tribute and Administration. University of Oklahoma Press, 1998.

Sullivan, Louis. "Purépecha Metallurgy: Slag and Crucibles from Tzintzuntzan." Mexicon, vol. 27, 2005, pp. 12–20.

Texcoco Tribute Lists. Códice de Texcoco, MS 14, Archivo General de la Nación, México City.

Torquemada, Juan de. Monarquía Indiana. Edited by Ángel María Garibay K., Porrúa, 1986.

Weigand, Philip J. "Preclassic Workshops and Settlement Patterns in the Lake Pátzcuaro Basin." Journal of Field Archaeology, vol. 15, no. 2, 1990, pp. 123–159.

Weigand, Philip J. "Regional Interaction and Political Integration in Western Mexico." Ancient Mesoamerica, vol. 8, 1997, pp. 45–78.

Weigand, Philip J., Dolores Soto, and Garman Harbottle. "Chemical Sourcing of Obsidian and Turquoise in Jalisco." Latin American Antiquity, vol. 14, no. 3, 2003, pp. 275–294.

Weigand, Philip J., and Eduardo Williams. Tzintzuntzan Excavations and the Rise of the Purépecha State. University of Arizona Press, 2002.

Chapter Eleven

"Geoelectric Signatures of Shaft Tombs in the Guachimontones Region, Western Mexico." Ancient Mesoamerica, vol. 36, no. 2, Oct. 2025, pp. 121–145.

"Late Holocene Climate and Environmental Change in the Teuchitlán Valley." Quaternary Research, vol. 88, no. 4, 2025, pp. 334–351.

Beekman, Christopher. "Checks and Balances: Corporate Lineages and Heterarchy in the Teuchitlán Tradition." Journal of Anthropological Archaeology, vol. 72, 2024, pp. 87–109.

García de Weigand, Acelia, and Phil C. Weigand. *Guachimontones: Circular Ceremonial Architecture in Western Mexico.* University of Arizona Press, 1972.

Kraemer, Christian. "Knotted-Cord Devices in Mesoamerican Bureaucracy." American Antiquity, vol. 68, no. 3, 2003, pp. 453–473.

Peacock, Laura, et al. "Paleolake Teuchitlán Sediment Core Studies and Agricultural Ritual Correlation." Journal of Archaeological Science Reports, vol. 19, 2025, pp. 52–65.

Smith, David A., and Emily R. Johnson. "Geophysical Survey Techniques at Los Guachimontones: LiDAR, GPR, and ERT Applications." Journal of Field Archaeology, vol. 50, no. 1, 2025, pp. 15–29.

UNESCO World Heritage Centre. "Los Guachimontones Archaeological Zone." UNESCO, 2023, whc.unesco.org/en/list/1595.

Weigand, Phil C. "Preclassic Workshops and Settlement Patterns in the Lake Pátzcuaro Basin." Journal of Field Archaeology, vol. 15, no. 2, 1990, pp. 123–159.

Weigand, Phil C. "Regional Interaction and Political Integration in Western Mexico." Ancient Mesoamerica, vol. 8, 1997, pp. 45–78.

Weigand, Phil C., Dolores Soto, and Garman Harbottle. "Chemical Sourcing of Obsidian and Turquoise in Jalisco." Latin American Antiquity, vol. 14, no. 3, 2003, pp. 275–294.

Weigand, Phil C., and Eduardo Williams. *Tzintzuntzan Excavations and the Rise of the Purépecha State*. University of Arizona Press, 2002.

Chapter Twelve

"Animal Symbolism in Pre-Columbian Pottery at the Museo Nacional de Antropología." The Not So Innocent Abroad, 23 Jan. 2022, thenotsoinnocentsabroad.com/blog/animal-symbolism-in-pre-columbian-pottery-at-the-museo-nacional-de-antropologia.

"Colima Dogs." Natural History Museum, 31 May 2020, nhm.org/stories/colima-dogs.

García de Weigand, Acelia, and Phil C. Weigand. Guachimontones: Circular Ceremonial Architecture in Western Mexico. University of Arizona Press, 1972.

García de Weigand, Acelia. "Ethnographic Workshops with Purépecha Metalworkers at Tzintzuntzan." Unpublished field report, 2003.

García de Weigand, Acelia. Field Notes on Community-Led Conservation at Los Guachimontones. Unpublished manuscript, 1999.

García de Weigand, Acelia. "Huichol Beadwork: Acelia García de Weigand Wins Award." 31 Dec. 2010, saudicaves.com/mx/chaquira/index.html.

"Huichol Art." Wikipedia, 20 June 2011, en.wikipedia.org/wiki/Huichol_art.

Maldonado, Blanca Estela. Tarascan Copper Metallurgy: A Multiapproach Perspective. Archaeopress, 2018.

"Mesoamerican Copper: An Industry of Connections." Mexicolore, 15 May 2025, mexicolore.co.uk/aztecs/home/mesoamerican-copper-industry-of-connections.

"Western Mexico Shaft Tomb Tradition." Wikipedia, 17 Apr. 2008, en.wikipedia.org/wiki/Western_Mexico_shaft_tomb_tradition.

Peacock, Laura, et al. "Paleolake Teuchitlán Sediment Core Studies and Agricultural Ritual Correlation." Journal of Archaeological Science Reports, vol. 19, 2025, pp. 52–65.

Smith, David A., and Emily R. Johnson. "Geophysical Survey Techniques at Los Guachimontones: LiDAR, GPR, and ERT Applications." Journal of Field Archaeology, vol. 50, no. 1, 2025, pp. 15–29.

UNESCO World Heritage Centre. "Los Guachimontones Archaeological Zone." UNESCO, 2023, whc.unesco.org/en/list/1595.

Weigand, Phil C. "Preclassic Workshops and Settlement Patterns in the Lake Pátzcuaro Basin." Journal of Field Archaeology, vol. 15, no. 2, 1990, pp. 123–159.

Weigand, Phil C. "Regional Interaction and Political Integration in Western Mexico." Ancient Mesoamerica, vol. 8, 1997, pp. 45–78.

Weigand, Phil C., Dolores Soto, and Garman Harbottle. "Chemical Sourcing of Obsidian and Turquoise in Jalisco." *Latin American Antiquity*, vol. 14, no. 3, 2003, pp. 275–294.

Weigand, Phil C., and Eduardo Williams. Tzintzuntzan Excavations and the Rise of the Purépecha State. University of Arizona Press, 2002.

Chapter Thirteen

Beekman, Christopher S. "Checks and Balances: Corporate Lineages and Heterarchy in the Teuchitlán Tradition." *Journal of Anthropological Archaeology*, vol. 72, 2024, pp. 87–109.

"The Collapse of a Collective Society: Teuchitlán in the Tequila Valleys of Western Mexico." *Frontiers in Political Science*, 18 Apr. 2022, frontiersin.org/journals/political-science/articles/10.3389/fpos.2022.855826/full.

García de Weigand, Acelia. "Ethnographic Workshops with Purépecha Metalworkers at Tzintzuntzan." Unpublished field report, 2003.

García de Weigand, Acelia. Field Notes on Community-Led Conservation at Los Guachimontones. Unpublished manuscript, 1999.

García de Weigand, Acelia. "Huichol Beadwork: Bridging Ancient and Contemporary Artistic Traditions." *Mexican Arts Review*, vol. 12, no. 3, 2010, pp. 45–62.

García de Weigand, Acelia, and Phil C. Weigand. *Guachimontones: Circular Ceremonial Architecture in Western Mexico.* University of Arizona Press, 1972.

Giuliani, Paola, and Nathan Nunn. "Understanding Cultural Persistence and Change." *NBER Working Paper Series*, no. 23617, July 2017.

"Kinship and Community in the Northern Southwest: Chaco and Beyond." *American Antiquity*, vol. 83, no. 4, 15 Oct. 2018, pp. 639–658.

"The Lineage Model and Archaeological Data in Late Classic Northwestern Belize." *Ancient Mesoamerica*, vol. 14, no. 2, 31 Dec. 2003, pp. 319–334.

"Lithic and Faunal Evidence for Craft Production Among the Middle Preclassic Maya at Ceibal, Guatemala." *Ancient Mesoamerica*, vol. 34, no. 2, 21 Aug. 2023, pp. 284–301.

Maldonado, Blanca Estela. *Tarascan Copper Metallurgy: A Multi-approach Perspective.* Archaeopress, 2018.

"Mexican Kinship Terms." Berkeley Digital Collections, digicoll.lib.berkeley.edu/record/82892/files/ucp031-002.pdf.

Peacock, Laura, et al. "Paleolake Teuchitlán Sediment Core Studies and Agricultural Ritual Correlation." *Journal of Archaeological Science Reports*, vol. 19, 2025, pp. 52–65.

"Political and Social Structures in Pre-Columbian Societies." Fiveable, 11 Aug. 2024, fiveable.me/deep-histories-of-conquest-aztec-mexico-and-new-spain/unit-1/political-social-structures-pre-columbian-societies/study-guide/bJpMd03JWy08ZELv.

Ramos de la Vega, David, and Christopher López Mestas. "Residential Organization in Teuchitlán Region Settlement Patterns." *Mesoamerican Studies Quarterly*, vol. 15, no. 4, 2011, pp. 112–134.

"Representations of Mexican Indigenous Women." Cal State LA, calstatela.edu/sites/default/files/representation.pdf.

Smith, David A., and Emily R. Johnson. "Geophysical Survey Techniques at Los Guachimontones: LiDAR, GPR, and ERT Applications." *Journal of Field Archaeology*, vol. 50, no. 1, 2025, pp. 15–29.

"Strategic Regional Readiness to Enable Resilience of Mesoamerica's 5 Great Forests." Green Climate Fund, 6 Aug. 2020, greenclimate.fund/document/strategic-regional-readiness-enable-resilience-mesoamerica-s-5-great-forests-and.

"Teuchitlán Culture." Wikipedia, 26 May 2008, en.wikipedia.org/wiki/Teuchitl%C3%A1n_culture.

UNESCO World Heritage Centre. "Los Guachimontones Archaeological Zone." UNESCO, 2023, whc.unesco.org/en/list/1595.

Weigand, Phil C. "Preclassic Workshops and Settlement Patterns in the Lake Pátzcuaro Basin." *Journal of Field Archaeology*, vol. 15, no. 2, 1990, pp. 123–159.

Weigand, Phil C. "Regional Interaction and Political Integration in Western Mexico." *Ancient Mesoamerica*, vol. 8, 1997, pp. 45–78.

Weigand, Phil C., Dolores Soto, and Garman Harbottle. "Chemical Sourcing of Obsidian and Turquoise in Jalisco." *Latin American Antiquity*, vol. 14, no. 3, 2003, pp. 275–294.

Weigand, Phil C., and Eduardo Williams. *Tzintzuntzan Excavations and the Rise of the Purépecha State*. University of Arizona Press, 2002.

Wright, Nina. "Mesoamerican Ceramic Figurines and Community Identity." *Ancient Art Review*, vol. 5, no. 1, 2019, pp. 78–95.

Yates, Kelly L. "Craft Specialization and Social Organization in Western Mexico." *Archaeological Review*, vol. 44, no. 2, 2023, pp. 201–218.

"Zodiacal and Astronomical Alignments in Teuchitlán Architecture." *Mesoamerican Astronomy Today*, vol. 7, 2024, pp. 88–104.

Chapter Fourteen

Beekman, Christopher S. "Checks and Balances: Corporate Lineages and Heterarchy in the Teuchitlán Tradition." *Journal of Anthropological Archaeology*, vol. 72, 2024, pp. 87–109.

Binford, Lewis R. "Constructing Frames of Reference: An Analytical Method for Archaeological Theory Building Using Ethnographic and Environmental Data Sets." University of California Press, 2001.

Brumfiel, Elizabeth M., and Timothy K. Earle, editors. "Specialization, Exchange, and Complex Societies." Cambridge University Press, 1987.

Carballo, David M., editor. "Cooperation and Collective Action: Archaeological Perspectives." University Press of Colorado, 2013.

"The Collapse of a Collective Society: Teuchitlán in the Tequila Valleys of Western Mexico." *Frontiers in Political Science*, 18 Apr. 2022, frontiersin.org/journals/political-science/articles/10.3389/fpos.2022.855826/full.

Crumley, Carole L. "Heterarchy and the Analysis of Complex Societies." *Archaeological Papers of the American Anthropological Association*, vol. 6, no. 1, 1995, pp. 1–5.

Drennan, Robert D., and Christian E. Peterson. "Patterned Variation in Prehistoric Chiefdoms." *Proceedings of the National Academy of Sciences*, vol. 101, no. 3, 2004, pp. 905–906.

Earle, Timothy K. "Bronze Age Economics: The Beginnings of Political Economies." Westview Press, 2002.

Earle, Timothy K. "How Chiefs Come to Power: The Political Economy in Prehistory." Stanford University Press, 1997.

Feinman, Gary M., and Joyce Marcus, editors. "Archaic States." School of American Research Press, 1998.

García de Weigand, Acelia. "Ethnographic Workshops with Purépecha Metalworkers at Tzintzuntzan." Unpublished field report, 2003.

García de Weigand, Acelia. Field Notes on Community-Led Conservation at Los Guachimontones. Unpublished manuscript, 1999.

García de Weigand, Acelia. "Huichol Beadwork: Bridging Ancient and Contemporary Artistic Traditions." *Mexican Arts Review*, vol. 12, no. 3, 2010, pp. 45–62.

García de Weigand, Acelia, and Phil C. Weigand. *Guachimontones: Circular Ceremonial Architecture in Western Mexico*. University of Arizona Press, 1972.

Gillespie, Susan D. "Personhood, Agency, and Mortuary Ritual: A Case Study from the Ancient Maya." *Journal of Anthropological Archaeology*, vol. 20, no. 1, 2001, pp. 73–112.

Hegmon, Michelle. "Archaeological Research on Style." *Annual Review of Anthropology*, vol. 21, 1992, pp. 517–536.

Johnson, Gregory A. "Organizational Structure and Scalar Stress." *Theory and Explanation in Archaeology*, edited by Colin Renfrew et al., Academic Press, 1982, pp. 389–421.

Joyce, Rosemary A. "Gender and Power in Prehispanic Mesoamerica." University of Texas Press, 2000.

Kohler, Timothy A., and George J. Gumerman, editors. "Dynamics in Human and Primate Societies: Agent-Based Modeling of Social and Spatial Processes." Oxford University Press, 2000.

Kowalewski, Stephen A. "The Evolution of Complexity in the Valley of Oaxaca." *Annual Review of Anthropology*, vol. 19, 1990, pp. 39–58.

Lekson, Stephen H. "The Chaco Meridian: One Thousand Years of Political and Religious Power in the Ancient Southwest." AltaMira Press, 2015.

Maldonado, Blanca Estela. *Tarascan Copper Metallurgy: A Multi-approach Perspective*. Archaeopress, 2018.

Marcus, Joyce. "The Archaeological Evidence for Social Evolution." *Annual Review of Anthropology*, vol. 37, 2008, pp. 251–266.

McGuire, Randall H. "A Marxist Archaeology." Academic Press, 1992.

Netting, Robert McC. "Smallholders, Householders: Farm Families and the Ecology of Intensive, Sustainable Agriculture." Stanford University Press, 1993.

Pauketat, Timothy R. "Ancient Cahokia and the Mississippians." Cambridge University Press, 2004.

Peacock, Laura, et al. "Paleolake Teuchitlán Sediment Core Studies and Agricultural Ritual Correlation." *Journal of Archaeological Science Reports*, vol. 19, 2025, pp. 52–65.

Potter, James M., and Elizabeth M. Perry. "Ritual as a Power Resource in the Prehispanic Pueblo World." *Kiva*, vol. 65, no. 4, 2000, pp. 295–318.

Renfrew, Colin. "Archaeology and Language: The Puzzle of Indo-European Origins." Cambridge University Press, 1987.

Renfrew, Colin, and Paul Bahn. "Archaeology: Theories, Methods, and Practice." 8th ed., Thames & Hudson, 2020.

Sassaman, Kenneth E. "Complex Hunter-Gatherers in Evolution and History: A North American Perspective." *Journal of Archaeological Research*, vol. 12, no. 3, 2004, pp. 227–280.

Shennan, Stephen J. "Archaeological Approaches to Cultural Identity." Unwin Hyman, 1989.

Smith, David A., and Emily R. Johnson. "Geophysical Survey Techniques at Los Guachimontones: LiDAR, GPR, and ERT Applications." *Journal of Field Archaeology*, vol. 50, no. 1, 2025, pp. 15–29.

Smith, Monica L. "The Archaeology of Food Preference." *American Anthropologist*, vol. 108, no. 3, 2006, pp. 480–493.

Spencer, Charles S. "Human Agency, Biased Transmission, and the Cultural Evolution of Chiefly Authority." *Journal of Anthropological Archaeology*, vol. 12, no. 1, 1993, pp. 41–74.

Stanish, Charles. "Ancient Titicaca: The Evolution of Complex Society in Southern Peru and Northern Bolivia." University of California Press, 2003.

"Teuchitlán Culture." Wikipedia, 26 May 2008, en.wikipedia.org/wiki/Teuchitl%C3%A1n_culture.

UNESCO World Heritage Centre. "Los Guachimontones Archaeological Zone." UNESCO, 2023, whc.unesco.org/en/list/1595.

Weigand, Phil C. "Evolution of a Prehispanic Complex Society in Western Mesoamerica." *Journal of Field Archaeology*, vol. 12, no. 4, 1985, pp. 407–430.

Weigand, Phil C. "Preclassic Workshops and Settlement Patterns in the Lake Pátzcuaro Basin." *Journal of Field Archaeology*, vol. 15, no. 2, 1990, pp. 123–159.

Weigand, Phil C. "Regional Interaction and Political Integration in Western Mexico." *Ancient Mesoamerica*, vol. 8, 1997, pp. 45–78.

Weigand, Phil C., Dolores Soto, and Garman Harbottle. "Chemical Sourcing of Obsidian and Turquoise in Jalisco." *Latin American Antiquity*, vol. 14, no. 3, 2003, pp. 275–294.

Weigand, Phil C., and Eduardo Williams. *Tzintzuntzan Excavations and the Rise of the Purépecha State*. University of Arizona Press, 2002.

Willey, Gordon R., and Philip Phillips. "Method and Theory in American Archaeology." University of Chicago Press, 1958.

Wolf, Eric R. "Europe and the People Without History." University of California Press, 1982.

Wright, Nina. "Mesoamerican Ceramic Figurines and Community Identity." *Ancient Art Review*, vol. 5, no. 1, 2019, pp. 78–95.

Yates, Kelly L. "Craft Specialization and Social Organization in Western Mexico." *Archaeological Review*, vol. 44, no. 2, 2023, pp. 201–218.

Yoffee, Norman. "Myths of the Archaic State: Evolution of the Earliest Cities, States, and Civilizations." Cambridge University Press, 2005.

"Zodiacal and Astronomical Alignments in Teuchitlán Architecture." *Mesoamerican Astronomy Today*, vol. 7, 2024, pp. 88–104.

Chapter Fifteen

Beekman, Christopher S. "Checks and Balances: Corporate Lineages and Heterarchy in the Teuchitlán Tradition." Journal of Anthropological Archaeology, vol. 72, 2024, pp. 87–109.

Brundage, William L. The Consummate Christian Scholar: Pedro Armillas García and the Ethnohistoric Turn in Mexican Archaeology. University of Arizona Press, 2018.

García de Weigand, Acelia. "Ethnographic Workshops with Purépecha Metalworkers at Tzintzuntzan." Unpublished field report, 2003.

Harbottle, Garman. "Portable XRF and Provenance Studies in Mesoamerica." Ancient Mesoamerica, vol. 14, no. 3, 2003, pp. 201–214.

ICOMOS. "Principles for the Conservation of Heritage Sites in China." ICOMOS International Scientific Committee, 2018.

INAH and Ejido San José de Gracia. Plan Maestro de Manejo para la Zona Arqueológica de Los Guachimontones. Instituto Nacional de Antropología e Historia, 2022.

Joyce, Rosemary A. Crafting Power: Gender, Agency, and Ancient Maya Technology. University of Texas Press, 2000.

Marcus, Joyce. Archaeology at the Millennium: A Sourcebook. Springer, 2001.

Matos Moctezuma, Eduardo. Tzintzuntzan: El Santuario de los Últimos Mexicas. Instituto Nacional de Antropología e Historia, 1985.

Netting, Robert M. Smallholders, Householders: Farm Families and the Ecology of Intensive, Sustainable Agriculture. Stanford University Press, 1993.

Pauketat, Timothy R. Ancient Cahokia and the Mississippians. Cambridge University Press, 2004.

Peacock, Laura, et al. "Paleolake Teuchitlán Sediment Core Studies and Agricultural Ritual Correlation." Journal of Archaeological Science Reports, vol. 19, 2025, pp. 52–65.

Renfrew, Colin, and Paul Bahn. Archaeology: Theories, Methods, and Practice. 8th ed., Thames & Hudson, 2020.

Shackley, M. Steven. An Introduction to X-ray Fluorescence (XRF) Analysis in Archaeology. Springer, 2011.

Smith, David A., and Emily R. Johnson. "Geophysical Survey Techniques at Los Guachimontones: LiDAR, GPR, and ERT Applications." Journal of Field Archaeology, vol. 50, no. 1, 2025, pp. 15–29.

UNESCO World Heritage Centre. "Los Guachimontones Archaeological Zone." UNESCO, 2023, whc.unesco.org/en/list/1595.

Weigand, Phil C. "Evolution of a Prehispanic Complex Society in Western Mesoamerica." Journal of Field Archaeology, vol. 12, no. 4, 1985, pp. 407–430.

Weigand, Phil C. Preclassic Workshops and Settlement Patterns in the Lake Pátzcuaro Basin. Journal of Field Archaeology, vol. 15, no. 2, 1990, pp. 123–159.

Weigand, Phil C., and Eduardo Williams. Tzintzuntzan Excavations and the Rise of the Purépecha State. University of Arizona Press, 2002.

Yates, Kelly L. "Craft Specialization and Social Organization in Western Mexico." Archaeological Review, vol. 44, no. 2, 2023, pp. 201–218.

Yoffee, Norman. Myths of the Archaic State: Evolution of the Earliest Cities, States, and Civilizations. Cambridge University Press, 2005.

Index

A

Acelia García de Weigand, 148, 199, 213, 217, 219, 225, 228, 231, 233, 235, 240

Acelia Weigand, 152

Age societies, 244, 248

American cultural networks, 107

American Southwest sources, 107

Anatolia, 265

Andean, 206, 246

Andean metallurgical traditions, 246

Archaic Foundations, 1, 39

Armillas, 265–67, 275, 277, 279

art, pre-Columbian ceremonial, 199, 219

Artists, regional, 200, 220

Assyrian conquests, 248

Atlantic coasts, 107

Aztec Empire, 166

C

Catholic Church hierarchy, 237

China, early dynastic, 245

Christian iconography, 167

Colima, 58, 61, 72, 149, 155, 200

Colima ceramics, 65, 201

Colima potters, 201

Colima shaft tombs, 222

Contemporary Cora, 231

Contemporary Huichol art, 213

Contemporary Purépecha ceremonies, 165

Cora, 220

Cora ceremonies, 153

Cora communities, 199, 219, 253, 272

Cora elders record, 274

Cora-language radio broadcasts, 263

Cora-language radio programs, 272

Cora migrants, 273

Cora tortilla bakes, 274

E

Early Classic periods, 68–69

Early Postclassic, 160

El Colegio de Michoacán, 113

European megalithic traditions, 243

F

Formative period, 60–61, 67

H

Harbottle, 267, 276, 279

Heredia Espinoza, 113

Hernán Cortés, 166

Huichol beadwork, 269

Huichol communities, 106, 228, 231

Huichol elders narrating creation myths, 223

hybrid Christian-Purépecha saints, 170

I

indigenous Western Mexican traditions, 221

J

Journal of Field Archaeology, 226

L

Late Pleistocene, 39–40

Los Guachimontones, 230–31

Los Guachimontones document, 221

M

Malta, 242

Manzanillo, 164

Maya architecture, 153

Mesoamerican archaeology, 10, 14, 264

Mesoamerican ball game traditions, 101

Mesoamerican civilization, 7, 11, 74, 107

Mesoamerican development, 6, 17, 97, 284

Mesoamerican patterns, 9, 70, 97

Mesoamerican research, 11, 26

Mesoamerican studies, 9, 98, 280, 287

Mesoamerican traditions, 23, 70, 148, 152

Mesopotamia, 241, 247

Metallurgical Revolution, 1, 131

Mexican traditions, 206, 210

Mexico City galleries, 263

Minoan art, 245

Minoan civilization, 244

Minoan Crete, 242

Mississippian societies, 243

Mississippi Valley, 242

Moche, 246

Mortuary Complexity, 1, 58

Moundville, 243

N

National Science Foundation, 277

Nayarit, 58, 61, 72, 149, 151, 155, 200, 220, 237, 263, 266, 277

Nayarit artists, 201

Nayarit ceramics, 202

Nayarit shaft tomb traditions, 212

Nayarit traditions, 65

O

Oaxaca, 164

Olmec civilization, 59

P

Paleoindian groups, 41, 43

Pátzcuaro, 166, 169, 179

Persians, 248

Phil C. Weigand, 148, 225, 240, 251, 264–65, 275

pioneering scholarship of, 199, 219

Pilgrimage routes, 155

Polynesia, 241

pre-Columbian, 200, 202, 213, 219, 237

pre-Columbian codices, 262

pre-Columbian heroes, 263

pre-Columbian Peru, 246

pre-Conquest lineages, 171

pre-Hispanic temple altars, 274

prehistoric Mesoamerica, 58, 64, 100

prehistoric Teuchitlán, 106

Pre-History, 59–279, 289

Purépecha, 163–64, 171, 173–74, 199, 219

Purépecha archaeology, 168

Purépecha artisans, 171

Purépecha state, 160–61, 167, 233

Purqpecha communities, 179, 181, 187, 189, 192, 194

enabled, 185, 188, 190, 193–94

S

Scandinavia, 266

South African plateau, 266

Southeast Asia, 266

Spanish chroniclers, 163

Spanish churches, 169

Spanish colonial institutions, 188, 194

Spanish colonialism, 175

Spanish colonial rule, 181, 186, 196–97

Spanish contact, 166

Spanish law, 181

Spanish rule, 186, 232

Spanish silver, 169

Spanish-style municipal governments, 168, 237

T

Tarascan, 167, 207, 225

Tarascan army, 166

Tarascan art, 200, 206

Tarascan art form, 208

Tarascan artists, 206

Tarascan capacity, 166

Tarascan copper ornaments, 207

Tarascan copper work, 210

Tarascan copper workshops, 206

Tarascan institutions, 166

Tarascan metallurgists, 206

Tarascan period, 108

Tarascan pottery, 60

Tarascan society, 208

Tenochtitlan, 175

Teotihuacan, 10–11

Tequila, 97, 101

Tequila volcano, 202

Teuchitlán, 61, 96, 98–99, 101, 104–5, 112–13, 171

Teuchitlán communities, 101, 103–4, 107, 114

Teuchitlán development, 108

Teuchitlán population concentrations, 102

Teuchitlán region, 102

Teuchitlán territories, 111

Teuchitlán trade relationships, 107

Teuchitlán tradition, 95–98, 103, 107–12, 114, 225

TeuchitlIn, 4

Texcoco, 166

Tlatilco, 60

Toltec regalia, 130

Tzintzuntzan, 160, 162, 164, 169, 172, 177, 233, 245

Tzintzuntzan Excavations, 233

Tzintzuntzan sites, 171

W

Weigand, 7–9, 16–17, 96, 101, 109–10, 112–14, 162–67, 170–73, 213, 226–27, 230–31, 233–36, 252–53, 265–66, 275–77

  Phil, 159, 161, 168–69, 174, 226, 231, 239, 252, 264, 267

WeigandjArmillasjHarbottle approach, 267

Weigand model, 267

Weigands' collaborative approach, 255

Weigand's discovery, 96, 114

Weigand's excavations, 100, 164

Western Mexican art, 208–11, 215–16, 222–23, 257

 evolution of, 200, 220

Western Mexican communities, 231, 236

Western Mexican copper, 140

Western Mexican guachimontones, 242, 245

Western Mexican metallurgists, 136, 141

Western Mexican metallurgy, 140, 144–45, 147, 245, 247

Western Mexican prehistory, 71–72, 96, 112, 251

Western Mexican shaft tombs, 59, 61, 69

Western Mexican traditions, 67, 212, 214, 216, 242, 286

Western Mexico, artistic traditions of, 199, 218

Western Mexico's prehistory, 19, 24, 28, 35–36, 95

Williams, Eduardo, 162, 171

Wixáritari dialect, 273

Wixáritari elder, 267

Wixáritari medicine-men, 262

Index Created with TExtract / www.TExtract.com

Made in the USA
Monee, IL
07 November 2025